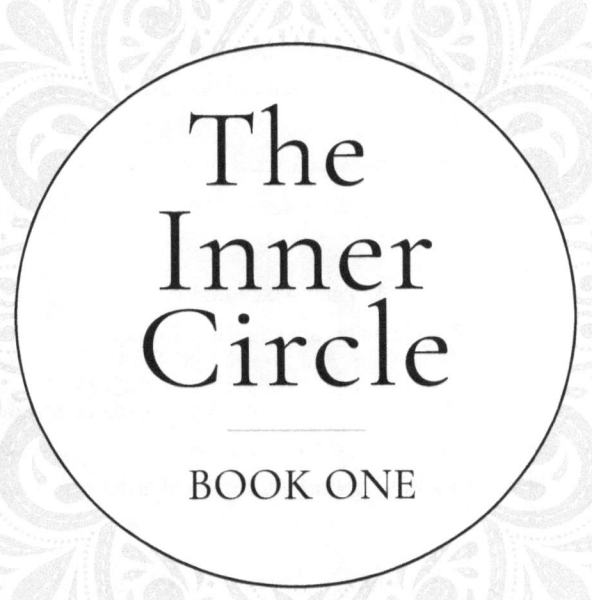

The Inner Circle

BOOK ONE

My Seventeen Years in the
Cult of the American Sikhs

PETER MACDONALD BLACHLY

The Inner Circle - Book 1
My Seventeen Years in the Cult of the American Sikhs

by Peter Macdonald Blachly
peter@peteralexander.us/

© 2021-2025 Peter Macdonald Blachly
Published by Sheep Island Press

All rights reserved. No part of this book may be used or reproduced by any means without the written permission of the author except in the case of brief quotations embodied in critical articles and reviews.

Book Design: Book Savvy Studio, Ashland OR

Library of Congress Control Number: 2025902183
ISBN: 978-1-7372280-3-5

First Edition
Printed in the United States of America

Praise for *The Inner Circle*

"Peter Macdonald Blachly's *The Inner Circle* is a very well-written memoir—easy to read, entertaining, and hard to put down. He manages to weave together his world-traveling adventures with his own spiritual journey as one of the first people to don a turban in the early days of the Yogi Bhajan cult, which he joined in 1970. Although Blachly pulls no punches about his gradual disillusionment with the moral failings of his Guru, the book does not come off as an exposé. Rather, it is his self-awareness and clear-eyed examination of his own vulnerable sense of identity, which made him susceptible to the manipulations of a malevolent narcissist, that sets the book apart from other memoirs. Whether practicing one of the world's religions, following a spiritual teacher, in an authoritarian cult, or in the thralls of a charismatic political leader, *The Inner Circle* provides valuable lessons for all of us."

    Steven Hassan, PhD, MA, MEd, LMHC, NCC
    Member of the Program in Psychiatry and the Law
    Freedom of Mind Resource Center, Inc., Newton, MA

"*The Inner Circle* is a magic carpet ride through a young man's quest for spiritual enlightenment. Like a modern day Siddhartha, Peter encounters the challenges, contradictions and harsh realities that occur when one surrenders to an immoral yogi.

With insight, humor and rigorous honesty, Peter gives us access into a unique time in American history—when the end of the utopian idealism of the 60s converged with the flow of East Indian wise men that came to America in droves. There is a wonderful nostalgia in his recollections, a wistful taste of simpler times with the ease of world travel and ever-changing circumstances. Peter embraces it all, with a combustible mixture of devotion, confusion and willing abandon. I highly recommend this captivating and poignant memoir."

    Suzanne Beth Jordan, Writer and advocate for *Beyond the Cage: The 3HO | Yogi Bhajan | Kundalini Yoga Aftermath*

"Like an exotic parasite for which his followers had no defense, Yogi Bhajan's cult has infected three generations of acolytes. Through this clear-eyed memoir, Peter Blachly walks us through how his life unfolded as a devotee of this malevolent con man. Seldom do we get such a detailed portrait of the damage cults inflict and the author's valiant steps to right himself."

    Stephen Josephs, Ed.D.

"*The Inner Circle* is a magical mystery tour that takes the reader through the spiritual Odyssey of a youthful musician's quest for self-discovery, enlightenment, and mystical awakening. His quest for identity begins with the innocence and naivete of the seeker as he devotes himself to a charismatic teacher and a new spiritual practice. It is a journey full of adventure and discovery that takes us across continents and coasts, and the author's gradual awakening that the Guru and his organization have a very dark side. After many years, as devotion devolves into painful disillusionment, the initiate finds his way out of the cult and into a new sense of himself. This is a great book, full of insight about the light and dark sides of devotion to a spiritual practice. A must read!"

    Dr. Ronald A. Alexander, Executive Director
the OpenMind Training Institute, Santa Monica,
author *Wise Mind Open Mind and Core Creativity:
A Mindful Path to Awaken your Creative Abilities* (2022)

"In *The Inner Circle*, Peter Macdonald Blachly offers a vivid and remarkably detailed account of his years in a yoga cult headed by Yogi Bhajan, a spiritual grifter with uncanny talents of group manipulation. The real gift of this book is not the account of yet one more manipulative guru, but of Peter's inner dialogue, struggles and self doubt as he navigates the whims and inconsistencies of Bhajan and the hierarchical group he created.

    This account is unflinching, self-revealing and brutally honest. Peter describes the longing and excitement related to achieving inner circle status, and the tremendously difficult pain of realizing that Bhajan was yet one more hustler seeking fame, fortune, status and sex. If you want to understand the mindset of an intelligent person who becomes trapped in a mind control cult, this is one of the finest accounts."

    Chris Kilham, medicine hunter, yogi, author of
The Five Tibetans and *The Ayahuasca Test Pilots Handbook*

"It is true, perhaps, that this instrument which had stood the test of a thousand years for the moral regeneration of a man from slavery to freedom and to moral perfectability may be a two-edged weapon and it may lead some not to humility and complete self-control but to the most Satanic pride, that is, to bondage and not to freedom."

—Fyodor Dostoevsky
(From *The Brothers Karamazov*—in reference to the system of "Elders" in Russian Monasteries)

Contents

Introduction		ix
A Note from the Author		xiv
CHAPTER 1:	Search for Wisdom	1
CHAPTER 2:	The Set-up	13
CHAPTER 3:	Meet Yogiji	19
CHAPTER 4:	A Deeper Dive	23
CHAPTER 5:	Wedding Day	35
CHAPTER 6:	Meeting the Parents	41
CHAPTER 7:	New Identity	47
CHAPTER 8:	Changes Afoot	55
CHAPTER 9:	My First Solstice Celebration	65
CHAPTER 10:	Tantric Yoga	71
CHAPTER 11:	A Dysfunctional Marriage	79
CHAPTER 12:	New Names	85
CHAPTER 13:	The Golden Temple Restaurant	91
CHAPTER 14:	Loss of a Parent	101
CHAPTER 15:	First Trip to India	109
CHAPTER 16:	Getting Around Delhi	115
CHAPTER 17:	Welcomed by Punjabi Sikhs	121
CHAPTER 18:	The Train from Delhi to Amritsar	127
CHAPTER 19:	The Golden Temple	131
CHAPTER 20:	The Magic of the Place	137
CHAPTER 21:	New Clothes	143

CHAPTER 22:	*Another New Identity*	149
CHAPTER 23:	*Get a Tabla Teacher*	155
CHAPTER 24:	*Key Relationships*	165
CHAPTER 25:	*The Khalsa String Band*	173
CHAPTER 26:	*Rise and Fall of the Band*	181
CHAPTER 27:	*A Stranger Back at Home*	189
CHAPTER 28:	*Danger*	195
CHAPTER 29:	*Conflict in India*	199
CHAPTER 30:	*Cracks Appear*	207
CHAPTER 31:	*A New Life in India*	213
CHAPTER 32:	*Big Yellow Bus*	221
CHAPTER 33:	*Making A Living*	227
CHAPTER 34:	*A New Life in Los Angeles*	243
CHAPTER 35:	*Closer to the Master*	255
CHAPTER 36:	*A New Livelihood*	259
CHAPTER 37:	*Disturbing News*	261
CHAPTER 38:	*Trying to Make it in Music*	265
CHAPTER 39:	*My Business Grows*	269
CHAPTER 40	*Shady Characters*	275
CHAPTER 41:	*Divorce*	285
CHAPTER 42:	*Disillusionment*	293
CHAPTER 43:	*Final Days*	299
Epilogue		303
Acknowledgements		306
Author		307

Introduction

When I was 20, I joined an eastern spiritual organization that was in its infancy in the US, and I grew with it for the next 17 years. It was a journey of self-discovery—or self-creation, perhaps—and, as Dostoevsky notes about the Russian Monastic tradition, it was a two-edged sword, promising spiritual growth and "liberation" but fraught with enormous challenges to my integrity and sense of self.

My unique experiences may appear exotic to a non-initiate. But since the 1960s hundreds of thousands of young people in America have participated to varying degrees in eastern religions and other spiritual groups. What was it that compelled so many to seek outside their own culture, coming under the sway of charismatic "spiritual teachers"—most of whom abused their followers in various ways? Although the ostensible reasons were likely idealistic and in reaction to the banality of American culture, did these spiritual seekers, like me, come from homes where emotions were stifled by denial, where parental affection seemed rare or non-existent, and where one's sense of identity was established by what they did, rather than who they were? Many of these spiritual teachers were adept at identifying and exploiting young people with attachment deficits. Yogi Bhajan even stated that all his students suffered from what he called "father phobia."

My own spiritual search grew from a quest for answers to the "cosmic questions" that are the basis of every high school and college philosophy class. It evolved into a search for integrity and the work of integrating into my own behavior a set of values, ethics, and ideals that I understood only intellectually at the time. More than anything else, however, it became a search for a strong sense of self that would overcome the nagging insecurity and inadequacy I had felt since my early childhood.

In *Book I*, I do my best to honestly describe the events and circumstances that led me to don a turban and white robes (even while riding a motorcycle through the streets of Los Angeles), to spend years traveling as a cultural liaison between the Indian and American Sikh communities, to live in India for months at a time studying sitar and tablas from the master musicians of the Golden Temple, to learn to speak Punjabi and to read and write the arcane Gurmukhi script, to help frame the administration of a new religion (new, at least, in its American form), to submit to an arranged marriage, to raise my children in a foreign country (at the behest of the Yogi) isolated from American culture, and to do many other things that were outside the norms of American society. I will also describe the circumstances that led to my gradual disillusionment, the break-up of my marriage, and my eventual departure from the community.

This is not easily done. Although this history is filled with adventure, the degree of my youthful naivete and impulsivity is shocking—even embarrassing. Married at 20, I was far too immature to be a responsible husband or parent, and in retrospect, my adventures often came at a heavy price to my wife and children. Further, many of the characters described herein are still involved in the American Sikh community, and—being naturally protective of their religion and history—may take umbrage at my perspective, though I have changed many of the names. I am not, however, writing this with any intention of it being an exposé. It is simply my own personal journey, as best as I can relate it.

There are millions of people who, like me, have given themselves over to a charismatic leader at some point in their lives—sometimes a political, rather than a religious or spiritual one. This book might serve as an eye-opener for them – encouraging a deeper examination of the internal forces and conditions that led them to submit to a sociopathic authority figure – but it is also intended to give value and honor to their intentions for a better life and a better world

My time with the American Sikh community—and my relationship with Yogi Bhajan—came to an end in 1987, but my troubles were just beginning. *Book II* documents my path of recovery from the detrimental impacts of having spent 17 years in a cult. Although the circumstances and events of my memoir are both individual and specific, there is a thread running throughout that I believe is universal: the struggle of every human being to find a sense of identity that is rooted in authenticity, integrity, accountability, compassion, and sensitivity to the needs of others. For those who are driven to do something worthwhile or great in life there is an added vulnerability: small egos rarely accomplish great things, but large egos can cause great harm when they go astray.

A key factor in the journey of recovery is that people who get immersed in cults tend to lose perspective about their own behaviors and motivations. They often develop a fabricated sense of identity and come to rely on the instructions of the cult leader for everything from how to use the bathroom to how to run their businesses. This "I'm just obeying orders" mentality creates a false sense of security and a general lack of accountability. It also enables an override of individual conscience, where service to the "mission" of the cult leader can justify behaviors that might be unethical, dehumanizing, or even illegal. After leaving a cult, most individuals are thrust into an identity crisis—and a new reality where they have to start making their own decisions and taking responsibility for their own actions. They also have to come to grips with ethical frameworks that probably did not apply in the context of the cult.

This is a journey that can be fraught with problems, due in part to the likelihood that the person's emotional life may have atrophied during their time in the cult—subordinated to, or replaced by devotion to the leader, or the pursuit of spiritual experiences such as elevated states of meditation. Most cults also instill a powerful set of norms that may be out of alignment with, antagonistic to, or even diametrically opposed to those of civil society. An example of this might be the subordinate role of women within most cults, or the devaluing or dehumanizing of individuals and groups outside the cult. Brain and behavioral scientists also note that trauma and abuse can cause neurological changes that distort perceptions and influence behavior patterns.

When one's moral compass and sense of self have both been compromised by adherence to a cult, the journey of recovery may begin, as mine did, with a descent into questionable behaviors, or an end-justifies-the-means approach to facing the challenges of life on the outside when deprived of the artificial bubble of protection provided—at however great a cost—by the cult leader or participation in the community. *Book II* does not cover all the moral challenges and failures of conscience I experienced in the years after leaving Yogi Bhajan's cult, but it focuses on some of the most dangerous people and situations I faced, and the more important of the many lessons I learned—lessons that healthy individuals usually learn a lot earlier in life than I did. My own journey into the cult, and back out 17 years later, was made more perilous by undiagnosed, high-functioning autism running through much of my family, which I only discovered many years later. The resulting naivete and feeling of social alienation left me highly vulnerable to the manipulative leadership of an authoritarian father figure like Yogi Bhajan.

I was fortunate to be with my own father when he died a few weeks short of his 99th birthday. The date was August 26, 2016, which also happened to be Yogi Bhajan's birthday. The irony of this coincidence was acute, for I realized that a significant part of my healing from Yogi Bhajan's influence coincided with my role as caretaker for

With my father, Frederick Johnson Oatman Blachly, August 23, 2016.

my father during the last eight years of his life. Although I had been violently thrown out of the house at age 18, and thereafter had only a distant and strained relationship with my father, I was the only one of his five children in a position to help in 2008, when he suffered a heart attack a few days after moving into a retirement home with his ailing wife. I was at his bedside in the hospital when, not knowing if he would survive the night, he gave me instructions for spreading his ashes in the cold waters of coastal Maine, in the same manner we had spread my mother's ashes thirty-five years earlier.

My father survived the heart attack, and in the following years came to trust and depend on me for the management of his living arrangements, finances, and medical care. For eight years I made the trip from Maine to Washington, DC at least once a month, and during that time our relationship bloomed in friendship, respect, trust, mutual appreciation, laughter, and the healing balm of love.

– PETER MACDONALD BLACHLY

A NOTE FROM THE AUTHOR

People change—not always for the better— but I believe that "the arc of the moral universe" cited by Dr. Martin Luther King, Jr. depends upon the majority of individuals in society changing for the better over time.

I began writing this book more than 25 years ago, when many of the relationships described herein were still raw and unresolved. In writing about them—particularly the relationship with my ex-wife—I did not try to re-write history or sugarcoat my perceptions and reactions, which were based on my experiences and lack of maturity at the time. As such, some of the characters, including myself, are not always depicted in a sympathetic way.

However, it would be unfair to conclude that behaviors and attitudes from more than 40 years ago accurately determine who we are today, or that anyone mentioned in this account—other than Yogi Bhajan, who died in 2004, and a few of his top lieutenants—should be judged for mistakes they made decades ago. Sadly, I learned only in recent years that Yogi Bhajan's behavior worsened over time after my departure in 1987, and that many people, particularly young women, experienced unspeakable abuses at his hand.

Fortunately, however, the opposite is true of most of the people described here. Some, whom I neither liked nor admired at the time, I can now say that I count as friends, and that they are contributing to the arc of the universe "bending toward justice."

The Inner Circle

BOOK ONE

Music was always a huge part of my identity, and probably my most meaningful contribution to the Sikh community.

CHAPTER ONE

Search for Wisdom

At the age of 20 I was desperate for wisdom. A burning desire for truth and meaning, ignited in my teens by reading Plato and Herman Hesse, had not been extinguished by two years of playing lead guitar for Claude Jones, a popular Washington DC rock band. The ego-gratification of heading the three-piece band I started in 1968 had faded with the addition over time of four other band members, so that by the end of 1969 I felt I was little more than a backup musician for our lead singer. At the time I had not articulated it this way, even in my own thoughts. But I grew painfully aware that the band would not fulfill my original idealistic vision of "saving the world" through music. I was also increasingly aware that my persona as a rock musician was an insufficient balm for the gnawing insecurity I felt about my own lack of real identity. In the peculiar slang spoken by our band members, I felt I didn't have "much of an act."

Our lead singer, however, seemed to have a great act. He was charismatic, funny, and self-assured, both on stage and off. Inevitably, I would measure myself against his powerful personality, and I could only take consolation by imagining that he was "shallow," while I perceived myself as "deep." However, this consolation was entirely unsatisfactory on another count: Joe was remarkably popular with the girls. His "act" was magnetic and evidently quite appealing to the young women in our circle. I, on the other hand, depended on being philosophy the first finger represents wisdom, the thumb is ego, and that these two are balanced in Gyan Mudra, which means 'sign of knowledge.' Now block your right nostril with your right thumb, fingers straight pointing to the ceiling, and begin long deep breathing through the left nostril." I gave it my best, trying to keep up with the enormous effort everyone around me put into breathing as deeply and powerfully as possible.

Larry encouraged us to "keep up," as we continued past the one-minute mark. While we huffed and puffed, he expounded about the *Ida*, *Pingala*, and *Shashumna*, the vital nerve channels of the "subtle body" that crisscross at the chakras up and down the spine. He told us to visualize the energy coming in at the 3rd eye (in the center of the forehead) with each inhalation, and out again with each exhale. I struggled to concentrate. The incense irritated my nostrils and made it painful to inhale. My knees were aching. On and on we went. I was feeling dizzy and couldn't concentrate enough to even pay attention to Larry's voice, which seemed to have faded into a drone in the distance. "Now switch sides, using your left thumb to block your left nostril." We had already been going for five minutes. I obeyed and tried my best. My right nostril was all stuffed up and I could barely force any air through it. My back and knees were now really hurting. Minute after minute we continued. I was not able to concentrate at all, just hoping for this exercise to end, counting seconds…

"Now begin Breath of Fire through both nostrils." The room erupted into a fantastic cacophony of rapid, forced breathing. Over the din Larry explained to the newcomers how to use the diaphragm to force the air rapidly in and out, and how Breath of Fire purifies the blood and strengthens the nerves. Breathing through two nostrils was a relief for me, and I increased my effort with new vigor. Another five minutes went by before we heard the blessed command, "INHALE!" I took an enormous breath and held it. My head started spinning. "Hold it, hold it," encouraged Larry. I was starting to tingle all over and feel faint. "Now Exhale. Inhale DEEP. Now Exhale ALL THE WAY OUT. HOLD THE BREATH OUT!" He shouted. I held my breath out, determined not to give in to the impulse to inhale. Longer and longer we held out, Larry demanding that we "Keep up." My entire body started shaking with the effort. "Inhale. Now exhale and relax. Stretch your legs."

I felt buzzed and couldn't help looking around at Anni and Mindi. In fact, everyone in the room seemed to be completely stoned and blissed out. Anni smiled at me as if to say, "I told you so." My body felt as if it was vibrating, and I was euphoric. "Now sit up straight and grab your shins with both hands," the command came after only a few seconds. Larry proceeded to take us through 40 minutes of intense physical exercise, flexing forward and back, side to side, stretching our legs, doing leg lifts, rolling our heads on our shoulders, holding our arms over our heads for three to five minutes at a time—all with vigorous long deep breathing or breath of fire. Some of the exercises were impossible for me, but I tried my hardest and felt increasingly invigorated even while my muscles got tired. "Your strength is not in your muscles," shouted Larry during one particularly strenuous exercise, "It's in your nervous system and your glandular system. The glands are the guardians of your health."

Throughout all the exercises, and moments of rest in between, Larry provided a constant monologue about eastern philosophy, natural vegetarian foods, and Oriental medical wisdom. Finally, he told us to lie down on our backs and relax. "Completely relax," he intoned gently, "From your head to your feet. Now we are going to concentrate on each part of the body and consciously relax. Start with your toes and feet. Breathe long and slow and relax. Now your ankles..." Over a period of several minutes he guided us through the entire body. Then he started playing the gong, softly at first, then

My band, Claude Jones, was quite popular in DC and was selected to perform along with Pete Seeger, Arlo Guthrie, and the Chambers Brothers at the Washington Monument for the first Earth Day in 1970.

"deep," though I was remarkably unfaithful for someone whose appeal to women was, in my mind, my "spiritual" nature.

My enthusiasm for the opposite sex earned me more than one unflattering nickname from my band-mates, and I couldn't help but feel guilty about my manic need for female affection, even while agonizing over my poor showing in this arena compared to Joe. Over time, guilt began eclipsing desire, and I considered making some substantial changes in how I lived and behaved. There were many other influences driving me to change, as well: disillusionment, anger, and fear about the war in Vietnam, and disgust at the Nixon administration's obvious dishonesty, even while I rejected the strident "down with the system" rhetoric of Abbie Hoffman. I was depressed by the gradual demise of the flower power ideals of the "Summer of Love," as the hip culture descended into the widespread use of hard drugs. The symbols of long hair and freaky clothes began to evoke more desperation, squalor, and crime than freedom and joy. By 1970 the dream of a better world through sex, drugs, and rock & roll was going sour. I was ready for a big change.

One February evening in 1970 I acquiesced to the entreaties of a group of my friends, and accompanied them to a yoga class in downtown Washington, DC. All I knew about yoga at that point was from reading *Autobiography of a Yogi*, which was more about miracles and extraordinary spiritual powers than specific yogic exercises or techniques. I was thrilled by the book, for it appealed to my sense of magic and recounted a life considerably more interesting and meaningful than the one I had created for myself. Also, in spite of the many warnings against such things, I could not help wishing I had the psychic powers described by the author: powers that could levitate objects, enlighten those around me with a touch on the forehead, and elicit the profound respect and reverence of men and women the world over. I knew those sorts of things were not going to come from playing lead guitar with Claude Jones.

I gave up smoking after Woodstock.

A large part of my social circle at the time revolved around the "Yellow Submarine," a house in McLean, Virginia, owned by a former CIA official whose children were fans of my band. A huge, street-facing mural of Peter Max's Yellow Submarine gave the house its name and advertised the kind of generous hospitality, friendship, and soft drugs one was likely to find inside. I loved the place. Most of the people there had read *Autobiography of a Yogi*, and many had begun attending Yoga classes in November 1969. Enthusiasm for the classes had spread rapidly through the group, and by February everyone seemed gripped with the kind of fervor one might expect among newly baptized born-again Christians or the book-peddling Hare Krishnas, who were just beginning to take over America's airports. I overcame my initial resistance to the tone that this fervor added to the many invitations I received, and finally agreed to go with my girlfriend, Anni, and her friend, Mindi.

As we walked up the steps of the Yoga Center, I was disappointed to see an unfamiliar triangular logo on a sign in the front window. It gave no hint of association with the Kriya Yoga mentioned in *Autobiography of a Yogi*. My first thought was that I had been deceived—that the "Kundalini Yoga" and "Healthy, Happy, Holy (3HO) Foundation" announced by the sign were just imitators of the real thing. But not wanting to let my friends down, and having no other way back to Virginia, I hid my concern and followed them into the front hall where we dutifully removed our shoes, or in my case a pair of smelly Red Wing boots.

In 1970, the Dupont Circle neighborhood, especially the residential area to the east of Connecticut Avenue, was in the throes of a slow transition. Like many once respectable inner-city neighborhoods, its glory had faded during the "white flight" to the suburbs that occurred after World War II. Abandoned by the white middle class, the long rows of stone townhouses had become low-cost rental housing, owned for the most part by absentee landlords, and occupied by "poor folks"—mostly blacks—until the beatniks and then the hippies moved in. Throughout the 1960s, Dupont Circle's reputation grew as a focal point of the hip scene in Washington, DC. On summer afternoons the grassy lawns and wooden benches of the spacious circle would be filled with conga drummers, guitar players, drug dealers, harmonica players, and all kinds of hippies, dropouts, and down-and-outers, along with a mingling of clean cut high school and college students, a cop or two on the outer edges, and an occasional businessman pretending to save time by cutting straight across the circle, a path which allowed a close, if surreptitious look at the many exotically, or scantily clad young women who made up a significant part of this motley assemblage.

As might be expected, the homes around Dupont Circle where many of these people lived or "crashed" reflected the general lack of money and lack of attention to cleanliness and order that so pervaded the counterculture. The yoga center was located at 17th and Q on the eastern edge of this enclave. It still bore the telltale marks of its transition from the hippie crash pad it had been only months earlier. Inexpensive oriental rugs had been laid on top of ragged carpeting that some miserly landlord had installed a generation earlier. A fresh coat of paint provided a thin disguise over cracks in walls and woodwork, and a thick pall of incense could not completely cover the faint mustiness that wafted up through the heating vents and the basement stairs.

The classroom consisted of what had once been the front parlor and dining room of the old row house. It was directly adjacent to the front hallway, accessible through a large arched doorway, giving the impression that the entire first floor, except for the kitchen at the back, was one large room. There was not a stick of furniture, except at the very front of the classroom where a sheepskin-covered ottoman served as the teacher's seat, and a low table behind it served as an altar of sorts. In the corner, a large bronze gong hung inside a wooden frame. The hallway wall was dominated by a vast, ancient mirror, below which was a low shelf running the entire length of the wall. On this shelf and beneath it was a clutter of shoes, jackets and other belongings, to which we added our own.

We were a few minutes early for the class and took places in the middle of the front room. I was uncomfortable sitting on the floor, and apprehensive of what was coming. People around me were either sitting in quiet meditation or stretching gently like runners before a race. Most were sitting on sheepskins or blankets they had brought with them. I felt unprepared, and nervously sought reassurance from Anni. She smiled beatifically at me and quietly signaled that I shouldn't talk out loud. People kept coming in—some through the front door, others from upstairs—so that soon both the front and back rooms were packed with a cross-section of Dupont Circle regulars.

A diminutive woman in white entered and sat cross-legged next to the teacher's seat facing the class. Putting her palms together at her heart and closing her eyes she began to chant in a sparse Gregorian melody. Experienced students, including Mindi and Anni, joined in and soon the entire room was reverberating with the sound. Even I joined in, attempting to imitate the strange eastern syllables *"Ek Ong Kar Sat Nam Siri Wahe Guru"*. I closed my eyes and tried to meditate, but my mind was far too active and I couldn't help looking up every time the front door opened to let in a new student. After five minutes my legs and back began to hurt. Then the teacher entered.

Larry was an authoritative looking 25-year-old with shoulder length brown hair, dark eyes, and a full beard and mustache. He was dressed in white Levi's and a loose white Indian shirt. He stood for a moment facing the altar, mumbling a short prayer, then sat cross-legged on the ottoman, closed his eyes and joined the chanting. After a few moments, as we came to the end of a round, he called out, "in-HALE," the last syllable rising with command and finality. Instantly the class fell silent, and for a long moment we all held our breath. "Exhale."

"We start each class by tuning-in to the teacher within," he began. "Place your palms together at your heart chakra, roll your eyes up to the third eye, and we'll chant *'Ong Namo Guru Dev Namo,'* which means 'Divine Teacher, I salute you.' Inhale." And so we started. After three repetitions he again told us to inhale, then to exhale and relax. I stretched my legs uncomfortably. I had done virtually no exercise for several years, and even though I was only 20 my body was stiff and unhealthy. I was six feet two inches tall and weighed only 145 pounds, the result of two years living as an impoverished, cigarette-smoking, psychedelic rock musician.

One year earlier the whole band and I had started eating a vegetarian, macrobiotic diet, not so much from mindfulness of healthy eating, but as the only affordable way to survive. My feeling of guilt and remorse at stealing a steak from the local grocery store had defined for me the limit of what I was willing to do in order to eat, and it did not include theft or shoplifting. Connie, our bass player's wife, suggested Macrobiotics, and since she offered to do all the cooking, we all agreed. Connie, her husband Jay, our "financial manager" Keith and I had all been students together at St. Johns College in Annapolis the year before, and had all dropped out at the same time to embark on the adventure of our rock band.

The whole band had been living together at the time in a ratty 2-bedroom house in northwest Washington that we rented for $165 per month. We called it "Little Gray," our answer to The Band's "Music from Big Pink." We had no money except what we earned playing gigs on the weekend. But with careful management it was enough. Keith would collect all the money, pay the rent, make sure Connie had enough for food, buy an occasional ounce or two of marijuana, and give us each a dollar a day for cigarettes.

"Now sit in easy pose—arms straight, resting on your knees, hands in *Gyan Mudra*: first finger touching your thumb, other fingers straight." Larry demonstrated and explained that in yogic louder and louder into a crashing crescendo, followed by a long period of dreamy, other-worldly overtones coaxed from the outer edges of the gong. A few minutes into this gentle phase, I drifted out of my body. It was the strangest experience! I was conscious that my actual body was lying flat on the ground, but I could also feel that I was literally outside of it, floating at an angle with my heels on the ground. Then I lost all consciousness.

"Roll your hands and feet." The voice was soft and distant. "Roll your hands and your feet from your ankles and wrists." I gradually came back to waking consciousness and recognized Larry's voice. Obediently, I rolled my hands and feet. "Now rub your palms together and rub the soles of your feet together." The room was filled with a gentle rustling as 30 people complied. "Now bring your knees into your chest, wrap your arms around your legs and rock forward and back. Now come sitting up straight, keep your eyes closed and sit in meditation pose with your hands in Gyan Mudra." As soon as we were settled, he explained the meaning of the chant we had been singing before class started. *Ek Ong Kar Sat Nam Siri Wahe Guru Ji.* "There is one Creator, His Name is Truth, Great is his Wisdom." He then started chanting, and we all joined in.

After five minutes of chanting, he instructed us to inhale, then relax. "May the power of God's life and breath inside you heal your body and mind," he began, "And may goodness fill your heart. May you find the strength to do what is right, to hold your consciousness high, and to spread love and light to all you meet. Sat Nam." He then started singing the refrain from the Incredible String Band's 'Very Cellular Song.' Everyone immediately joined in—especially me, since my band had been playing the song for a couple of years and often used it to close our concerts. "May the long time sun shine upon you, all love surround you; and the pure light within you guide your way on; guide your way on; guide your way on…"

As soon as the song was finished, Larry stood up and left the room. I sat in awe. Never had I experienced anything so powerful and essentially pure. I looked at Anni, my eyes overflowing with love and joy. Gradually, people started talking in hushed and gentle voices. The entire room seemed to have been transformed into a gathering of angels, a virtual love-fest on the highest plane of purity and soulfulness. I believed we had transcended our personalities, our weaknesses, our negativity and fears. "This is it!" I thought. "This is what I've been looking for. This will give me the power to change my own life and effect positive change on the planet." I was determined to learn this discipline and teach it. It was as simple as that. My mind was made up.

The woman in white, who had started the chanting before class, now walked through the crowded room dispensing dates and almonds from a basket. Another beautiful, raven-haired woman came from the kitchen with a tray full of assorted teacups, brimming with delicious Chai, an Indian spice tea. I was in heaven. Everything was beautiful. It was as if the highest aspirations of the flower power scene had all come together in this sanctified and loving place. Each detail of this exquisite scene reinforced my conviction that I was going to be a yoga teacher.

Later, as I went to get my boots, I picked up a flyer with an explanation of mantras on one side and a class schedule on the other. I was not going to miss any classes if I could help it. I was already a devotee. I left my dollar (I was no longer buying cigarettes) in the donation basket near the back stairs and walked out with Anni and Mindi. My euphoria extended to them both, but especially to Anni. The tsunami of love I felt for her was overwhelming. The die was cast. I knew my future.

My band, Claude Jones, was featured on the front page of The Washington Post's *"Style" section. This photo, by Steve Szabo, won a nationwide award for photo journalism, which was presented by the President of the United States. We loved the irony of the hippie-hating Richard Nixon having to make the presentation.*

CHAPTER TWO

The Set-up

During 1969 my band's fortunes had improved. We had outgrown Little Grey as the band took on new members. Responding to advice from the *I Ching*, "... the southwest brings good fortune," we had sought and found a wonderful old house on 160 acres of rolling farmland tucked inside a horseshoe bend of the Rappahannock River. The place was just past Warrenton, Virginia, 50 miles to the southwest of Washington: an hour's drive. At this point our retinue included Jay, our bass player, and his wife, Connie (who was like a mother to the whole group), our drummer Reggie, rhythm guitar player, Francis (also a classmate of mine since 1959 at St. Albans School where we had both served as choirboys in the National Cathedral Choir), our lead singer, Joe, keyboard player, Mike, financial manager, Keith, equipment manager, Claude Jones (after whom the band was named), his girlfriend, Debbie, and two "roadies" and part time percussionists (the "red-ass rhythm section"), John and Steve. We also had a second keyboard player and songwriter, John, who didn't live with us. Economics and camaraderie had played equal roles in bringing us together into a communal household. For the most part, we had a good life together.

We set up one of the old barns as a practice room, and in this congenial atmosphere expanded our repertoire and honed our musical skills so that our performances were consistently excellent. Our stature in the DC community rose enormously, and we had a large following that regularly packed the Emergency, a non-drinking nightclub on M street in Georgetown that was THE place for the hip crowd. No one cared that they served no alcohol, since no one in this crowd was into booze. Mind-altering drugs, however, were another matter. The band and its audiences at the Emergency always developed a special kind of rapport that made us feel like one big family. And indeed, it was, for wherever we played, even high school proms at private schools in the suburbs, we dragged along a huge retinue, demanding that since our "family" was a vital part of the Claude Jones experience, they should all get in free.

After I started going to yoga classes, it was not long before I convinced most of the Claude Jones family to come as well. For a few blessed weeks in March and early April, our band's routine changed. Everyone stopped smoking, drugs were shunned, and instead of "toking up" before our gigs at the Emergency, we would come freshly invigorated from doing breath of fire and Kundalini Yoga. I was extremely happy. Not only did I have my own life-transforming practice of yoga, I was also sharing it with my closest friends; and our music and stage presence were becoming an expression of the things that meant the most to me. My original dream of saving the world looked like it was back on track again. But things were about to unravel.

I had met Anni one week before the Woodstock festival in 1969, when Claude Jones was playing its first-ever club gig at a dive called the Showboat Lounge. This formerly first-rate jazz club in the Adams Morgan area had hosted such greats as Charlie Byrd. But like the neighborhood around it, it had fallen on hard times, a victim of "white flight." By the time we played there it was on the way back up, but was still a pretty rough place. However, the acoustics and layout were fabulous, and while we played there, our sound started coming together in extraordinary ways. We were a pretty good group of musicians, and from time to time in our practice sessions we had touched on a kind of magical sound that we felt would elevate us to greatness if we could only maintain it consistently. Our gigs at the Showboat gave us the opportunity to reach those almost transcendental moments more and more often. Word spread, and soon we were drawing audiences who came not for the booze, but to hear the music.

Anni showed up one night, and we immediately became friends, then occasional lovers. But there was a problem. Anni was married and had a young son. Her husband, Stew, was the bass player in another band. I had met him only once and did not like him. I saw him as a dark and foreboding presence for whom long hair was a style, not a statement. But Anni managed to arrange things so that I never had to cross paths with him, and I'm not sure he was even aware that she and I were seeing each other. Occasionally Anni would speak of him, and it was not good. He was abusive, both verbally and physically, and her descriptions made me afraid for her wellbeing. One day, shortly after starting yoga classes, I drove to her apartment in Georgetown and found her alone with her two-year-old son, Nate. "Pack up," I said, "I'm taking you away from here. Get Nate's things. Just bring what you need. Let's go."

I suppose I should have been surprised that she acquiesced, but I didn't think twice about it. I felt so strongly that it was the right thing to do. Whether or not Anni was having second thoughts, she did not display it. She packed two suitcases, got Nate into her car and followed me out to the farm in Virginia. Unfortunately, my room at the farmhouse was too small to accommodate us, but within a day I found a place we could live together on the second floor of a house in Warrenton, just five miles from the farm. We moved in immediately, got Nate enrolled in the Montessori School one block away, and for several weeks were extremely happy together.

The band was doing better than ever, and I actually had a little money for the first time in two years. The high point was Earth Day, when we played on an outdoor stage at the Washington Monument for a crowd of 20,000-30,000 people. But with the warm weather, disaster struck. An allergy that had first surfaced for a few weeks the previous spring, hit me again with a vengeance. It manifested whenever my body heated up from exertion. If I walked up a flight of stairs, ran even a hundred feet, or did any yoga at all, my whole body would start itching unbearably. The only remedy I found (without the benefit of medical advice) was to take "Contac," a powerful anti-histamine that had mild side effects. But deferring to my newfound ideology about health and natural foods, I held off taking the drug, and instead simply stopped going to Yoga classes for a few weeks.

The combination of my moving away from the farm and breaking the routine of attending yoga classes into which I had drawn my friends had a chilling effect on the band. Most of them stopped attending classes, and soon they were smoking again and toking up before gigs, just like the old days. I was devastated and felt betrayed, never thinking that they might have felt betrayed by me, too. We continued playing together, but it was different. On stage and off I was acutely aware of their being stoned, and though I still loved them all as my friends, I no longer felt bonded with them as I had before.

Then Yogi Bhajan came to Washington, DC. Yogiji, as he was affectionately known to the students at the Ashram (yoga center), was an Indian Guru who had brought to America the teachings of Kundalini Yoga that were transforming my life. Everyone had been speaking of him with awe, and Larry had done an excellent job of promoting his upcoming visit. Larry asked me to bring my guitar to Washington National Airport and lead the whole group in chanting to welcome Yogiji as he got off the plane. I was flattered at the request, and didn't much mind the disbelieving stares of the people in the airport as I stood at the gate leading 40 devotees in chanting. At that moment, it seemed a lot more meaningful to me than playing lead guitar for Claude Jones.

When Yogiji walked through the gate, everyone rushed to surround him, leaving me standing awkwardly alone with my guitar. Yogiji was certainly impressive. He was well over six feet tall, regal in bearing, and dressed completely in white. His dark complexion was accentuated by a full, jet-black beard and mustache, and a brilliant white turban wrapped impeccably on his head. From one hundred feet away he looked at me above the heads of devotees pressing in on all sides. When his eyes met mine, I felt like an explosion occurred inside me. My world went sideways, and I literally had to hold on to the pillar next to me to keep from collapsing. I had read of powerful psychic phenomena in *Autobiography of a Yogi*, but I was not expecting anything like this.

Yogiji had looked at me for only a second, but one glance from this "master" had shaken me to my core. Simultaneously, I felt ecstatic and terrified, as if I had been given the power of flight while losing control of something essentially my own. I didn't try to define the feelings going through me. I just hung tightly to the pillar and watched as if in a dream. I stood there for several minutes while Yogiji and the mass of devotees made their way out the door. When I recovered, I followed them out to the parking lot. Yogiji had already driven off in Larry's car. I found the friends with whom I had arrived, got into their car, and we headed back to the Ashram.

Yogi Bhajan inspired great devotion in the early days. I often introduced his classes and lectures by leading the group in chanting beforehand.

CHAPTER THREE

I Meet Yogiji

That evening Yogiji taught class at the Ashram. For the first time in several weeks, I attended. He gave us a particularly difficult workout with many exercises that required holding our arms straight at various angles from our shoulders. It was torture, but everything he talked about resonated with me. He told us that long hair is God's gift, mankind's antennae for cosmic energy and divine consciousness, that the body is the temple of the soul, and other spiritual concepts that may sound like clichés today. By the end of class, the combination of breathing, exercise, relaxation, and meditation had put us all in that peculiarly elevated "love space." We were also entranced by the charismatic power of this man.

My feelings about Yogiji were mixed. I was in awe of him: I admired and looked up to him. But I was also terrified. In his presence, I felt completely exposed and helpless. I attributed this to his all-seeing power, and in my mind I endowed him with supernatural qualities I imagined were appropriate for an enlightened Guru. I sensed that his power and wisdom would be instrumental in purifying and strengthening my own inner being, and I was willing to subject myself to any ordeal, including my fear of him, to achieve that.

After class he went upstairs with Larry and a few of the longtime devotees who lived at the Ashram. I was jealous of them for the special privilege they enjoyed. To my surprise, however, after a few minutes Sonya, the woman in white from my first yoga class, came down and told me that Yogiji wanted to meet me, and that I should come upstairs. He wanted to meet ME? My ego soared. I climbed the stairs to the 3rd floor where Yogiji was sitting with Larry and the other followers gathered at his feet.

Before I even entered the room Yogiji looked up at me, riveted me with his eyes and said, "You have to fight!" What in the world did he mean? I struggled to understand, seeking a deeper meaning. All I could do was stammer out a pathetic question, "You mean... with my fists?" He laughed heartily. "Any way you can. You just have to fight!" he repeated. I was no less confused. "Yes, sir," I answered weakly. I had never felt so small, so intimidated. I knew there must be some deeper meaning in this inscrutable exchange. But Yogiji's attention was already diverted to one of the other devotees. I stood at the door for a moment, no longer the center of attention, wondering if I should come in and sit at his feet like the others. I couldn't bring myself to do it. After a few seconds, I just turned and walked back down the stairs.

I don't know if there is any way to adequately describe the impact this brief meeting had on me. I had already decided that I would be a yoga teacher. Now it was clear that this ambition would also involve some kind of relationship with Yogiji. Among my other feelings about him, I already knew that I was envious of his incredible power. I wanted to be his equal—even his superior. And I did not ever again want to submit to the kind of intimidation I had just experienced at his hands. Yet I also respected and was in awe of him. I was flattered that he had noticed me at the airport and had asked for me alone among the 50 or 60 other students in the class.

Later that night Anni told me she thought she was pregnant. At first, I was overjoyed. Then she told me that the father was Stew, her husband. "Have you been seeing him?" I asked incredulously. We had been happily living together for several weeks. She admitted that she had. For the third time that day, I was speechless. I loved her so deeply that I was willing to forgive anything, even this. I rationalized that she was confused, that her emotions were naturally still torn between Nate's father and me. I thought back with guilt to a week earlier and my admission that I had been attracted to a girl at one of our gigs. I had told Anni how the girl came up to me between sets and gave me a very affectionate hug, and that the sensation of her large breasts pressing against me was a big turn on.

Stupid! How could I have been so insensitive of Anni's self-esteem? I could still hear the dead silence with which she had responded, could still see the tears in her eyes. Even now, in the face of the unspeakable betrayal she had just revealed to me, I tortured myself for what I perceived as my own lack of fidelity. I kissed her and said everything would work out. I said that I loved her. I said that she was an angel. I swallowed my pride and my hurt, and we went to bed.

The next day, Yogiji taught class again. Afterwards I managed to get a brief, semi-private audience with him—meaning that Larry and Sonya were both there and heard every word I said. I didn't care. I was desperately confused and needed some strong advice. "My girlfriend thinks she is pregnant, Sir," I began. "Should I marry her?" Yogiji looked at me with enormous compassion, as if I was a three-year-old coming to him with a hurt finger, and answered that it was the right thing to do. "But she thinks it is someone else's child," I protested weakly. Yogiji, Larry and Sonya all looked at me with a mixture of exasperation and contempt. "Well, Sonny," said Yogiji, "You'll need to do whatever you think is right." He turned, putting his arms around Larry's and Sonya's shoulders and dragged them away, leaving me standing stupidly in the center of the room. He departed for the west coast the next day.

The Ashram and the wider community of yoga students were all in a bustle during the second week in June. There was going to be a big Summer Solstice Celebration in New Mexico. For ten days, students from all over the country would be camping out, and Yogiji would be there, teaching every day. Most of my friends from the Yellow Submarine were going, and Anni had been telling me for some time that she was going as well. I regretted that I would be stuck in Washington for a number of gigs with the band. But Larry made it a lot more palatable by asking me to teach the classes at the Ashram while he was away. I had already taught a couple of the morning sessions and was doing well. I was a good student and in just a few months had learned enough to do a respectable job of teaching. I was thrilled with the recognition and privilege Larry was thus bestowing on me.

A day before leaving for New Mexico, Anni dropped another bomb on me. "When I come back from Solstice, I'm going back with Stew," she said. We were sitting in her car in the driveway at the Yellow Submarine. It was a beautiful day, and a gentle summer breeze rustled through the leaves around us. I was not prepared for this—had not for one second suspected it was coming. I was so naive! "No!" I exclaimed. "I love you. I want to marry you. I'll take care of you." Birds chirped merrily nearby and fluttered past our open windows. "I'm sorry," she said, and I could tell that she really was. "I've been thinking about this for a long time, and I haven't been fair to you. He's my husband. I took vows with him. He's Nate's father."

I continued to protest and beg, but it was hopeless. Anni, the only woman I truly loved, the only person I could dream of marrying, whose son I treated as my own, was leaving me. Defeated and stung to the quick, I eventually got out of her car, and she, with tears rolling down her cheeks, drove away and out of my life.

CHAPTER FOUR

A Deeper Dive

THE LAST TWO WEEKS OF JUNE dragged on interminably. I devoted myself to teaching two classes a day at the Ashram and to playing the few gigs with Claude Jones that had kept me from going to Solstice. Yoga classes were small, but I made them more interesting for myself by bringing my guitar and making up new melodies for the *Ek Ong Kar* mantra. These seemed to go over well with the students, and I gained confidence. Larry had told me I shouldn't play the gong until he had instructed me how to do it. There was a great mystery about the gong, and a profound sense of reverence for the instrument. It was kept protected in a deep blue velvet cover that one of the devotees had made for it. Throughout the time that Larry was gone, I respected his wishes and never played it.

Instead, I started experimenting with my guitar during the deep relaxation period of each class. I knew I had something of a gift in this regard, for one night at the farm a few months earlier I had cured Francis (our rhythm guitar player) of a migraine headache by playing some gentle, improvised melody. We were both sitting in the living room and, at first, I was just doodling. But I became aware that Francis was lying back with his eyes closed, and I knew he must be listening intently. I started playing with more attention to detail, carefully articulating the inner melodic voices, the length of sustain of each note, the harmonic and melodic interplays of my improvisation. I went on for about fifteen minutes, and when I stopped was surprised to hear Francis say "Thank you." I was actually feeling grateful to him, for I was acutely aware that he had been listening with an artist's ear, and this had caused me to play exceptionally well. He then told me that he had been suffering from a horrible headache when I started playing, and it was now completely gone.

So, I tried playing in yoga classes during the deep relaxation periods, attempting to accomplish with my guitar what Larry had been able to do with the gong. I found that I had to simplify things tremendously, because intricate melodies were distracting to the students. It was actually more challenging than almost anything I had ever done musically. I was richly rewarded for my efforts, however, by the gratitude and praise of the students.

At the same time, my gigs with Claude Jones were growing more strained. The more I got into yoga and the circle of friends that made up the Ashram community, the less I felt connected to my band-mates. One day, while walking near Dupont Circle, I was stopped by a teenager who asked me, "Hey! Aren't you that guy in Claude Jones…"—I felt my ego soaring at the recognition—"…who looks like a chicken?" I wasn't thrilled with the comparison. In fact, I was flooded with a crisis of identity. What was I doing, anyway? Who was I? A skinny lead guitar player who looked like a chicken? How devastating and embarrassing. I knew that none of the yoga students would dream of saying something so disrespectful. I knew they appreciated the way I led the classes.

During the first week of July everyone came home from the Summer Solstice celebration in New Mexico. I wanted desperately to be included in their circle, to hear the stories, to share the excitement. But it seemed most people were just exhausted from the experience and the traveling, and wanted to be left alone. It also seemed that there was a chasm between those who had gone to the solstice and those who had not. It was as if the solstice people had gained several levels of spiritual advancement—perhaps they had experienced things too profound to even communicate with the unfortunate ones who stayed behind. Larry was more aloof, and seemed more powerful, somehow. I felt intimidated by him now, as I had by Yogiji a few weeks earlier.

Two days after the group returned to Washington, I went in to teach the morning class, which Larry no longer condescended to do, since it was not as well attended as the evening classes. I was

Ganga entranced me with her beautiful eyes, devotion, and intellect. Our friendship has remained intact for more than 50 years.

30 minutes early, so I went back to the kitchen to see if anyone was hanging around. I drew the doorway curtain to one side and looked directly into a pair of unbelievably beautiful golden-green eyes. I was only vaguely aware of the woman's other features. Our eyes had locked, and it felt like several hundred thousand volts of electrical

energy were passing back and forth between us. I heard a voice say, "I'm Peter, what's your name." Another voice, a beautiful, musical voice said, "I'm Ganga, I'm Larry's wife."

"Oh God!" I thought. "How could you do this to me? Ganga is so beautiful! How could she be married? And to Larry!?" I knew Larry had gotten married while at Solstice. But there must have been a mistake. I sensed that Ganga was as stricken with me as I was with her. "We must be meant for each other," I thought. "There must have been some cosmic mix up. Larry was such a cold character. This woman was all alive, creative, sensual, spiritual. She was just like me," I thought. What a disaster. I had fallen in love at first sight with my yoga teacher's wife. I had been told that this was the worst sin imaginable.

But Ganga, evidently attuned to what I was thinking, assumed just enough formality in her voice to let me know that she was not going to be vulnerable to the flights and fancies of our hearts. She was married to Larry, and she was going to play that role with devotion and fortitude. She finished putting together the tray of tea and snacks she had been preparing for him, gently said goodbye and disappeared upstairs. I don't know how I got through the yoga class, or anything else for the next several days. All I could think about was Ganga, her beautiful eyes, her gentle demeanor, and her radiant spiritual energy. A few days later she and Larry drove to New York, where Yogiji was teaching a week-long "intensive" on Staten Island. Again, I was left in charge of teaching the classes in his absence.

Three days later I had just finished the evening class and said goodbye to the last student when the phone rang. I picked it up and said, "Sat Nam." (Sat Nam was the standard greeting among the yoga students, translating roughly as "God's name is Truth." It was meant to recognize the divine in each person.) "Sat Nam," said a voice on the other end of the line. It was Larry. "How are things going down there?" he asked. "We had almost thirty students tonight," I said. "Everything seems to be going pretty well. How is it in New York?" I asked. "It's incredible," he replied. "There is no question that Yogiji is the Living Master of the Aquarian Age. I can't tell you about it now, but will fill you in when I get back to DC." His voice conveyed the solemnity of a deeply held secret, as if he had the inside story on the universe and he was letting me in on a little piece of it. I took the bait. "Wow!" I responded in awe.

"Listen," he continued, "I'd like you to move into the Annex (a house several blocks away where a number of yoga students were living in a loose commune) and take over managing it for me." There was a long silence while I tried to digest this information. "Are you still there?" he asked. "Yes," I said. "Are you ready to make that kind of commitment?" "I think I can do that," I stammered. "Good, and there's another thing. I want you to command the proper respect as the head of that household, and in order to do that you'll need to get married."

"Married!" I responded, incredulous. "But who should I get married to?" "You'll find someone," he said coyly, as if he had someone in mind. I immediately thought of the dark-haired woman who had served tea after my first yoga class. I was under the impression that she was living at the Ashram, though I hadn't seen her for a week or two. I knew nothing about her except that she was of Egyptian heritage and was stunningly beautiful and sensual. "I'll look around," I said. "Are you sure about this?" "It's what Yogiji wants," he answered. "We'll be home in a few days. See what you come up with and let me know." He said, "*Sat Nam*," and hung up.

In order to understand how I could even consider agreeing to such an arrangement, it is necessary to explore some of the ideological framework that Yogiji and Larry had been teaching. We were admonished that emotions were bad—that they should be channeled into devotion. We had also been told that lasting relationships had to be based on shared spiritual commitment, not emotional and physical attraction. Duty and commitment were the highest values, while ego gratification and attachments that came from emotional or sexual relationships were bad, for they led one away from spiritual enlightenment. Numbed by my breakup with Anni, frustrated at the inaccessibility of Ganga, and guilty about my own sexual drive, I was prepared to believe all of this. I was ready to get married to anyone who shared my spiritual beliefs, and it would be even better, I thought, if it was someone I was *not* physically attracted to, for I didn't want sex to play a corrupting role.

In this warped state of mind, I wasted no time in trying to find a wife. For two days I looked for the Egyptian girl, pretending to myself that the attraction was purely spiritual. Just before teaching Yoga class on the second night, I asked one of the other students if he knew where she was. "Yeah," he said. "She went down to Greenbelt, Maryland with David (another yoga student) and a couple of other guys to do an LSD aura cleansing and transcendental transformation." That was more than I wanted to hear, and I immediately ruled her out as a prospective wife.

After class, I searched through the Ashram to see who was there. If I was going to take over as director of the Annex, I could only marry someone who was already committed to the yogic way of life. Why did Anni have to go back with Stew, I lamented. And now that the Egyptian girl was out of the picture, the selection was narrowed to the women living in the Ashram. On the 3rd floor I found two young women – girls actually, as they both appeared to be about 18. Janet and Rose were uncomfortable in my presence, and as little attracted to me as I was to them. I spoke with them for a few minutes about Yogiji and Ashram living, not revealing my purpose. Both were reticent to speak, and seemed painfully insecure. Janet, in particular, was so shy and hesitant that I felt ill at ease even talking with her. She had been to hear Claude Jones play at the Emergency, and I remembered she had been out to the farm once, earlier in the spring for a picnic with a group of yoga students. I recalled seeing her sitting in a corner most of the time with her legs pulled up and head on her knees in fetal pose.

Rose was sweet, but even less communicative than Janet. She sat stiffly like a nun during my brief reconnaissance, as if to say that it was "inappropriate" for a man to be visiting in the ladies' bedroom. "Is this what Larry had in mind?" I wondered. "He had to know that these were the only two women in the Ashram, so he must have intended that I marry one of them. And Larry had said it's what Yogiji wanted, too. And it's bad to base a relationship on sexual attraction," I reminded myself. A wave of guilt swept over me. Only a week earlier, out in the woods behind the Yellow Submarine after one of my band's gigs, I had slept with the little sister of one of my best friends. As we lay in her sleeping bag, she told me I was like salt in her wounds. I didn't know what she meant, but years later learned that she had been raped a week before by members of a motorcycle gang. My sexual drive had become a torment to me, pulling me away from my spirituality, as I saw it, and causing me to inflict pain on people I cared about. Maybe by marrying someone I had no attraction to, I could conquer the demon that was ruling so much of my life—but one of *these* two? I looked back and forth between them. I felt it was a sad choice, but they were the only females in the building, and I was an impulsive and immature 20-year old, determined to obey my spiritual teacher and find a wife.

After a few minutes, I walked back downstairs and stood in the front doorway, contemplating my next move. Was I ready to jump off this cliff? I needed help, a sign from God—something, anything! A thunderstorm was blowing in, and the rain and lightning were just starting to hit. In my experience, nothing could be more romantic than a thunderstorm. I stood there for several minutes as the storm grew in intensity. It was magnificent. I heard someone coming down the stairs behind me and turned to see Janet on her way to the kitchen. I walked to the foot of the stairs as if in a dream and met her as she reached the bottom, spontaneously putting my arms around her and holding her in a long, gentle embrace. Thunder crashed outside.

"Come with me," I said, and led her to the vestibule so we could watch the storm together. Confused and fearful, she complied. I stood behind her and put my arms awkwardly around her waist. For several minutes we stood in silence as the storm raged. Lightning and thunder were all around us. After some time, I stammered nervously, "Let's go to Staten Island and ask the Yogi if we should get married." I could feel her body stiffen in response. "Well, um, you know, I'm not really ready for anything like that," she said meekly. "It doesn't matter," I said. "Let's just see what he says." Another flash of lightning struck nearby with a deafening peal of thunder, and the rain unleashed itself, coming down in torrents while we stood warm and dry just inside the vestibule. "Well," she said. "I guess we could, like, um, you know, just ask."

Later that night I borrowed a car from Ed, an older student who lived on the 3rd floor. I ushered Janet into the passenger seat and we drove to New York. Earlier I had called Larry to get directions and to let him know we were coming. Our destination was a houseboat on the north shore of Staten Island. It was a grueling drive in the dark of night. Janet tried to stay awake to keep me company, but ended up sleeping most of the way. We finally arrived at 4:00 AM. On the roof of the houseboat sat a solitary figure, silhouetted against the pre-dawn sky, with arms outstretched doing breath of fire. We were certainly at the right place! Inside there were dozens of people sleeping, scattered about the floor. Janet and I found a little unoccupied space, lay down in borrowed sleeping bags and went to sleep.

When we awoke at about 6:00 AM, everyone was already up doing yoga. I was proud to see that Larry was leading the group. Larry was Yogiji's chosen favorite, and I now felt privileged and superior because of my close association with him. His prestige was so elevated among the rest of the students that when he taught it was considered "almost as good as Yogiji." Janet and I stayed in the background for a while, but about 9:00 AM, after the morning yoga session had broken up, Yogiji came up from a downstairs bedroom. Larry was with him, and he was looking for us. "So, you're the couple that wants to get married?" Yogiji demanded. "Yes sir," I answered, trying to be strong and decisive. Janet mumbled something incomprehensible and looked at the floor. "Be ready at 11:00 o'clock," he said, and walked past us as if we were of no further importance.

A WEDDING! What a joyous event. And Yogiji was going to perform it himself! Everyone at the houseboat was excited, and the morning was spent making preparations. While Yogiji was occupied downstairs with other devotees, Larry took me to the side and told me some of the secrets of a spiritual marriage that Yogiji had shared with him: that sex was a sacred thing which should only be shared once a month; that Janet should massage my feet with almond oil each evening; that if ever we had a disagreement, I should not condescend to argue, but should hold myself in silence until she gave in and apologized by saying, "You're right, I'm sorry, it is the will of God." He loaned me a pair of white Levi's and a white shirt he borrowed from one of the other yoga students. Larry, who was usually so aloof and distant, was treating me like his younger brother. I basked in the attention. I didn't mind that the pants were six inches too short.

Janet, meanwhile, was also getting a lot of attention. Sonya and

Ganga were helping her find clean, white clothes, and doing up her hair with flowers. They shared with her the same type of "lessons" that Larry was sharing with me, educating her about the woman's duties in a spiritual marriage. Janet, only 18, was swept along by it all, and like me was too insecure to object or say no.

At eleven o'clock everything was ready. All the sleeping bags and sheepskins were rearranged to face an altar that had been hastily assembled in the center of the room. Janet and I were ushered in, along with another couple who, just a few minutes earlier, had decided to take advantage of the opportunity to get married, too. We sat on our heels in a line facing the altar, the two happy couples, side by side. Janet's shoulders were slumped forward, her eyes fixed on the floor. Yogiji came in and sat in front of the altar facing us. The seventy-five yoga students chanting softly in the background fell quiet at a signal from his hand.

"Today," he announced to the assembled crowd in his heavy East Indian accent, "these two couples will join in sacred union. This kind of union is the highest form of Yoga. The saints and sages have said, *'Grust Ashram Mahan Ashram Heh,'* which means there is no higher state than the state of spiritual marriage. Today you leave your egos behind. Your neurosis and psychosis have no place. You will turn your emotion to devotion and you will rise together in the duties and spiritual bliss of this divine union. Do you understand what you are doing?" He glared at us one at a time. Sheepishly, we nodded. "Yes, sir," I mumbled, not sure if it was appropriate to speak at this time.

"Now we will all chant together as you take the holy vow by doing the *Prakarma*, walking slowly around the altar, the woman following the man." Six or seven women, including Sonya and Ganga, stood ready to usher us around the altar. Both couples stood up, and we began the solemn procession, guided by a dozen helping hands. As I passed Ganga, our eyes met. What was I doing marrying

Janet, with whom I felt no connection whatsoever, when the woman with whom I thought I shared the deepest possible connection was standing in front of me, gently touching my hand as I walked by? This was insane! But we were both resigned to our fates and had put duty and devotion above the love we knew we could never consummate. Janet and I and the other couple completed our short circle and sat back down.

The wedding ceremony consisted of four 'rounds' commemorating the vows we were taking. Between each round, Yogiji explained a new level of the commitment we were making. These were vows that could not be broken, he explained, no matter what. Each successive vow was deeper and more binding than the last. With each one, he gave us the opportunity to say no. The burden of taking these vows was on each of us, individually, and each affirmation we made was done in full awareness of the gravity of what we were committing to…at least it was supposed to be. I was overwhelmed at what I was agreeing to, but could not possibly say no. I felt like I was being led to the slaughter.

Yogiji reached into the deepest part of our souls and tied a string of knots from which there would be no escape. The vows were eternal, beyond life and death, never to be torn asunder, even by God himself, he said. I held my head high, trying nobly to submit my soul to the sacrifice that he laid out before me. In this moment my devotion to Yogiji and to the spiritual discipline and ideals he spelled out for me, was absolute. So, too, was my fear of him. There was no turning back. When the last round was complete, the tension in the room finally broke with the celebratory singing of "May the longtime sun shine upon you." Yogiji glanced at Janet, her shoulders still slumped, then fixed a loving gaze on me. "You are a very brave boy, my son," he said. In response I bowed forward, stretched out my arms and touched his feet, just as I had seen Larry do many times.

Janet and I were "married" by Yogi Bhajan on a Staten Island houseboat, July 17, 1970.

CHAPTER FIVE

Wedding Day

AFTER THE CEREMONY, the newlyweds and wedding guests were treated to an informal reception. The devotees on kitchen duty had made a great quantity of Yogi Tea, a delicious, five-spice concoction designed by Yogiji himself, and a wedding cake of the "health food" variety, which hadn't risen. By its consistency and flavor, it more closely resembled an icing-covered energy bar than a wedding cake. But I was grateful for the effort that had been made. Larry then announced that the newly married couples were invited to join a select group who would be going by boat that evening to the Randall's Island Rock Festival, where Yogiji was scheduled to address the crowd.

After the Woodstock festival in 1969, it became 'de rigueur' for the organizers of big music festivals to include talks by Indian holy men. There were many to choose from, but some of the more popular ones were Yogi Amrit Desai (Kripalu Yoga Centers), Maharishi Mahesh Yogi (Transcendental Meditation), Swami Satchitananda (Integral Yoga Institute), Swami A.C. Bhaktidevanta (Hare Krishna), Sant Kirpal Singh (Ruhani Sat Sang), Bhagwan Shree Rajneesh (Auroville), Sant Charan Singh (Radha Soami Sat Sang), Maharaji (Divine Light Mission), and our own Yogi Bhajan. Also present were American counterparts of these spiritual leaders, like Timothy Leary, Steve Gaskin (The Farm), Wavy Gravy (Hog Farm), Baba Ram Dass (Lama Foundation), and Ken Keyes (Loving Light Center). Notably, there were few, if any women on this list of spiritual celebrities.

Most of these dynamic, charismatic spiritual teachers, whose teachings all included the transcendence of the ego—and most of whom were known to their followers as the ONLY "living master of the age"—invariably competed, both personally and ideologically. Sometimes the competition became heated, even violent. Tonight, however, Yogiji's competition would be limited to a stellar array of rock stars and, as it turned out, a drugged-out audience that had little or no interest in the spiritual message he carried. I was thrilled that Janet and I were chosen to be a part of his retinue—it seemed like a privilege of gargantuan proportions.

As soon as the wedding festivities were completed, Janet was given the great honor of being allowed to iron the robes that Yogiji would wear that night. This special privilege was usually reserved for Yogiji's "secretaries," a group of women who, in various numbers, accompanied him everywhere. Janet was even allowed to go downstairs for this task. After mingling with the other yoga students for a while and hearing from them how "special" the ceremony was, how lucky I was to get married in a ceremony performed by Yogiji, and how Janet had looked so beautiful, I was filled to overflowing with goodwill and generosity of spirit. I decided to find Janet and keep her company while she worked. She was in the hallway at the base of the stairs, hunched over the ironing board with a hurt and angry look on her face. I came down the stairs and affectionately put my arm around her.

"What's the matter," I asked tenderly. "I can't do it right," she lamented, full of self-recrimination. She twisted to the left to get away from my proffered arm, and continued in a pouting, frustrated voice, "I can't get these wrinkles out, and I've scorched the fabric." I felt stung by her rejection of my affectionate overture, but let it pass. I looked closely at the garment on the ironing board and saw the slightest discoloration on a tiny area of the hem. "It's not even noticeable," I encouraged her. "It'll be OK."

"No, it won't!" she retorted angrily. "I've ruined it. I can't do anything right." "Sure, you can," I continued, valiantly trying to lift her out of this funk. "That little discoloration will wash right out, and nobody's going to notice anyway. We're going to be on a boat." She was not to be consoled. "You don't know!" she said, "Just go away." I stepped back, alarmed that she would turn her anger and frustration on me. I regarded her silently for a moment. She wouldn't look up, but remained slump-shouldered, dejected and apparently convinced of her own worthlessness. I considered trying once more to help her, but decided against it. Without another word, I turned and climbed back up the stairs.

The yoga intensive had ended with the wedding, and many of the local students had already packed up their things and left. The houseboat was still full of devotees waiting for private appointments with Yogiji, as well as those who would be going to the rock festival. I was in no mood to talk with anyone and climbed up to the roof where I could be alone for a few minutes. I found an obscure corner and tried to meditate, chanting mentally for a while, coordinating the syllables of the mantra with my long deep breathing. It was a challenge to keep my mind from wandering, even though I had been practicing this technique for several months. Soon, the heat of the sun, the excitement of the day, the dizzying effect of the breathing, the weight of the wedding cake, and my lack of sleep conspired together: I leaned back against the railing and slipped into a dreamy sleep.

I was an eagle flying high above the earth. Below me I spotted a lamb grazing on the hillside. Swooping down, I clamped my talons into the lamb's thick wool, intending to fly off with my prey to my aerie haunts. But the lamb was too heavy. I couldn't lift it. I flapped my wings powerfully, then frantically, for my talons were entangled in the fleecy wool. More and more I struggled, exhausting myself with the effort. Realizing I could neither lift my prey nor escape, a wave of panic swept over me. I suddenly awoke. I was sweating and my head was throbbing.

The symbolism of this dream could not have been more to the point. I had made a terrible mistake and was now in big trouble. If only I had not jumped so blindly into getting married. If only I had mustered the courage to say "no" as Yogiji spelled out the real implications of the marriage to which I was committing myself! But it was too late. I had thrown myself off the cliff and there was no going back. I groaned at the thought. I would just have to make the best of it. "Fake it and you can make it," Yogiji had quipped in his yoga classes. It was a modus operandi that was profoundly integrated into the philosophy and lifestyle he taught. I gritted my teeth and resigned myself to the disturbing thought that I would have to spend the rest of my life with Janet.

That evening, just before dusk, about fifteen of us accompanied Yogiji up New York's East River aboard Louie Moonfire's motor launch. Louie was another celebrity fixture at most of the major rock festivals of the day. He was famous for showing up with a following of sheep, goats and other barnyard friends, and a huge sign that proclaimed, "Love Our Animal Friends, Don't Eat Them." He was an icon of both the counterculture and the burgeoning vegetarian movement. He was also quite wealthy, and his motor launch added a level of prestige to Yogiji's arrival—with his entourage—at Randall's Island. It was already dark when we disembarked at the large, concrete landing, and for ten minutes we milled around in confusion while Larry and Louie negotiated with security guards and stage managers for our entry into the festival. I found an empty seat at the end of a concrete bench and sat down. Next to me was a black guy with an enormous Afro. The random beam of a flashlight in the hands of a nearby security guard revealed that my neighbor was Jimi Hendrix.

I was stunned! No one—no one else in the world of rock & roll came close to Jimi Hendrix in my esteem. He was the BEST. For years I had idolized and tried to imitate his phenomenal technique, the amazing tonal range he was able to wrest from his Fender Stratocaster electric guitar, his extraordinary melodic and harmonic sense, and the sheer animal power of his guitar playing and singing alike. I was sitting only six inches away from him! Should I say something, I wondered. Was there any way to engage in a conversation?

"OK. Let's go!" Larry had gotten things worked out with Security. Like a small army, our entourage re-assembled and marched through the gate. Swept into action this way I didn't get a chance to even say hello to Jimi. I glanced back as I joined the group, but he was already lost in the shadows. So, too, I reflected, was my career with Claude Jones. Earlier that afternoon I had made my decision: I was going to leave the band. No longer would rock & roll be the vehicle by which I expressed myself to the world. The rest of the evening only confirmed my resolve. The music at the festival, even Jimi's performance, seemed listless and self-indulgent, the audience jaded and degenerate. The whole scene was dead, a thing of the past. It was time to move on. I was sure I had made the right decision.

My mother was something of an aristocrat. This photo from "The Washington Post" shows her with the plaster model of a stone carving, or boss, that was installed in the ceiling of the "Peace Bay" of the Washington National Cathedral, honoring my grandmother and her family.

CHAPTER SIX

Meeting the Parents

THE NEXT MORNING, before departing for Washington, I called home. I had not spoken with my parents for over three months since the first of April, when I tried to bring Anni with me to my mother's birthday party. My father was waiting for us on the street as we drove up. "Pete," he said, standing at my driver's window, "I think you better just keep on going." "What do you mean, Pop?" I asked. He cleared his throat. "Your mother just isn't ready for this," he said, alluding to the fact that Anni was older than me and was a married woman with a child. There was no arguing with him. After delivering the message, he simply walked away, barely acknowledging Anni's presence. I was mortified. I apologized profusely to Anni, and we drove back to Warrenton.

My mother answered the phone. "Hello, Mom," I enthused. "I've got some good news!" "Oh?" she answered stiffly. "Yeah. I've decided to leave Claude Jones (pause); I've stopped smoking cigarettes and using drugs (pause); I'm moving into the Ashram (long pause); and I just got married (dead silence)." My mother never knew, even if she suspected, that the band members were pot heads and acid-freaks. But it was the part about getting married that upset her the most.

Finally, she responded icily. "Where are you?" "I'm on Staten Island, but we're coming home today. By the way—it's a big drag—but did you know that a man has to be at least 21 in New York to get married? I need to get your signature on the marriage license." I didn't tell her there was no marriage license, nor that Yogiji was not registered in New York to perform marriages—or anywhere else in the country, for that matter. "Who's the girl?" demanded my mother. Her voice was dripping with disappointment and anger. "Her name is Janet, and she's one of the main students at the Ashram," I exaggerated. "How old is she?" Her voice was turning cold. "She's almost 19," I lied. Janet wouldn't turn 19 until October. "Well," she sighed, "Bring her by when you get back, and we'll see."

"It'll be late this afternoon, 'cause we have to go by and visit her parents first. OK?" There was no answer except the sound of the phone hitting the receiver. It had gone about as well as I could have expected.

Janet's parents lived in Bladensburg, Maryland, in a nondescript, two-story, brick apartment complex. My heart sank as we drove into the neighborhood. It was joyless and barren. The inside of their apartment had polyester shag carpets, Sears & Roebuck couches, dime store picture frames, light green Formica counter tops, plastic and aluminum kitchen furniture. Janet's parents did not appear to have much interest in music, art, or literature, but at least they were kind.

Janet's mother, Hazel, welcomed me as best as she could, though her relationship with Janet was strained. Janet had run away from home three years before, when she was 15. She and her mother rarely, if ever, had a conversation that did not end in an argument. Al, Janet's step dad, was a big lumbering fellow, easily three inches taller than I. But he slumped his head and shoulders forward to such a degree that he appeared like a caricature of defeat, and he was so uncertain of himself that he seemed afraid even to shake hands. He only spoke when spoken to, and his voice had a strange drawling tone that made every quavering statement sound like a question.

I felt bad for sizing them up this way. "I'm just an arrogant elitist," I thought. But their home was so oppressive I felt I was suffocating. No wonder Janet ran away. At least she had a survival instinct. As soon as it was decently possible to get away, we said goodbye amid a flurry of gratuitous comments from Hazel about how happy she was to have a new son-in-law.

The next stop was my parents' house in Chevy Chase. The contrast to Bladensburg was so severe that I truly felt sorry for Janet. Even the main thoroughfare, Connecticut Avenue, was magnificent with towering trees and wide sidewalks. Raymond Street, where my parents lived, reflected the fine architecture and planning from the early 1900s when the "Cities Beautiful" movement infused grace and aesthetic appeal into private and public buildings alike. Each home on Raymond Street had charm and individuality. Each yard had trees, gardens, and artistic landscaping. My parents' place looked like a small estate. The three-story house was set back from the street behind a line of ancient maple trees. A generous porch wrapped around the entire front and side of the house, its Ionic columns and railings providing a pleasing offset to the lines of the slate roof above. The front stairs were so wide that when I was younger, our entire family of seven was able to sit side by side for photographs. Everything about the house was artfully designed to be comfortable and gracious without being ostentatious.

I pulled into the driveway and parked at the side of the house. My mother met us at the front door, courteous but restrained. I had not seen her in about six months, and this was not the best of circumstances. I certainly did not feel like the Prodigal Son. Her discerning eye assessed Janet in a glance, and I could tell she was not pleased. This was going to be an ordeal. After serving juice and cookies she invited us to sit with her in the living room. I could see that Janet was both impressed and intimidated by my mother's formality and by the surroundings.

My parents were not rich; they had sacrificed any pretension at wealth in order to provide a first-rate education and music lessons for their five children. But my mother was a well-educated and refined woman who had impeccable taste. She had decorated carefully over the years, enhancing the natural, architectural elegance of the house with fine carpets, classic and antique furnishings and high-quality oil paintings and watercolors, including four magnificent 19th century American portraits of distant ancestors that she had inherited from her mother. Their aristocratic faces looked down on us from within their imposing gilded frames, reminding us sternly of the nobility of our family's heritage. I later learned to my chagrin that one of them had been captain of a slave ship out of South Carolina.

The centerpiece of the living room—in fact, the centerpiece of the house and of our lives growing up there—was an 1881 Steinway grand piano. My mother was an excellent pianist. She was also an artist, writer, poet, and an avid reader of the classics. But her greatest love was music. She and my father, who was a concert cellist, often played together. Even now, some of the richest memories of my childhood are of falling asleep at night to the sound of them performing works for piano and cello by Beethoven, Mozart, and Bach.

The downside of my mother's fine aesthetic sense, however, was a tendency to be aloof and judgmental of those who didn't measure up to her standards. To this shortcoming in my mother's personality, Janet now fell a hapless victim. My mother's incisive questioning revealed that Janet had only a ninth-grade education, that she had spent the previous three years as a hippie, hanging around Dupont Circle, that her parents had divorced when she was only two years old, that her mother lived in Bladensburg, and that, in my mother's opinion, she had a general lack of ambition to do anything with her life that my mother might have found cultured, or useful to humanity.

I looked on with horror. Although Janet came from a disadvantaged childhood that included time in foster care, she was quite intelligent and artistic—and the most powerful ideal we shared was to do something good for humankind by teaching yoga and meditation. From time to time I would try to interject something in poor Janet's defense. But my mother was merciless. She made it clear that she thought her youngest and dearest son was throwing his life away. Instead of seeing that Janet had been traumatized in her youth, and treating her with compassion, she only reinforced the trauma. But her cruelty had the opposite of its intended effect. I refused to acknowledge Janet's "deficiencies" as my mother uncovered them through this interrogation, and only resolved more firmly to see things through.

Janet, whose self-esteem even more compromised than mine, was devastated by the interview with my mother. I was grateful that she did not break down crying, as I was afraid she might. That part she held off until we had said goodbye and were safely in the car on the way back to Dupont Circle and the beginning of our unhappy lives together.

It never occurred to either of us that in the absence of a marriage license we could have walked away from the impending disaster at any time. Instead, we regarded Yogiji's authority as superior to the legal authority of the state, and we were resigned to stay together.

When Claude Jones performed for the second Earth Day in 1971, I was in the audience, bravely sporting a turban, though I felt very conspicuous and foolish that I was not on stage, performing with my former band members.

CHAPTER SEVEN

New Identity

Upon our return to Washington, DC, Janet and I tried to get settled into a third-floor bedroom at the Ashram Annex, a townhouse on T Street, five blocks away from the main Ashram on Q Street. We were the only couple, and Janet the only female living there. Our assigned task was to bring a new level of discipline and dignity to the house and its occupants. All ashram residents were expected to rise each morning at 3:30 AM for 2-1/2 hours of group *sadhana*, a spiritual practice based on yoga, meditation and prayer. In those early days there was no prescribed format, and many of the ashram members, especially those at the Annex, valued the absence of structure, for it allowed them to do their own thing—up to and including sleeping straight through the hours designated for sadhana. I was supposed to get everyone together and make sure they participated. Janet and I were also supposed to make sure that everyone did their part to keep the house neat and clean and abide by the strict vegetarian diet, do no drugs or alcohol, smoke no cigarettes, and have no extramarital sex. The day we moved in, Larry called to tell me that since Janet and I were not legally married yet we, too, should abstain from having sex. It was to be a house full of celibates. It did not occur to me to ask Larry if being married by Yogiji wasn't enough, considering the vows we had taken.

The thrill of being put in charge of the Annex wore off the very first day as I came face to face with the miserable duties laid out for me. I was not a good sadhana enforcer and took no joy in depriving the Ashram anarchists of their freedoms. But I believed in the rules and prohibitions and tried to do my duty, even though it put me in an adversarial position with everyone else in the house. When there was open conflict, which was often, I pulled rank by citing the authority given me by Larry. I even claimed that my mandate came from Yogiji himself. The one good thing about the responsibility was that it motivated me to get up each morning at the appointed time to complete my 2-1/2 hours of sadhana. My duties also entailed teaching the morning classes at the Ashram. Further, I attended the classes each evening that Larry taught. As a result, my body gradually recovered from the years of neglect and abuse, and I soon gained mastery over many of the *asanas* (yogic positions) and certain techniques of meditation.

Janet and I, restrained from consummating our "marriage" by Larry's dictate, developed a kind of friendship borne out of nearly constant companionship and the shared adversarial role into which we were thrust. We lived in the same room, and though we shared little if any affection and never even saw each other undressed, we did manage to connect and to agree on issues of spiritual ideology, as well as on the practical issues of trying to reform the Annex household. The prospect of getting our marriage legalized, however, did not look good. My mother refused to sign the non-existent papers, Yogiji was not yet legally recognized in New York or anywhere else, and I felt ideologically opposed to going to a Justice of the Peace. Even that option would not be available until I turned 21. Mostly, however, I was just not motivated enough to wend my way through the red tape. As a result, we didn't get a valid marriage license until early 1972, just before our first daughter was born.

In late August, Larry and Ganga flew to Los Angeles to attend Yogi Bhajan's birthday party. This was promoted as a huge event, and all of us who were left behind once again felt as if our spiritual destinies had somehow been compromised. I was jealous of the close relationship that Larry had with Yogiji and dreamed of going out to L.A. to be one of Yogiji's special students. I would dedicate my life to his service, live in his household and do anything he told me, even if it meant sleeping two hours a night and meditating for 10 hours a day. I would welcome the discipline, and my spiritual power and authority would grow with each passing day. But it wasn't to be. Instead, I was given the "honor" of driving Larry and Ganga to Washington National Airport for their flight to the West Coast.

Ten days later, I drove back out to the airport to pick them up. That morning I had a dream in which Larry came off the airplane wearing a turban just like Yogiji's. It was a prophetic vision, for just as in my dream, Larry showed up crowned with an impeccably tied, brilliant white turban. He looked great, but my reaction upon seeing him was a mixture of admiration and jealousy. It seemed that he was strengthened and elevated by every interaction he had with Yogiji. I saw the turban he now wore as a special badge of authority and favor. I wanted the same contact and attention from the "master," and was determined to get it one way or another.

A month later, Yogiji was in Washington again. Increasingly, in his classes, he talked about the Sikh Gurus and the teachings they had brought to humankind. The Sikh religion had been started by a spiritual radical named Guru Nanak some five hundred years before. He was the son of a Hindu but was schooled by a Muslim. Rejecting both religions in his teens, he started practicing—then teaching—a way of life based on a daily discipline of prayer and meditation. He traveled by foot throughout India and the Middle East, sharing his wisdom and teachings through songs and parables. His followers became known as *Sikhs*, which means "students." Guru Nanak was followed by a succession of nine other Gurus over the next 200 years, each of whom contributed one or more new facets to the Sikh way of life, until the 10th Guru, Gobind Singh, formalized both the religious practice and the peculiar dress that has distinguished the Sikhs since the early 1700s. The foundation of the Sikh religious service, and the primary activity in a Gurdwara, or Sikh temple, has always been the singing of sacred hymns based on the poetry of the Gurus and other saints and sages from India and the Middle East.

On Saturday evening word spread among the Ashram residents that we were all going to accompany Yogiji the next morning to a religious service at the house of a prominent Indian Sikh. At that time there were two guests at the Ashram who had come to see Yogiji: Lawton and Mark, from Atlanta and Detroit respectively. They had both been to Solstice and were as committed to the yogic way of life as I was. They were also fun-loving and good-natured, and Lawton was a fellow musician. We immediately became friends. That evening they told me they were both planning to get initiated into the Sikh religion the next day. I decided I would join them. The three of us would put on turbans and take whatever vows Yogiji spelled out for us. It seemed to me a natural progression of my commitment to the spiritual path, and I was in good company. It would also put me on a more equal footing with Larry, whose authority over me often felt humiliating, despite my admiration for him.

The next morning Larry helped all three of us wrap turbans on our heads. Mark and Lawton looked fantastic, I thought. They both had full beards and mustaches, which seemed a natural, masculine complement to the ornamental effect of a turban. But I had absolutely no facial hair, and was mortified, when I looked in the mirror, to see that with a turban, I looked exactly like a 15-year-old girl. But I was already determined to go through with this. Beard or no beard, I was going to wear the turban. It was to be a long ordeal: I would have almost no facial hair until I was nearly 30.

The Sikh religious service is a remarkably simple affair, comprised of an hour or two of sacred music, followed by a group *Ardas* or prayer, and finally a *Hookum* or reading from the *Guru Granth Sahib*, the Sikh holy book. The Sikhs do not believe in a living human Guru, but consider the teachings embodied in the Guru Granth Sahib to be their living guide and highest spiritual authority. As a result, this weighty 1,400-page volume of sacred poetry is an object of the highest veneration. The Guru Granth Sahib takes the place of an altar in a Gurdwara and is the focal point of every religious activity. Most of the rituals that have crept into the Sikhs' religious practice over the past 300 years are related to the handling of the Guru Granth Sahib. It is always kept wrapped in regal raiments and, as the living embodiment of the original ten Gurus, is afforded the deferential treatment of royalty.

After getting dressed in our finest white Levis, imported Indian shirts, and newly tied turbans, the Ashram devotees accompanied Yogiji in a caravan to the house of Ganga Singh Dillon in the Maryland suburbs where the service was taking place. Removing our shoes at the front door we solemnly entered the living room, and following Yogiji's example bowed our foreheads to the ground in front of the Guru Granth Sahib, left a dollar offering, and took our seats on the floor—men on one side, women on the other, with an aisle in between.

The floor of the living room was covered with sheets. The Guru Granth Sahib, wrapped in brightly colored material, rested on a low platform behind which sat an elderly Sikh woman who from time to time waved an ornately-handled fly whisk of the purest white horse hair. Above the platform, suspended like a floating pavilion, was a richly decorated piece of material, replete with tassels along its edges and four corners. To the side, facing the congregation, sat two musicians. One played a harmonium, the other a set of tablas, the

Indian hand drums used to accompany most classical Indian music.

I was fascinated with the music. It was being performed in a call and answer style, with the *Ragis* (musicians) singing a line which the congregation then repeated. After each verse, the entire group would join in singing the chorus. I could not follow the words at all, but couldn't help humming along with the chorus, each time it came around. The music was infectious, driven by the exciting, undulating rhythms of the tabla. All around us were seated Indian men in turbans and western clothes, and women in their traditional Punjabi dress. The whole scene was strange and exotic, but I felt at home with it all, especially with the music. Within moments of sitting down, I had determined that someday I would learn how to play the tablas.

As one of the hymns came to a conclusion, Yogiji, speaking in Punjabi, made some arrangement with our host that resulted in Lawton, Mark and me being introduced and ushered to the front. The moment had arrived for the initiation by which we would become Sikhs. The three of us were directed to assemble at one side of the Guru Granth Sahib and sit on our heels. Yogiji sat in front of us and began in heavily accented English: "We are here to initiate you into the holy path of the Sikh. This is a path of Dharma where you lay down your ego and give your heart and head in service of the Guru Granth Sahib. From today onward you will look only to the Guru Granth Sahib as your Guru. If you understand this vow, you must now bow your forehead to the floor." In unison we complied, remaining with our heads bowed until Yogiji told us to sit back up. "Guru Nanak teaches us," he continued, "that a Sikh will rise in the Amrit Vela, the early hours before dawn, and after bathing in the cold water will chant and meditate on God's name. After singing God's praises, you will then carry your prayers in your heart throughout the busy hours of the day. If you understand this vow, you will bow your forehead to the floor." Again, we bowed and waited for Yogiji's instruction before rising.

"As a Sikh you will practice kindness to everyone, remembering that all men and women, and all religions are equal in the eyes of God. You will respect the body that God gave you, leaving your hair uncut. You will not eat meat, drink alcohol, or smoke cigarettes. And in public you will always wear the turban of Guru Gobind Singh (the 10th Guru who formalized the attire of the Sikhs). If you understand and agree to these vows, you will bow your head to the ground." In unison, we bowed. Yogiji let us remain there for nearly a minute before he instructed us to sit up again. I didn't know it at the time, but Yogiji was improvising the whole affair. There was no formal procedure like this for initiating people into the Sikh Religion. There is a baptism ceremony called *Amrit Chakna*, comparable to the Christian confirmation or Jewish Bar Mitzvah, by which Sikhs are formally inducted into the religion when they reach puberty. But no one had ever seen or had to deal with westerners converting to the Sikh way of life.

"You have taken these vows," Yogiji said, "Before God and Guru, and before the *Sadh Sangat* (congregation) of the Sikhs gathered here today. These vows may never be broken, for once on the path of truth there is no turning back. Now you will take your places in the Sadh Sangat and they will welcome you into the *Panth of the Khalsa* (gathering of the pure ones)." This last statement seemed directed to the Indians in the congregation, as if to tell them to accept us as their own. When we stood, beaming with pride and devotion, and went to resume our seats in the congregation, I could see tears in the eyes of some of the old ladies. As I sat down an elderly Sikh gentleman sitting behind me patted me on the shoulder and said in a loud whisper, "Very good, very good!" I turned to acknowledge him and was struck by the look of kindness and love in the old man's eyes. It was a look of such complete acceptance that I felt as if I had come home at last from a journey of many lifetimes.

CHAPTER EIGHT

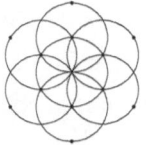

Changes Afoot

Two months later Yogiji was back on the East Coast—this time to take a group of 84 students on an 84-day *Yatra* or holy pilgrimage to India. Larry and Ganga, and two of my friends from the Yellow Submarine were going, as well as a couple of the better-off students in the Ashram. Janet and I were to be left behind this time, with the promise that we would get our chance on the next trip. "Besides," Larry appeased with flattery, "I need you to keep things together here at the Ashram while we're gone. No one else is qualified." They were to be gone for 12 weeks.

I drove Larry and Ganga to New York, where we met up with the rest of the group. The scene at Kennedy Airport was almost riotous. By late 1970, Yogiji had sent teachers to start ashrams in at least 50 cities throughout the US, and most of the Ashram directors were now wearing turbans. Most of them were also joining the Yatra, so that about half the group already looked like Sikhs.

Yogiji was returning to India "victorious," the only Sikh in history to carry the message of the Sikh Gurus to westerners on a massive scale. He was already claiming that there were over 100,000 American "Sikhs," which might have been true if every student who had ever attended at least one yoga class could be counted as a Sikh. This trip would turn Yogiji into an instant celebrity and hero among the Sikhs in India. It would also prove to be a defining moment for him and for us in several other ways.

Since coming to America, Yogiji had been promoting his own teacher, Maharaj Virsa Singh, as the "living master of the age," the person under whose guidance Yogiji had found liberation while chanting the same mantra he had been teaching to all his American Yoga students. Even the flyer I had picked up at my first yoga class had cited Maharaj Virsa Singh as Yogiji's teacher and the source of the mantra I had just learned. Most of the yoga students going on the Yatra held the expectation that Virsa Singh was going to be even more incredible than Yogiji. They were disappointed.

After a warm reception by the Maharaj and his followers upon landing in Delhi, the group of Americans rapidly became aware that things were not entirely Kosher. According to Larry's account, Virsa Singh demanded that Yogiji turn over to him all his students, as well as any money they had given him. Yogiji refused on both counts. It struck me as odd that the American students' money was an issue for discussion. The implication that Yogiji had control over it was also not lost on me. This issue caused an irreparable rift between the two spiritual giants. There was another dark side to the antagonism between them: Yogiji later claimed that Virsa Singh had seduced his wife. Not only was Yogiji no longer welcome at Virsa Singh's Ashram, the tension between them threatened to play itself out in violence perpetrated by Virsa Singh's followers. The members of the American Yatra quickly relocated to a mango farm on the outskirts of Delhi, where they camped in tents. Attempts were made to negotiate a peaceful settlement with Virsa Singh, but to no avail. The antagonism and threats of violence lasted for years.

The group of Americans eventually left Delhi for a visit to the Golden Temple in Amritsar, eight hours to the north by train. Here, Yogiji and his followers were welcomed with open arms. The Shriomani Gurdwara Prabandak Committee (SGPC), the chief administrative body for all the historic Gurdwaras in India, provided housing for the entire group and treated them as VIP's. To cement the status of the newly converted Americans even further, Yogiji arranged for several of his students, including Larry and Ganga, to be formally baptized into the *Khalsa*, the "company of the pure ones," in a ceremony at the *Akal Takhat*, the holiest shrine in all of Sikhdom.

Ganga later recounted the circumstances. "We were never told about it; we were just following Yogiji around the Prakarma (a broad marble walkway around the Golden Temple compound) when he instructed a bunch of us to go up a narrow flight of stairs. We thought he was coming with us but an armed *sevadar* (servant) closed the door, and when we got to the top of the stairs, there was a small room with 5 fierce looking Sikhs with their swords drawn. We were instructed to take off our pants and stand there in our underwear. I thought we were going to be murdered or raped or both. Instead, we got roped into some very hefty vows. There wasn't one of us who wasn't shaking with fear."

This formal induction ceremony called for strict observance of the Sikh way of life, including the daily reading of five *Banis* or prayers (about 2 hours'-worth), and the wearing of the "five Ks"— *Kara* (a steel bracelet to signify strength), *Keshas* (uncut hair to signify acceptance of the body given by God), *Kanga* (a comb worn to signify personal cleanliness), *Kirpan* (a small dagger to signify willingness to defend the truth at all costs), and *Kacheras* (a loose fitting underwear to signify chaste behavior). The vows involved in this ceremony were so severe and so well respected among the Sikhs that the Americans who took them were afterwards accorded celebrity status. And the prestige this brought to Yogiji gave him access to the political elite of India. On future trips we would meet variously with Prime Minister Indira Gandhi, President Giani Zail Singh, Governor of Rajasthan and former Speaker Sardar Hookum

Singh, and many other political leaders and celebrities.

In a ceremony at the front of the Akal Takhat, Yogiji was formally recognized and thanked for his work in bringing so many Americans into the folds of the Sikh Religion, and it was after this that we began referring to him as "Siri Singh Sahib"—a title that he said had been bestowed on him by the SGPC (a claim hotly disputed by researchers and the SGPC itself).

With the growing visibility and fame, it was a challenge for Yogiji to maintain the image of his American students as a group of devoted Sikhs. Many of them were little more than tourists, coming along for an inside look at India, and only a few were devoted students of the caliber of Larry or Ganga. While staying at the mango farm outside Delhi, several had succumbed to the temptation offered by the cannabis that grew abundantly between the trees. Among the group were also several unmarried couples, a potential public relations disaster in the rigid moral environment of Indian culture at the time. Yogiji arranged a group wedding to solve this dilemma. Most of the couples complied, but my friends from the Yellow Submarine wouldn't do it. When I heard about it later, I was shocked at their lack of devotion. How could they refuse a direct request from Yogiji, I wondered? Anyone who had read *Autobiography of a Yogi* should know that liberation only comes as a result of absolute and unquestioning faith in one's spiritual teacher.

By the time the group came back from India six weeks later, it seemed that we had turned a new chapter in our evolution as an organization. Not only was Maharaj Virsa Singh out of the picture, replaced by Yogiji as the foremost living master of the Aquarian Age (in our estimation, at least), our loosely strung together family of ex-hippie yoga students was also quickly being reshaped into a viable religious group. Instead of just the 3HO Foundation (Healthy Happy Holy Organization), which existed to teach Kundalini Yoga and Meditation, we were now "Sikh Dharma of the Western Hemisphere."

Yogiji quickly leveraged his assumed title of Siri Singh Sahib into a new hierarchy within the American Sikh community, first by using it to gain legal recognition for himself as an "ordained minister" based on Sikhism. This opened the door for the heads of ashrams and their lieutenants, as well as Yogiji's own secretaries and the regional directors to become ordained and to bear their own titles. Larry became a "Mukhia Singh Sahib"—as did the heads of the other geographical "regions" Yogiji had created within 3HO ("Mukhia Sardarni Sahiba" in the case of women). The heads of ashrams became simply Singh Sahib or Sardarni Sahiba. Within a year or two I was also "ordained" (by decree from Yogiji) and became "Singh Sahib Sat-Peter Singh Khalsa," legally registered as a minister of the Sikh Religion in DC, Maryland, and Virginia to perform weddings, funerals, and other religious functions.

The transition from secular yoga organization to a recognized religion was an awkward one. Many people who were drawn to yoga and meditation, even within our existing family of students, were turned off by any reference to religion. It was difficult, therefore, with our now highly visible religious affiliation, to appeal to the public on the basis of yoga and meditation alone. In my own yoga classes I would try to downplay the religious part, claiming that Sikh Dharma was not a religion, but a "way of life." At the same time, we were trying to gain respect, credibility, and acceptance in the media and on Capitol Hill based on the Sikh Dharma being the "fourth major religion" of the world. "With fifteen million Sikhs worldwide," we would claim, "The Sikh religion has more adherents than the Jewish faith." (As of this writing there are more than 22 million Sikhs worldwide.)

There was another pressing issue driving our need to be recognized as a legitimate religious organization. Yogiji was coming under fire from the "anti-cult" groups. Throughout America there was a growing fear about the dangers of cults. Charismatic "spiritual leaders" were "brainwashing America's youth," and using their personal power to take over the minds, bodies, and finances of their students. So great was the power of these cult leaders, it was feared, that their students would do virtually anything they were told—up to and including having sex with the 'master,' giving him (or her) all their money, even killing people or committing mass suicide at his command. There were (and are) dozens of frightening examples, from Charles Manson to David Koresh and Jim Jones. Was Yogiji one of these? "No way!" we exclaimed. "Sikh Dharma is a legitimate religion, and Yogiji its highest religious authority in the Western Hemisphere, as recognized by the SGPC." It was an important argument, not only with the media but also with the parents of almost every yoga student and Ashram member.

In my mind I ran through the key criteria that defined cults, but never questioned whether Yogiji actually fit the profile of a cult leader. Did he take his students' money? He didn't take mine, because I didn't have any. But, yes, I knew of quite a few people who willingly gave large sums of money to him, even their entire inheritance in some cases. But this was done out of their own free will. They were responsible, intelligent adults and knew what they were doing. Did Yogiji have sex with his students? There were always allegations, but this was something I could never believe. He was a perfect living Master and would never do something like that. Besides, he denied every allegation, and I believed him. Would his students do anything he told them to do? I acknowledged that this was a difficult question for me. I couldn't deny that my belief in him was so strong that I might do almost anything he asked. I was glad that I was never really tested by this question. For many years Yogiji never asked me to do anything that I could question on moral grounds, such as doing harm to someone, and I believed that he never would.

In the spring of 1971, Yogiji was in Washington DC again. Our Ashram community had grown steadily, and we were now the second largest Ashram in the country, deserving of a great deal of Yogiji's attention. This time he brought his wife, Bibiji. Bibiji had been left behind in India for nearly two years when Yogiji first came to America by way of Canada in late 1968. They had a strained relationship, a fact that was obvious when they were together, and which Yogiji even alluded to from time to time. Bibiji's loyalties had been caught in the middle of the conflict with Maharaj Virsa Singh. We never knew the details, but Yogiji had publicly stated he would never again have sexual relations with his wife. I was struck by how strange it was that this would be an item for public knowledge—especially after I met Bibiji, who I thought was wonderful. But I refrained from trying to understand my spiritual master in normal human terms. He was, after all, a liberated being, and not subject to the rules by which we judge ordinary men—at least so I believed.

When Yogiji and Bibiji visited the Ashram, I got a chance to spend some precious time alone with them. My reputation as a musician had been conveyed to them, and Yogiji thought it would be a good idea for Bibiji to teach me some *shabads* or sacred hymns of the Sikhs. The following morning, we were all going to Gurdwara (the term refers not only to a Sikh Temple, but also to the religious service, which can take place virtually anywhere), and Yogiji wanted me to perform a shabad. For several hours Bibiji worked with me, helping me transliterate from a small book of hymns written in the Gurmukhi script of the Punjabi language. I struggled with the words and the pronunciation: *Ik Ardas, bahaat keerat kee, Guru Ram Das rukho sernai.* ("I have one prayer oh Lord: Guru Ram Das protect your servant.") I set the lyrics to a melody and chords that I made up on the spot, and tried to memorize it all so that I could play it at the service the next morning. Yogiji and Bibiji seemed pleased with my efforts.

The next morning an army of young American Sikhs descended on the house of Ganga Singh Dillon (by now most of the people living in the Ashram had put on turbans.) Halfway through the service, I was called upon to sing. I sat next to the Guru Granth Sahib, placing on top of a harmonium the transcribed words I had scribbled out the evening before. I felt nervous under the scrutiny of the Indian Sikhs in the congregation, who seemed to regard me with a mixture of disbelief and bemused tolerance. Turbans on westerners were still a novelty, but an American playing the holy music of the Sikhs on a guitar was unheard of. They seemed simultaneously thrilled and threatened. I played a few chords, tuned the guitar quickly and began. I had completely forgotten the melody I made up the previous evening and was forced to improvise. I struggled with the words, squinting at my own messy handwriting, trying to fit the syllables into some logical musical phrasing. "*Hum avgun bhareh, Ik gun nahi, Amrit Chaad, Bickeh Bikh Kai.*" There was no call and answer, and no one sang along with me.

Verse after verse I encountered like a wave of adversaries, each one prepared to stymie me. I limped along, not even able to maintain a consistent melody from line to line. But my skills at improvisation, honed from the years of playing with Claude Jones (I used to brag that I had never played the same solo twice) came to my rescue. I finished the last verse with an artistically rendered instrumental ending and bowed my head respectfully. I did not know how my musical offering had been received. The solemnity of the occasion prevented any expression whatsoever, either of praise or criticism.

But after the service, during *langar*—a delicious North Indian meal that follows every major Sikh service—a number of men and women congratulated me. One even told me that my pronunciation had been excellent. I had to laugh, for I knew only too well that it had been terrible. But that would change. Many of us in the Ashram were about to start learning to read, write, and speak Punjabi. And within 18 months I, too, would be traveling to India as a representative of Yogiji and the American Sikh community.

We American Sikhs were embraced by our native Punjabi counterparts, and many warm and friendly relationships evolved. Here I am shown with Larry and Giani Mohinder Singh, one of the top administrators of the SGPC, the main religious authority of the Sikhs that oversees the administration of all the historic Gurdwaras in India.

Janet and I were invited to speak about our "life lessons learned" to the 300 or so participants of the summer solstice celebration in 1971 at the end of an intensive 4-hour session of yoga. I was 21 and Janet only 19. I remember saying that I had learned not to count on my own plans coming to fruition, since life continually throws us curve balls.

CHAPTER NINE

My First Solstice Celebration

As the summer of 1971 approached, Janet and I began making arrangements to attend the Summer Solstice celebration, which that year was being held in Paonia, Colorado, 9000 feet above sea level in the middle of the Rocky Mountains. This was doubly exciting for me, for not only would it be my first Solstice, Paonia was also only a few miles from the town of Delta, where my grandfather had grown up as a cowboy in the late 1800s. In my early childhood I had heard from him wonderful stories about his adventures "out West." His brother Clarence, my great uncle, had lived with us in Chevy Chase for several years after his wife died, and he, too, had told me stories. When my grandfather heard that I was going to Paonia he gave me a color-coded, molded-plastic topographical map of the area and recounted to me some of my family history.

My great-grandfather, Andrew Trew Blachly, had tried to make his fortune as a rancher in the old west, but had been unsuccessful. He and his wife, Adele, were both connected through their parents to Oberlin College and Adele was an alumna, but their marriage had not been approved by either of their parents, for Trew and "Dellie" were first cousins. Colorado was a refuge for them, away from the social pressures of their disapproving families. But life was hard. By 1893, Dellie had eight children and another one coming. My grandfather, the second oldest, was 13. They were living in a two-room, dirt-floor shack and had not enough money for either clothes or food. After a terrible winter in which many of his livestock died, my great-grandfather took work as cashier and part owner of the First Farmers and Merchants Bank, the only bank in Delta. That August, while on the way back from a trip to Oregon, the country was facing one of its worst financial crises, and banks were failing everywhere. Anticipating a run on his own bank, Andrew Trew stopped in Grand Junction and was able to borrow enough cash from a bank there to prevent the First Farmers and Merchants Bank of Delta from folding.

It might have been better if he had not saved the bank, for a couple of weeks later on the morning of September 7, 1893, the infamous McCarty brothers, an offshoot of the James Gang, robbed the bank. During the robbery my great-grandfather was shot and killed, leaving his wife and eight young boys to fend for themselves.

Hearing these stories had made me curious and excited to learn more. When I got to Delta, I found there was still a plaque on the wall of a local bank commemorating the robbery, and a small historical society that displayed the guns used in the robbery and photographs of two of the bandits who had been shot and killed while trying to make their getaway. Apparently, it was the biggest thing that ever happened in Delta, before or since.

For the trip to Colorado, I would be driving a 1955 Chevy station wagon I had bought for $75 from one of the yoga students. What a great car! It had a 265 cubic inch V-8 engine and a Hurst shifter on the floor (known among drag-racing circles for its ease and speed in shifting gears). To help pay for the trip we were giving a ride to two of the other women from the Ashram, and to save money we would be staying at various Ashrams along the way. One of the great joys of being a part of the 3HO family in those early days was that by 1971 we were never more than a day's drive from an Ashram, and the feeling of family among us was generally so close that we were always guaranteed a warm welcome, especially at the smaller "outposts" in places like St. Louis or Kansas City.

Most of these smaller Ashrams were in low to middle-income, inner-city neighborhoods that were, like our Ashram at Dupont Circle, on their way back up. All were set up as communes with the head teacher in charge, usually along the same kind of authoritarian model that we had in Washington, DC. There were some advantages to this model. The ashrams were always fairly clean, the meals communal and well organized, and the logistics of overnight stays easy to arrange. In every Ashram the largest common space was the living room, which served as both the classroom for public yoga classes and the communal space for morning sadhana. As the religious aspects of Sikh Dharma gradually gained dominance, this space also served as a temple, and both before and after Solstices it served for several days as a kind of hostel for travelers visiting from other Ashrams. In most cases it was a lot of fun to travel by car to a solstice celebration, for it gave an opportunity to visit with old and new friends along the way, and the people in smaller towns were usually as glad for the company as the travelers were for a place to spend the night.

Except for our overnight visits to the Ashrams along our route, and a blown clutch near Evergreen, Colorado—which caused an unscheduled camping trip on the side of a mountain and an arduous solo effort on my part to remove and replace the transmission to install a new clutch plate—our trip to Paonia was uneventful. But the Solstice celebration was incredible. We were camped out in a cherry orchard—over 300 of us rising each morning in the frosty pre-dawn to bathe in a frigid irrigation ditch and do our morning sadhana as one large group under the trees. The first morning, like the band of ex-hippies we were, everyone stripped naked—men and women together—and bathed in the same area. Word came down from Yogiji later that day that we were required to wear swimming trunks or underwear while bathing, and that men and women had to bathe in separate sections of the ditch.

Our diet was intense: spicy potato onion soup in the morning, super-spicy beans and rice in the evening, both served with a wedge of iceberg lettuce. Yogiji directed the food preparations and delighted in dumping box after box of cayenne pepper into the giant woks in which dinner was cooked. It was a "cleansing diet," he laughed, though for the first three days virtually everyone was constipated. On the third day, as if by magic, everyone had to go at once, making a comical scene as 300 people simultaneously lined up at the latrines.

But the biggest excitement was that Yogiji was, for the first time ever, teaching Tantric Yoga. Every afternoon we gathered, sitting in long rows, men and women facing each other to do exercises as couples under his direction. Never before had I experienced anything either so difficult or so rewarding. Each exercise seemed harder than the last. We would hold our arms straight out with our palms turned up, or our legs raised to 60 degrees, or our arms with palms together stretched above our heads—and hold these difficult positions for 31 minutes, or even 62 minutes at a stretch. Combined with the positions would be long, deep breathing, breath of fire, or chanting of a mantra. And the entire time we would stare into our partner's eyes. People were collapsing or just giving up right and left, only to be coaxed back into the exercise by "monitors" who navigated between the rows to keep everyone in line.

By the end of each day, we were all completely wiped out, but in such an altered state that everything about the experience took on epic, if not magical proportions. On several evenings we broke into spontaneous celebration, with guitars and drums seeming to appear out of nowhere to drive a frenzied release of pent-up emotions in dance and song. These were the moments I loved the best. I would join fellow musicians in improvising rhythms, chords, and melodies to accompany the various mantras we had learned. With 300 enthusiastic voices joining in we could go for an hour or more on the simplest melody. Our shining faces, reflected in the firelight, revealed the ecstasy we all felt. Eyes met eyes with love and absence of judgment. We were, each one of us, "clear channels." Together as a group, we felt we could transform the world. As things wound down each evening, the music would take on more meditative tones, and by the time we ended with the obligatory "May the long time sun shine upon you," our collective spirits felt indescribably transcendental.

In my experience, no solstice celebration ever recaptured the fire and passion we shared at Paonia, though I was always hoping for it and trying to recreate it. The experience re-energized me and confirmed in my heart and soul the absolute correctness of my path. Another important thing had happened: I had met and played with a number of excellent fellow musicians. We had written songs together, played for the group, been recognized, and had received validating praise from Yogiji. The new friends I made and the musical endeavors upon which we would soon embark would play an incredibly important role in my life for years to come.

When Yogi Bhajan first started teaching what he called "White Tantric Yoga" in June 1971, each course would last for 10 days, 4-hours per day. It was exhausting, but incredibly exhilarating and inspiring.

CHAPTER TEN

Tantric Yoga

BACK IN WASHINGTON, DC, we did not have to wait long for Yogiji to come for another visit. In August he was there to teach a course in Tantric Yoga, the first in a long series that would take him all over the world. The Tantric Yoga courses were particularly successful, not only in drawing many more people into the 3HO family, but also for bringing money into the organization's coffers. There were a lot of expenses. Yogiji's staff had grown to about ten women, and only Shakti Parwah, the "mother" of 3HO, earned her own living with an "outside job." She worked tirelessly as a waitress and gave selflessly of her time and energy to support the mission of the organization. The rest of the "secretaries" were housed, clothed and fed, and their Mercedes and travel expenses paid for by the money Yogijii was able to bring in. His teaching schedule was understandably rigorous.

The Tantric course in Washington was held in the auditorium of a local church. It was an enormous success. About 150 people came, each paying $100 for the four-hour-per-day, ten-day course. Not only local students and ashram members attended; students came from all over the East Coast, and from as far west as Missouri. It was wonderful having people come from far and wide. Yogiji was like a magnet for young people of shared intentions and ideals, and at each of his courses I would meet new friends. Most of us were in our late teens or early twenties. My particular job at this course, and at most other functions I participated in for years to come, was to lead the group in singing and chanting before Yogiji's arrival. It was a high-visibility position to which I was well suited. Not only did it gratify my need for creative musical expression, it also satisfied my ego, for I thrived on the attention of the students and Yogiji alike. At the time it was for me quite gratifying when meeting new people to be recognized as someone "important," especially if the new people were attractive women.

Yogiji had given us instructions in advance that during the ten days of the course the participants should eat only fruit that grew at least four feet above the ground. This was a difficult challenge. After four days, most of us were feeling so spaced out or low on energy that we begged for a remedy. He told us to hold out as long as we could, and that if we felt the practical demands of our daily lives required our being more "grounded" we could eat an avocado. I held out until the seventh day. When I finally gave in, just the taste of the avocado on my tongue sent a tingling, electrical sensation throughout my entire body, and with each bite I felt more energized. By the time I finished eating, I felt like Superman.

A lot of Yogiji's teachings revolved around food and health. His storehouse of knowledge in this area was immense. He was adamant about eating organic foods, abstaining from meat, and using food to cure all manner of physical ailments. Onions, ginger, and garlic were high on his list of curative roots, and our diet was generally loaded with them. Yogiji would often give students special diets whose healing effects, he claimed, ranged from purely physical to emotional and spiritual. The effects were often noticeable and highly beneficial. Sometimes these special diets were horrible, like a week of nothing but daikon radish juice. But they were often delicious and naturally healing in their simplicity, like a month of nothing but mung beans and rice cooked according to Yogiji's own spicy recipe. So powerful were the healing qualities of Yogiji's dietary prescriptions that we were able to help long-time heroin addicts quit their habits and go through detox with no withdrawal symptoms using only Kundalini Yoga and diet.

There was certainly no question that the fruit-only diet during the ten days of the Tantric Yoga course had an enhancing effect on the exercises and meditations we did. Toward the end of the course, the meditative states we were reaching were more and more profound. It was usually in these most "cosmic" moments—when everyone was feeling blissful from the rigors of exercise, breathing, and chanting or singing together—that Yogiji would elicit deeper levels of commitment from his students. Towards the end of the ninth day, he asked several of the Ashram members—both from our own Ashram and from other cities—to stand up. He looked the group over for a few seconds, then started matching men and women up as couples. All the rest of us looked on and cheered. This was great fun! Within a few minutes, Yogiji had "engaged" three new couples—men and women who had never even met before—and announced that they would get married the next day. We believed that he was a master who could see our auras and read our destinies. No one was better qualified to make spiritually appropriate matches. The chosen couples looked at each other and gulped.

A similar match-up, but on a much larger scale, had just occurred in Paonia. About a dozen couples had left Paonia in brand new, arranged marriages, including several of my fellow yoga students from Washington, DC, and my new friend, Lawton, who got married to Rose, as well as several other of my fellow yoga students from Washington. It was evident that a big part of Yogiji's agenda was to get all the single people in the Sikh Dharma securely married to each other. As it turned out, this strategy filled a number of purposes. It generally kept the single men from certain indiscretions with their female students; it protected single men and women from the potential risks involved in looking for partners outside of the Dharma (mainly the risk of being pulled away from Yogiji's influence); and it helped jump-start new Ashrams: instead of just one person being sent to a new city to start a yoga center, it was a lot more effective to send a highly committed couple; and it helped to consolidate relationships and distribute human resources between various Ashrams around the country. For example, our Ashram had lost at least four people to other cities because of the marriages at Paonia. But with these new marriages we were gaining six—for a part of Yogiji's instruction to them was that they should move to DC to live in Ahimsa Ashram where they could study with Larry and Ganga.

There was another, more insidious "benefit" to these arranged marriages. Most of these couples, like Janet and me, were not in love. Their relationships were ideological rather than emotional. Their true emotional attachments, disguised as spiritual devotion, were not for each other, but for Yogiji. As such, he was able to manipulate and control almost every couple in the organization by exercising his influence with one or the other, and often both of the partners. But we didn't see this as manipulation. Those of us who were most devoted, accepted his interference in our private lives as an honor. We were delighted to have the personal attention of our spiritual master turned to even the most mundane and intimate details of our lives.

The last day of the Tantric Yoga course was a very special one for me. Yogiji had already described to us the process he had to go through while teaching Tantric: He would extend himself in his psychic body to every student in the class, and during the exercises would be working with each one of us individually on the spiritual plane. Because of this deeply empathetic relationship, he explained, he was extremely vulnerable to any changes in the magnetic field of the group. When someone gave up in the middle of an exercise, or got up to go to the bathroom, or did anything else that was out of sync with the rest of the group, Yogiji could feel it, he claimed, and it was physically painful to him. His entreaties to us, therefore, to "keep up" in the exercises, had an added level of force, for none of us wanted to be responsible for causing him pain. After nine days of teaching, the ravages of this form of psychic self-sacrifice had apparently taken their toll. Yogiji said he needed a quiet place away from the noise and energy of the Ashram where he could rest and recuperate for a few hours. My parents were spending a few weeks in Maine at the time, so I suggested their house in Chevy Chase. I was amazed and overjoyed that he accepted. No one else would be going except Yogiji, Premka (his top secretary) and me.

I immediately called my parents in Maine to get their permission. I knew it might be difficult. Three years earlier, while they were on vacation, I had moved the entire Claude Jones band into the house for a month without their knowledge or permission. By the time they came back, there was no hiding the fact. Cigarette burns marred the carpets, and the place was filthy despite of our half-hearted efforts to clean it up. My mother had found an odd pair or two of women's underwear stuffed into unlikely hiding places. But the worst physical damage was upstairs, where the plaster ceiling in the second-floor guest bedroom had fallen in. Frank, our bass player, and his wife, Connie, had been in bed at the time, and it had fallen on top of them. There did not seem to be any particular connection, or reason why it should have happened. It was just bad luck for me and bad timing that it was while we were all in the house. More damaging than the physical evidence, however, were the reports from neighbors who had witnessed the steady parade of hippies and beat-up cars that were in and out, and the incredibly loud music emanating from our basement at all hours of the day and night.

My parents were so livid when they returned, they would barely talk to me. A few weeks later they threw me out of the house. I had borrowed my brother's car to visit some friends at St. Johns College in Annapolis, promising I'd be home by 9:00 PM. When I called at about 11:00 PM to tell them I wanted to spend the night, my father got on the phone and told me in no uncertain terms that I was to drive home immediately. When I walked in the front door at about 12:30 AM he was waiting for me with a belt in his hand. He cursed and swore at me while swinging away, backing me into a corner where I tried to cover my head and face from the blows he was raining down on me. I was appalled at the injustice and malice of this extreme response. I had never seen my father do anything so brutal, and in my recollection, this was the first and only time in my life that he physically beat me. I yelled back at him that I wouldn't fight back, "Because I'm a PACIFIST!" He wasn't impressed. Ten minutes later I was on the street with a suitcase, walking the mile and a half to "Little Gray" on Military Road to join my friends from Claude Jones.

My mother answered the phone at the cabin in Maine. When I explained what I wanted, I could feel the chill. But before she could actually say "no" I continued, explaining that it was only for a couple of hours and that it was really important to me. Understandably reluctant, she finally agreed, warning me that the place better be perfect when she got home. I assured her that it would be, thanked her and said goodbye. I had partially redeemed myself three months earlier by going up to Maine and replacing a pier that had been carried away in a winter storm. It had been a week of hard work cutting trees, building a crib and filling it with several tons of rock. Under the circumstances, the use of her house for two hours seemed like a relatively small favor.

When we got to my parents' house, I set Yogiji up in the guest bedroom on the second floor. It was a lovely room with a comfortable queen-size bed. I was sure he would find it to his liking. He was going to take a nap for a few hours, then the three of us would have some lunch together before heading back downtown to the Ashram. I offered to give him a foot massage to help him sleep. Massage, especially foot massage, was another key component of Yogiji's healing methodology. I was already well versed in the techniques from studying two of the leading books on the subject, Eunice Ingham's *Stories the Feet Can Tell* and *Stories the Feet Have Told*, and with my strong hands and mostly intuitive sense of touch I was quite good at it. Yogiji accepted my offer, so I got a towel and some almond oil and went to work while he laid down with his head propped on the pillow. For a long time, I concentrated on my work. Yogiji was a big man. His legs were like tree trunks and he had enormous feet. Foot massage, the way he liked it, required deep penetration of the muscles, which required a great deal of physical and mental effort.

I spent about a half hour on each of his feet and was just finishing up when I became aware that he was peering at me through half-closed eyes. Yogiji said nothing, but I felt strangely compelled by him. A shock of ill ease jolted me as I realized that the energy in the room, and in my thoughts, was tangibly sexual. I freaked out. "It must be me," I thought. "He has a pure aura. He is a liberated living master, and the only reason I'm having these thoughts is that he has uncovered in me some latent homosexual tendency." I was terrified. I resisted the thoughts, banished them from my mind. "No way!" I told myself. "I'm not gay! And he wouldn't be putting out sexual energy, least of all towards me!" As I went through this agonizing mental process, I felt that he could see straight through me, that he knew exactly what was going on in my mind. I continued to massage his feet and gradually regained my composure. A few minutes later, I got up to leave. "Tell Premka to come up and see me," Yogiji said as I was closing the door. I went downstairs, found Premka sitting in the kitchen, sent her upstairs, and went out in the backyard for a while to think through this very strange incident. It was very disturbing to me, for I internalized the cause of it entirely, never thinking for a second that Yogiji could have had anything to do with it other than providing a pure "mirror" upon which the impurities and corruption of my own mind would stand out in stark relief.

About an hour later Yogiji and Premka came downstairs looking oddly refreshed. Yogiji was in an excellent mood and insisted on cooking us some lunch. Premka and I helped in little ways, cutting up the onions and garlic, but it was Yogiji's meal. I felt deeply privileged and blessed to be eating food prepared specially for the three of us by the hand of my master. "Did your father die recently?" Yogiji surprised me as we sat eating. "No," I answered, "He's in Maine with my mother." "Is there someone else who died here?" he probed, "An old man?" I thought for a moment. "My uncle Clarence died recently," I answered, "and he used to live here. He even tried to commit suicide one day by swallowing a bottle of aspirin. But he's been living for the past few years in Silver City, New Mexico." "Well," said Yogiji, "He's here now."

I was deeply impressed. I believed that Yogiji was sensitive to psychic phenomena. He had told us of the special work he did during the early morning hours when we were doing sadhana: he would sit in meditation, contacting lost souls and guiding them through the astral planes so that they could be either liberated, or reborn for another lifetime. It did not surprise me that he had sensed a ghost in my parents' house. I was surprised only that he had not been able to identify it accurately—especially that he would think it was my own father, who was very much alive. "Is there anything we can do to help him get liberated?" I asked innocently. "Your parents should feed the poor," he answered. "They should have poor people come to the house and they should feed them." I always meant to tell my parents how they could liberate Uncle Clarence, but I never got around to it. I just never quite knew how to bring it up.

CHAPTER ELEVEN

A Dysfunctional Marriage

It was now more than a year since Janet and I had gotten married. It was a most difficult relationship. Other than our shared devotion to Yogiji and our commitment to the Sikh way of life, which to us was synonymous with the teachings of Yogiji, we did not see eye to eye on almost anything. I was an extrovert who loved social interaction with all kinds of people. She was so insecure and introverted that Yogiji mockingly nicknamed her "Paranoia Kaur," (Kaur, which means "Princess," is a standard surname for all Sikh women). At the time I felt vindicated by this, little realizing how his cruelty only retraumatized her. All her friendships were challenged, and in most cases destroyed by her propensity to escalate petty disagreements and misunderstandings into major, irresolvable conflicts. Although she was so self-negating as to inspire pity and compassion, she would invariably redirect blame for any conflict upon the other party or parties. As a result, she was eventually left with almost no one she could turn to as a friend or even as a counselor. Ganga had been like a big sister to her, but Janet's jealousy and resentment of Ganga's energy, wisdom, and feminine grace, as well as the close friendship that Ganga and I shared, soon poisoned their relationship to the point that Ganga disengaged almost completely.

From the very start of our relationship, I had an active and engaging social life, while Janet had virtually none. Larry, Ganga and

I were close friends, in spite of my issues with Larry, and we spent a lot of time together going to movies or social events, sharing meals, or representing Yogiji, Sikh Dharma, or 3HO at official functions. As the Ashram community grew over time, other students joined our core social group. But Janet never did. Every week I was out doing things with other people, while Janet, uninvited, stayed home. From time to time I would take her out alone to a movie, but it was from a sense of compassion and obligation, and I usually had to sacrifice some other more appealing social activity that I would have done without her. The only thing we regularly did together was go to sadhana or Gurdwara, and even there we sat separately. We were mismatched and both of us were miserable.

Within a few days of getting married, I had realized that being with someone to whom I was not attracted was NOT a solution to what I considered my out-of-control sexual energy. In fact, it only made things worse. The only thing that changed was that instead of acting overtly and honestly on my impulses and needs, I simply went into denial. I would seek physical contact with women, pretending to myself that it was not sexual in nature. The role of massage in Yogiji's teachings gave me innumerable opportunities to disguise my need for contact as an altruistic and selfless act of massaging the feet, hands, head or shoulders of any attractive woman who was willing. Since I had "good hands" my offers were often accepted and usually greatly appreciated. The conflict between my genuine altruism and hidden agenda raged in my soul. In conversations with women, I would engage in eye contact that was overflowing with desire. Unappreciated by Janet, who was as little attracted to me as I was to her, I sought validation in the eyes of other women. I was so overt in this behavior that it made Janet even more insecure. I protested my loyalty and spiritual commitment, and though I remained technically faithful, it was plain to everyone that my relationship with Janet was not fulfilling a number of very basic needs for either of us.

Janet and I had abided by Larry's prohibition against sex for several months, but eventually I broke down. Janet could hardly have been described as an enthusiastic participant, and I was tormented by guilt at having caved in to my own weakness. I tried forever after that to at least abide by the "once a month" dictum that had become one of the official teachings of 3HO. But it was a hopeless and miserable restraint. Once an hour would have been a more appropriate guideline at that point in my life. I suffered unbelievably. I was a walking time bomb, a danger to myself and to others. And in the secret life of my thoughts, I lived in constant shame. Eventually, I confided my problem to Yogiji. He prescribed a diet of rice and vegetables completely devoid of protein. It didn't work.

Yogiji promoted Kundalini Yoga as the "Yoga of creativity." Through the exercises and meditations of Kundalini Yoga one is supposed to be able to transmute sexual energy into creative energy. I gave it my all. No one practiced with more vigor. I worked especially hard on a technique called *Laya Yoga,* in which the muscles of the lower abdomen are rhythmically contracted and released in conjunction with the chanting of a mantra, and with a mental focus on raising energy from the base of the spine through key chakras and out the top of the head. It was complicated and a difficult process to learn, and one slip of the mind could ruin the whole thing. But I practiced diligently, and within a few weeks was feeling dramatic effects. Most notable was the sensation that my body was either microscopically small, or larger than the Universe.

It was a wonderful transcendental space, for while in it I was completely happy, carefree, and liberated from the details of daily life. It also bordered on physical ecstasy. The first time it happened, I was amazed. "It must be an anomaly," I thought. But it happened again and again. Soon, I was able to achieve this remarkable state after just a few repetitions of the mantra. I could literally "feel" the energy go up my spine and out the top of my head. It created a vortex like the field of a magnet, with the top of my head and the base of my spine as the two poles. "This is it," I thought. "I don't need anything else."

But liberation, I discovered, was not to be found in a cosmic experience of meditation. Years earlier Timothy Leary had tried an experiment with LSD. He told of spending a week in a remote farmhouse tripping with his friends, hoping to make permanent the heightened and ecstatic state achieved through acid. But when the week was over and everyone came down from the effects of the drug, he was disappointed to find he was still basically the same old Timothy Leary, with the same personality, problems, and neuroses that he had started with a week before. That is exactly how I felt.

I realized that liberation was going to be a long, hard process of integrating into every thought and action of my daily life the same feeling of "connectedness" with my soul that I experienced in meditation. The daily sadhana, then, was not a goal in itself. It was a form of practice, a way to train my mind so that I could consciously control my thoughts and actions, and bring them into alignment with my highest ideals. Much later I would realize that neither was my religion a goal in itself, but a way of establishing a new identity that could break through the bonds and limitations of my former self. I also overlooked the most basic instructions in Patanjali's Aphorisms (published in English as *How to Know God*), which admonished students to get their ethical life in order before attempting the spiritual path.

Early on, I took to heart the idea that sexual energy could be transmuted into creativity. Since there was no other legitimate outlet for me, creative activities were to be my salvation. I found many places to put my existing talents to work, and I set about developing and honing new ones as well. I was playing music every day,

CHAPTER ELEVEN: A Dysfunctional Marriage   83

In spite of the general unhappiness of our marriage, Janet and I did find moments of friendship and mutual affection, especially at the solstice celebrations when we were in the company of many like-minded friends.

practicing, writing new melodies, leading meditation and deep relaxation, and working on new songs from time to time. I got a job teaching music and yoga at a private school for troubled teens in Leesburg, Virginia. I was regularly teaching yoga classes at the Ashram. I was fixing cars, doing everything from minor tune-ups to complete engine rebuilds. I did handyman activities at the Ashram, from fixing plumbing leaks and replacing light fixtures, to maintaining the furnace. And as Washington, DC, increasingly became a focal point for Yogiji's courses and activities, I took a primary role in designing publicity, advertising, and public relations materials.

Larry acted as a mentor for my writing and design efforts, and though he didn't do any writing himself, he had a keen eye and was an excellent critic for everything I produced. Although my grammar was excellent, I discovered that good grammar alone is not sufficient for writing compelling prose. Larry would point out phrases or sentences that he didn't like, explain why he didn't like them, and send me off to try again. This relationship lasted for ten years as my assignments grew to include publicity and advertising materials for a number of businesses that the Ashram members started together. It was often painful, for Larry was unforgiving in his critiques. But I was keenly aware that my writing skills were improving over time, and gradually I took more and more satisfaction in being able to write good, clean, expository prose.

All of my creative activities brought me satisfaction and a sense of self-worth, for I felt I was making valuable contributions to the Ashram and to Yogiji's mission. I imagined that I really *was* doing something positive to make the planet a better place for humanity, and I felt embraced by the growing family of friends and yoga students. Life was pretty good. But I was in agony about my relationship with Janet. Every attractive yoga student or new female Ashram member was like salt in my wounds, reminding me by her presence that I had made a terrible choice, not only for myself, but for Janet. Ganga consoled me once by saying that with the kind of energy I had, I needed someone like Janet to act as a pair of brakes. Without her dampening influence, Ganga joked, I would have spun out of control long ago. I had to admit that there might be some truth to this observation. But for me, for whom intimacy and affection were so deeply important, Ganga's rationale was little comfort.

CHAPTER TWELVE

New Names

DECEMBER, 1971 marked the first time the 3HO family celebrated the Winter Solstice together. The ten-day celebration was held in Orlando, Florida in an RV campground, an absolutely flat and featureless compound of several acres enclosed by a ten-foot chain link fence. The bleakness of the facilities was depressing. But, fortunately, this was in the days before Disney World took over the City of Orlando, bringing millions of visitors per year—which is to say that we had the campground completely to ourselves. About 300 people showed up, mostly from the East Coast, but also including nearly all the Ashram directors from around the country.

The Solstices were by now taking the place of vacations in the lives of most Ashram members. Very few of us had much money back then, and it was cheaper to drive than to fly, especially if expenses could be shared with a couple of extra passengers. By the time we had driven round trip, with 10 days of camping sandwiched in between, each solstice celebration required at least two weeks off from work. I don't know quite how we managed, but for many years Janet and I attended nearly every summer and winter Solstice celebration.

For me, Orlando in 1971 was notable for two things: my musical friends and I started writing and performing real songs—not just the mantras we accompanied in yoga classes—and Janet got a new name. The "new name syndrome" had actually started two years before. Quite early in 3HO, Yogiji had renamed most of his closest students, among them Premka, Sat Simran, Balwant Singh, Ganga, Sonya, Sat Singh, Shaki Parwah, and others.

Then, slowly at first—like popcorn on a low flame—one student after another began asking for, or was just assigned a spiritual name. At first Yogiji seemed to base the names on astrological and numerological calculations. He would ask each recipient's birthday and somehow arrive at a numerical configuration that suggested to him a Sikh name. I never understood how it worked. At first the names were relatively benign, drawn mostly from mantras we already knew: Ong Kar Singh, Wahe Guru Kaur, Sat Siri Kaur, Ram Das Singh and so forth. To save effort, or perhaps to further cement their destinies together, Yogiji often gave married couples the same name. Sat Jiwan Singh and Sat Jiwan Kaur, for example. "Singh" means Lion in Punjabi, and since the time of Guru Gobind Singh in the early 1700s has been taken by all Sikh men as a last or a middle name. It was one of Guru Gobind Singh's ways of eliminating the caste system within his growing Sikh community. Women all take the name "Kaur," which means Princess.

It wasn't long before almost everyone was asking Yogiji for a spiritual name. Having a Sikh name, like the wearing of a turban, quickly became a yardstick by which a person's commitment was measured. I had toyed with the idea, but never asked for one. A couple of Yogiji's Indian friends had suggested that I should become Pritam Singh, but I wasn't really interested. I was fairly happy with "Peter," and was wary of the uncertainties involved in the naming process. There was no indication in advance what name Yogiji might bestow, and once given there was no going back. Many of the names were fine, but some were cumbersome, and others quite odd-sounding to a western ear. I didn't want to end up as a "Seva Simran Siri Sat Nam Singh," or a "Guru Karta Poorak Singh." Sometimes it even seemed that Yogiji used his name-giving power with a sense of humor, or perhaps as a weapon. One unlucky woman walked away as "God Kaur." And I couldn't help wondering how "Christ Singh" was going to explain his new name to his Jewish parents and friends.

So, I held back, perfectly happy to be known as Peter for the rest of my days. But Janet had no such patience, and she had little attachment to the name she had carried since birth. In fact, she was quite anxious to be rid of it. One day after the Tantric Yoga exercises, Yogiji was relaxing on stage. It was an uncharacteristically informal setting, and several people took advantage of the opportunity to ask for spiritual names. As others realized what was going on, a line formed. One person after another came off the stage after a brief interview with Yogiji, either glowing with delight, or in some cases looking a bit less than enchanted. Dharma Kaur, Raj Kaur, Akal Singh, Prakash Kaur, Kirpal Singh, Sarabjit—it was a flurry of new identities. The newly named were comparing notes as they came off the stage, "oohing" and "aahing" as if they had just received a new piece of exotic jewelry.

Eventually Janet joined this parade. When her turn came up, she stepped forward uncertainly, as if she were approaching the high dive at a shallow pool. For a few minutes she consulted privately with Yogiji. I watched from a distance and noticed that she had a strange look on her face as she came away. She didn't seem happy. "Did you ask Yogiji for a new name?" I asked as she rejoined me. "Yes," she answered, looking down at the ground. There was a long silence. "Well?" I asked. In the 3HO tradition, a name given by Yogiji is like a new destiny. It is supposed to provide a target for the highest aspirations of one's soul, break the ties of old karma, and establish the student firmly on the path to liberation. There is hardly anything more meaningful or important to the sincere seeker of truth. "What is it?" I demanded, unable to contain my curiosity.

"Sat-Peter Kaur," she replied.

There was a long pause. I realized that this was probably not the greatest name in her view. It seemed to be somewhat lacking in feminine grace, and being a hybrid of Punjabi and English, didn't exactly have the feeling of a "real" Sikh name. It also sounded dangerously close to "saltpeter," and I realized it was likely to be both inadvertently and intentionally interchanged with it. There was something else about it that I knew disturbed her: instead of providing a new and independent identity, the name seemed to just tie her destiny to mine. It was like saying that her highest aspiration was to be connected to me. I didn't like it much, and couldn't blame her for her lack of enthusiasm. On the other hand, I realized I might use the opportunity to get off pretty lightly in this new name business: I could simply be Sat-Peter Singh. It was almost like keeping my original name, and at least it wasn't something with eighteen syllables that sounded completely ridiculous in its English transliteration. It was also unique.

"Well, I'll just be Sat-Peter Singh, then," I said.

The hard part about getting a spiritual name, assuming you even like the sound of what Yogiji has bestowed, is convincing everyone you know to address you by it. Your close friends and those who respect you usually go along with the change, though even they will stumble along for a few weeks or months until they get used to it. But there are always those who resist, or who intentionally refuse to make the shift. Former teachers and classmates from high school are likely pockets of resistance, as are one's parents unless they are incredibly liberal. When Cassius Clay changed his name to Mohammed Ali, there were sportscasters who for years refused to call him that. Prince seemed to have an easier time when he became "The Artist Formerly Known as Prince," but perhaps that was because people recognized his quirky name-change was a political statement rather than a religious one. How would the media and the public have reacted if he had changed his name to Hari Dayal Singh Khalsa, Mushtaq Ali Mohammed, or Krishna Das?

Getting people to acknowledge and remember a new name might be even harder than getting them to accept the change to white clothes and a turban. In the 17 years I was with the Sikhs, I don't think my father once called me "Sat-Peter," though he was reluctantly willing to be seen in public with me from time to time in my Sikh regalia. And when I went to my high school class' 5th reunion in the Summer of 1972, it seemed my old friends and classmates reacted much less to my turban than to my insistence that they call me Sat-Peter Singh. Later on, when I was running an advertising agency in Los Angeles, I used to introduce myself to potential clients over the phone simply as Peter. I tried using Sat-Peter for a while, but it was a struggle just to get past the reaction to my name ("What did you say??" or "Hahaha, did you say SALTPETER?" or "I'm not interested." Click…). So, I resorted to using the "simplified" form of my name. It did not present a moral crisis for me to revert to "Peter," but what would I have done if my name had been Sat Sampuran Narayan Singh? Perhaps carrying around a name like that and inflicting it on my friends, family, and business associates would have signified a higher level of commitment to the Dharma. I felt lucky.

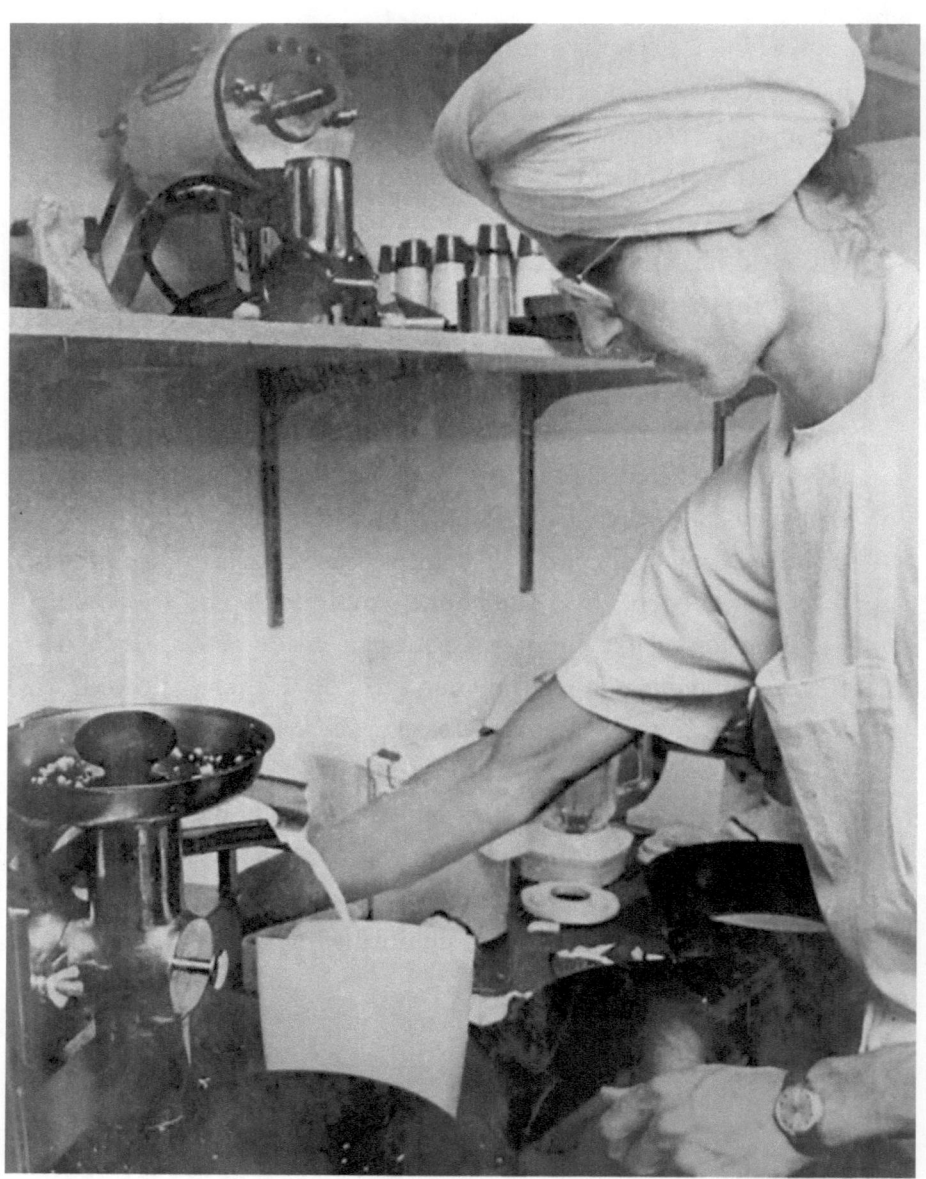

This photo from "The Washington Post" in 1971, shows me operating a juicer in the kitchen of the YES! restaurant and health food store in Georgetown. I managed the place for a time before Larry, Ganga, and I joined forces to create the Golden Temple Conscious Cookery, which opened in 1972.

CHAPTER THIRTEEN

The Golden Temple Restaurant

Throughout 1970 and 1971 significant changes had been taking place both in my personal life and in the Ahimsa Ashram community in DC. In early 1971 Sat-Peter Kaur and I moved back into the Ashram on Q Street. The Annex, with only three students, had become economically unsustainable, and a room had opened up at the Ashram due to the departure of a couple who left to join another spiritual group. Such defections were fairly rare at the time, and always stirred those of us who remained into a frenzy of accusations, speculations, and slander against the departed. Their destiny was "cut," according to Yogiji. They would be reborn as cockroaches. The spiritual group to which they had defected was "nothing more than a cult," and the leader of the group a "charlatan." We reassured ourselves that Yogiji was the one and only Living Master of the Age (even though there were dozens of other Indian Swamis and Gurus claiming the same unique status), and that we were the lucky and blessed ones who would carry humanity to glory. After all, were we not the manifestation of George Washington's secret spiritual vision—the one in which he saw ranks of angel soldiers dressed in white coming to the rescue of freedom and the American way? Yogiji had told us about this vision, so it must have been true.

The American public was by this time becoming obsessed with cults. So many Eastern and New Age spiritual groups were active that it was almost impossible not to know someone who was involved, or whose child or cousin was involved in a group like the Hare Krishnas, the Children of God, Jews for Jesus, Transcendental Meditation, the Farm, the Premies, the Scientologists, or dozens of others. Some of these groups were seriously into mind control, with charismatic leaders who demanded absolute devotion and obedience from their students.

Most of the groups prescribed spiritual regimens that included vegetarian diets (called "protein deprived" by the press), minimal time for sleep, and long hours of yoga, chanting, meditation, or other spiritual disciplines. They were also built on a system of communal living that often left the members isolated from contact with the outside world. Most of these groups were headed by men, and most of these "teachers" were known, suspected, or accused of sleeping with their female students. Sometimes horrible abuses and tragedies came to the attention of the American public: the Manson family (not exactly a spiritual group) with its murderous rampage in Hollywood; the Kripalu Yoga Center, whose beleaguered leader, Yogi Amrit Desai, publicly confessed to sleeping with his students; or the Hare Krishnas, pilloried in the press as drug traffickers, money launderers, and child abusers.

A new industry sprang up to help middle-class families wrest their children away from the cults. Called "deprogrammers" these individuals' and organizations' first weapon against the cults was kidnap, followed by imprisonment, starvation, sleep deprivation, mental and emotional harassment, a variety of tortures, and many other techniques of coercion up to and including sexual abuse and rape. The deprogrammers' method was to dehumanize their "clients," tearing apart and vilifying their belief systems, unmasking and reinforcing the presumed sinister motives behind the cult leaders, discrediting friendships and even marriages with other cult members, until the victim—alone, helpless, and terrified—broke down or caved in. A successful deprogramming rendered a "normal" individual who could be returned to his or her loving parents so the happy family could get on with their own particular version of the American dream. Sometimes there were accidents, however: permanent or long-lasting emotional damage, psychotic breakdowns, even deaths.

With our high-visibility turbans and white clothes, our group was an easy target for the anti-cult hysteria, and we were desperately anxious to establish our identity as a legitimate world religion. We tried to position ourselves as "mainstream." The Sikh religion, after all, was the world's fourth or fifth largest religion. There were more Sikhs in the world than Jews, we would say. We weren't like those other groups. Yogiji even said publicly that he wasn't a "Guru," though we all secretly thought he was. We were sure that we didn't fit the criteria by which cults were identified, for our highest authority was the body of teachings of the Sikh Gurus as embodied in the Guru Granth Sahib—not some megalomaniac, charismatic leader whose every word was our command, for whom we would jump off a cliff, steal, or commit homicide if he told us to.

We were individuals, fully in control of our own decisions and our own destinies. It was by our own free will that we sought and accepted Yogiji's advice on everything from what to eat, to whom to marry. If he pre-empted our questions by telling us what to do, it was out of our own free will that we obeyed. Some of us even tacitly agreed with the deprogrammers' view of the cults, though not their methods. The Hare Krishnas and the Children of God, and most of the rest really were cults, after all. And of all the new spiritual groups, only we were truly legitimate. Comforted by these thoughts, I tried not to give much time and energy to the issues of cults and deprogrammers. I had too many other things going on.

Just after we returned from the Summer Solstice of 1971, Sat-Peter Kaur got pregnant. It was for me one of my more cosmic life experiences, for I was fully aware at the moment it happened that Sat-Peter Kaur had conceived. I felt my heart bursting with an inexplicable joy and sensed that we were surrounded by a strange white light that seemed to emanate from within me. Tears rolled down my face, and I simultaneously laughed and wept with joy. Sat-Peter Kaur asked with a concerned look on her face, "What's going on?" "Don't you know?" I demanded through my tears, incredulous that she could be so oblivious. But I couldn't explain. I just knew that she was pregnant, and that it must be a special child to have been accompanied by the extraordinary experience I was going through. "This is what liberation must feel like," I thought. "Utter and unbelievable happiness, so super-charged that it translated into a feeling of physical ecstasy and an aura of white light." I lay in bed reveling in the thoughts and feelings for a long time until I drifted off into a delicious sleep. Sadly, when I awoke the next morning, the sensation was gone. But looking over at Sat-Peter Kaur, still asleep in the bed next to me, I knew that the experience had been real, and I knew that she was pregnant. A visit to the doctor six weeks later confirmed it.

I had been working at *YES!*, a local vegetarian restaurant and health food store, for a few months at this point, but wasn't earning enough money to support a family. Larry and Ganga, meanwhile, had been talking about starting our own vegetarian restaurant. Ganga was an exceptional cook. She had lived in Yogiji's household prior to getting married, and had been chiefly in charge of the food preparation for Yogiji, his secretaries, and his guests. Before that, she and Larry had worked at the Source Restaurant in Los Angeles. In fact, they had met there when the entire staff, including the owner, Jim Baker, started attending Yogiji's classes together in Los Angeles in 1969. Larry's father had also owned a restaurant—a Denny's, of all things—so Larry had grown up with a great deal of personal experience in the restaurant business. With our Ahimsa Ashram family now numbering about 15 people, all of whom worked at various odd jobs around the city, it seemed like we had a ready staff. If we could just pull together all our resources and focus our efforts, we might be able to create a business that could support the entire Ashram while providing a way to share with the general public Yogiji's teachings about food.

One morning while walking around the Dupont Circle area, I came upon a dress shop that had just gone out of business. It was on Connecticut Avenue, half a block north of the circle, and only two blocks from the Ashram. It was the perfect location! I took down the number of the realtor whose sign appeared in the window and ran back to the Ashram to tell Larry. He and Ganga were as excited as I was, and we immediately called and made an appointment to preview the building that day. As we walked through it later in the afternoon, we knew it was just what we wanted, even though it was a little narrow: 90' long and only 13' wide. The building had three floors plus a full basement. It was more space than we really needed, for the kitchen and dining room would occupy only the first floor. But we could make use of the basement for a walk-in refrigerator and dry-food storage, and the second floor for an office. As we walked through, we planned the layout of the place. We could modify the old dressing rooms into private booths, put the kitchen at the back with a pass-through window, install a few sinks and a stove, and be in business within a month or two. We were ecstatic. Larry handled all the legal and business details with the realtor, and upon the signing of a six-year lease the next day, our dream of starting a restaurant was suddenly a reality.

But it didn't take a month or two to get the place ready. It took nine months of hard work. In order to meet codes, we had to replace the ceilings in the first and second floors with two layers of 3/4" drywall. It entailed completely replumbing the building and reworking the heating and ventilation system. We had to add a bathroom, fire doors, lighting, and an exhaust hood over the stove. The kitchen design and dining room floor plan would need to take into account predictions about "time and motion" of waiters, bussers, and kitchen staff, integrating the functions of kitchen equipment with the demands of the menu that Ganga was putting together. We had to acquire kitchen and dining room equipment and appliances, chairs, tables, china, and silverware. Finally, we had to work out prices, design and print menus, develop relationships with suppliers, and somehow make the monthly rental payments until we were able to open for business.

After we had laid everything out on paper with the help of one of the yoga students who was an architect, I took on all the mechanical work while Larry supervised the construction activities. I had no experience in plumbing other than clearing an occasional clogged drain or replacing the washer in a leaky faucet. But I was undaunted by the prospect of connecting hot and cold-water lines to at least seven sinks, and I happily took on the task of designing and overseeing the construction of custom stainless-steel sinks, countertops, and a commercial dishwashing station, as well as a hood and exhaust system for the ten-burner stove, and electrical hook-ups for a huge walk-in refrigerator and freezer.

I had worked a summer job five years earlier building and installing air-conditioning and heating ductwork for my uncle's air conditioning company in New York, and I had been mechanically inclined since my childhood summers in Maine where I had repaired outboard motors and almost anything else that got broken. When I was 12, I had built a hydroplane. So, although I knew next to nothing about the assignments I was undertaking, I was brimming with confidence at my ability to get the job done.

I worked for weeks getting all the drains, vent-stacks and copper supply lines installed. Each piece of copper pipe had to be soldered perfectly to avoid leaks. The man at the hardware store told me how to clean the copper, brush on the flux, heat the pipe with a propane torch and apply the solder. He also told me about the repercussions of failing to perform any one of these steps perfectly. But I was new at the job and a little more impatient than was advantageous for such tedious work. There was also no easy way I could think of to test the system until it was completely finished. It actually would have been relatively easy to devise a system to test things as I went along, but it didn't occur to me at the time. I worked at a frenetic pace, doing most of my soldering in the semi-darkness of the basement under the kitchen floor, my arms stretched uncomfortably over my head and the hot flux splattering into my face. Finally, after weeks of effort, I was finished. I proudly regarded my work, using a flashlight to trace the long parallel lines of hot and cold supply pipes. Then I went out to the street to turn on the water main.

As I walked back into the building, I could hear an ominous hissing sound emanating from the basement. It got louder as I descended the stairs. To my horror and dismay, when I reached the bottom stair, my flashlight revealed an enormous shower from my pipes under the kitchen floor. Nearly half the soldered joints were leaking. I started counting leaks, making mental note of which joints needed to be re-soldered. Then I ran back upstairs, soaking wet, to turn off the water main. By now the entire building's supply pipes were filled with water, right up to the fourth floor, and they would all have to be drained before I could hope to repair even one soldered connection. Up and down the stairs I went, opening every faucet to allow the water to drain out. After half an hour, I started to work again on the leaky connections. I could hear the residual water boiling out of the copper lines as I applied the propane flame. I quickly discovered that even one drop of water is enough to prevent the solder from "taking." I could melt the solder onto the pipe with a direct flame, but unless the pipe itself was dry, clean, and heated appropriately, the solder would just ball up on the surface and fall off.

I worked for hours, carefully redoing every joint that I could remember as having leaked. My efforts yielded only an incremental improvement. When I had gotten to all the joints I could remember, shut every faucet on all four floors, and once again turned on the water main, I still had at least a dozen leaks to contend with. Up and down the stairs I went again, repeating my earlier efforts, with more boiling off water in the lines, more bad connections, more flux splattering in my face, and more leaks when I again tested the system. I was frustrated beyond belief, but I was making progress, and there was no way I was going to admit defeat or even let Larry or anyone else know how hard a time I was having.

I worked for two more days, draining the system and fixing leaks at least six more times before the entire system held. When it was done, I was so overjoyed and proud that I insisted on having Larry turn on the hot and cold water in every one of the seven sinks and come down to the basement so he could admire the symmetry of my handiwork hanging under the kitchen floor. He was duly impressed. Only after he offered me his congratulations did I reveal the difficulties I had gone through. Now that the job was successfully completed and my plumbing ability clearly established, it was easy to laugh at the earlier incompetence and setbacks through which I had struggled. My next job was the heating and ventilating system.

The months dragged on, and by the beginning of 1972 we were getting close. Ganga started trying out her recipes in the restaurant kitchen, refining and reworking quantities and ingredients to accommodate serving several hundred people per day. Then we started organizing actual kitchen staff, with Larry and Ganga developing procedures for everything, and training those of us who would be handling each workstation. Ganga designed aprons for the wait staff and assigned consecutive numbers to each waiter. We got the menus back from the printer. Larry and I went to restaurant auctions in Baltimore and Glen Burnie, Maryland, and procured a used walk-in refrigerator and some extra pots and pans for the kitchen. The varnish had just dried on the natural wood tabletops, and a large, hand-painted sign installed outside the second-floor front window proclaiming our existence, when we finally opened our doors for business. It was the middle of March.

"The Golden Temple Conscious Cookery" was an immediate success. It had seating for sixty-six people, but the very first day when we opened for lunch there were well over two hundred lined up around the block to sample our cuisine. We had an ideal location, within walking distance of thousands of office workers, and thousands of "upwardly mobile" local residents—more than enough to ensure good crowds for both lunch and dinner. We also had a great idea whose time had come: vegetarian food that did not sacrifice taste for healthfulness. Ganga's cuisine was delicious, and most people didn't seem to mind waiting for up to an hour just to get seated and a lot longer to get served.

We stumbled through our first day, celebrating with songs and chanting after the last customer left. Each successive day we got our systems better organized. Our kitchen and dining staff quickly improved, and within a few weeks we had a humming operation that was the talk of the town. There were only 18 of us living in the Ashram at the time, and most of us were working 18 hours a day. Sat-Peter Kaur, in the last days of her pregnancy was assigned to teach the classes at the Ashram so the rest of us could work in the restaurant. Then on March 29, 1972, just a few weeks after opening

Managing the workflow in the kitchen was an intense and highly stressful job.

our doors, Sat-Peter Kaur gave birth to our daughter at home in Ahimsa Ashram. I was there, and, under the guidance of a midwife, received my darling daughter into the world in my own hands. We named her Amrit Alexandra. She was the first baby conceived and born within the 3HO family anywhere in the world, and the only one who was given a name by her own parents. From then on, Yogiji assigned names to every new child.

CHAPTER FOURTEEN

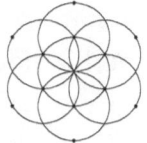

Loss of a Parent

MY MOTHER WAS DYING. In 1965 she had undergone an operation for breast cancer, and for a time it seemed she had recovered. But throughout 1972 she had been in and out of the hospital. The cancer had metastasized and was attacking her entire body. I had no idea how serious it was. I was so busy with my own life and still so distant from my parents that there were a number of operations and hospital visits of which I was not even aware. After Christmas, however, she began a protracted stay in the hospital. My father called to tell me where she was and invited me to go visit her. One day in early January, I convinced Larry to let me have the afternoon off. I found my mother lying in her hospital bed, looking incredibly pale and drawn. She was glad to see me and had tears in her eyes as she held my hand. After asking how things were going with me, to which I replied in short but glowing terms, she started talking about herself and her feelings.

"I just can't help wondering 'Why me?'" she said. My mother was deeply religious, and I knew her life, like mine, had been underscored by a search for meaning and truth. However, I saw her beliefs and expressions of faith as conventional: she attended church on Sundays, regularly sought personal and religious counseling from the Dean of the Washington National Cathedral, where my older brother and I had both sung as choirboys, and she maintained a liberal fair-mindedness about poor, "colored", and disadvantaged people. Yet, she had never shared with me any meaningful thoughts or insights about religious or spiritual subjects. I was completely surprised, therefore, as I stood beside her bed, to hear her say, "Through all of this I have come to realize that Jesus was not just a person we worship as the Son of God. It's his spirit that is important. His spirit is alive, and I know now that it lives inside me, and inside you, too." She squeezed my hand weakly. "I know," I replied gently.

This was, in my eyes, the greatest revelation I could ever hope for her or anyone else to have. It was the essence of my own spiritual belief, though I conceived of it slightly more impersonally than she had expressed it. In my view, Jesus was just one of many human beings who had manifested "Christ Consciousness." I agreed with her that it was the consciousness, rather than the individual human being, that was important. It was the hope of manifesting this consciousness in my own life that had led me to my spiritual practices. I didn't tell her all this, however, or use the opportunity to open up a broader discussion that might justify my own life-style and religious practice as a Sikh. I just held her hand and let her talk.

"I know I am dying," she continued. "But the worst thing is leaving Fred." It was strange to hear her speak of my father by his first name. I thought that she might be disoriented, and I was uncomfortable at the idea that she was feeling sorry for herself. But I was wrong. She was only concerned about my father's wellbeing. "He won't have anyone to take care of him, and I hate the thought of leaving him alone," she said. I felt terrible. I knew—all my siblings knew—that my father had been having an affair with another woman for almost 15 years. It was one of those family secrets no one would ever talk about, and to which my mother would never have alluded or admitted. My father had stayed with my mother through it all—or she with him. Even now he visited and spent time with her every day in the hospital. But the irony of her concern for him jarred me. "He'll be all right," I said, with more certainty than I wanted her to hear.

I came back for another visit a week later. My mother was in a different room and she didn't appear well at all. I was surprised that she looked up at me with accusing eyes as I walked in. "I don't like what you're doing," she said sternly. "What are you talking about?" I replied defensively. My mother's accusations were the one thing I couldn't stand. They had started when I was very young. One spring afternoon when I was three or four years old, she had confronted me in the backyard, demanding to know what I had been doing behind the garage. "Nothing," I said. It was true. I really hadn't been doing anything except exploring. But she wouldn't believe me. "Did you go to the bathroom back there?" she demanded heatedly, as if that would have been a terrible thing for me to do. Her suspicions were usually ill-founded, and as I grew up, I felt I could never expose to her censorship and judgment anything about my activities or my true feelings. I was dismayed that here on her deathbed she was once again accusing me of doing something bad. "What have I done wrong?" I implored. "And Alex, too," my mother continued, including my older brother in her sweeping condemnation and carrying on as if she had not even heard me. "You and he have both been having affairs, and I DON'T approve."

"That's not true," I protested. I really was taken aback. Of all the things to accuse me of when it was my father who had been fooling around all those years! "I haven't done anything like that, and neither has Alex!" The conviction and anger in my voice disarmed my mother. "You haven't?" she asked, looking confused and defeated. "No," I said. "And where did you get that idea?" "I can't really remember," she said weakly. "I was sure it was true. Maybe I dreamed it." There was a distant and wild look in her eyes. Her pupils were heavily dilated. I lied, assuring her that everything was fine with my marriage. But she was too weak and disoriented to carry on a conversation. I held her hand in silence for a long time until she stirred uncomfortably and said, "You should go now."

A week later came the call from my father. I was hard at work rerouting some heating and air-conditioning ductwork in the restaurant when Larry called me to the phone. "Pete," said my father in a somber tone, "Your mother passed away this morning." I listened impassively as he cleared his throat. "The doctor told her a couple of days ago that he had run out of his little bag of tricks. All he could do was give her pain medication so she wouldn't have to suffer."

It was typical of my father to focus on technical details as a way to avoid discussing anything deeply emotional. If any conversation edged even close to an emotional issue, he would abruptly change the subject, asking about the weather or something equally innocuous or ridiculous.

Ten years earlier he had picked me up at the bus stop on my way home from school one day with the news that his own mother had died that morning. I had tried to express my condolences with a sympathetic look, imagining how sad I would feel in his place. "Why do you have that look on your face?" he asked. "Aren't you sad?" I suggested. "These things happen," he responded, clearing his throat. "So, how was school today?"

Was it stoicism, I wondered, or a character flaw? My father was certainly not unique among his generation in this respect. He had lived through the Great Depression as a teenager and had risked his life passing out anti-Nazi pamphlets while studying cello in Munich in 1936. He had served in the Army during World War II. He had made great personal sacrifices to provide his family not only with financial security but also with the advantages of music lessons, art, and private schools. He was intelligent, well educated, musically talented, and gifted with a wry sense of humor. But at the time he seemed completely incapable of dealing with anything that involved emotions.

The news about my mother touched me deeply, but in deference to my father's mode of avoidance, I simply thanked him for calling me and asked when the service would be. As soon as I hung up the phone, I retreated to the basement. It was the only place in the building that felt like my own, for I had spent so much of my time there working on the plumbing. It was also the only place where I could be alone. I stood for a long time in silence, trying to sort out my conflicted feelings. I was sad at my mother's passing, yet felt a strange sense of relief. It was as if a weight of oppression and judgment had been lifted from my shoulders. There would be no more scolding or accusing looks, no more interrogations, no more cold condemnations of my decisions. The severity of her personality slowly melted from my memory as I stood there in silence. After a while, I sensed only her love. I imagined her watching over me, and could almost feel her presence. I tried to make contact with her spirit, closing my eyes and trying to still my thoughts. I immediately experienced a feeling of vertigo and sensed that my mother was with me there in the dark.

I tried to tell her that I would be good, that I would not disappoint her, that she would be proud of me. I asked for her help and her forgiveness for everything I had done wrong in my life. A wave of guilt swept over me that I'd only visited her twice during her illness. I tried to still my mind. I focused on our summer home in Maine, the place my mother loved more than anywhere else. I thought of sailing with her in the "Royal Tern," the gaff-rigged sloop she had commissioned in 1956. Sailing on the New Meadows River was her greatest delight. I could almost see the sparkle of the afternoon sun on the dappled water, and the look of attentiveness and expectation on her face as she scanned the horizon, watching the water's surface for telltale signs of gusty wind. I could see her fingers curling and uncurling as she gripped the tiller. She was happy.

I remembered all the things she had done to give my life creativity and meaning—how she had begun teaching me piano at the age of four, bought me a guitar and found a classical guitar teacher when I was ten. I thought of the encouragement she had given me for my earliest watercolors and musical compositions. I had artist's hands, she had said when I was six, praising the way I played an arpeggio on the piano. I remembered when I was very young the softness of her cheek as she kissed me goodnight, the sweet strains of her beloved Chopin etudes, or the Bach, Mozart, and Beethoven sonatas for cello and piano that she and my father would play together well into the evening.

I was comforted by these thoughts and filled with warm affection, and began to welcome the idea of her guardian presence. I thought to myself how comforting it would be if I could count on her spirit being forever accessible to me. I was torn, however, for according to the teachings of the Sikh religion, the soul after death needs to be freed from the chains of its earthly existence so that it can progress to a new birth. I didn't want to hold back my mother's soul, no matter how emotionally comforting it might be to me. So, I began quietly chanting *Akal*, the death chant of the Sikhs. Akal means, "immortal" and is supposed to liberate the soul of a departed one. It is chanted with a full breath, with the emphasis on the second syllable. I had never chanted it alone before, and the darkness and solitude of the basement added an air of mystery to the experience. After three repetitions, I stood in silence again, realizing I really did not want my mother to be gone so soon. The insistent noise of the kitchen upstairs pulled me out of this reverie, and with a promise to come back later, I climbed the stairs and resumed my work.

Four days later Sat-Peter Kaur, baby Amrit, and I attended my mother's memorial service in the Bethlehem Chapel of the Washington National Cathedral. The place was full of people and full of memories for me, for I had sung there as a junior choirboy in 1958. Francis Sayre, Dean of the Cathedral and my mother's spiritual counselor, conducted the service with heartfelt emotion. Afterwards there was a reception at my parents' house in Chevy Chase. It was a blur of relatives and family friends, and I was grateful when it was all over. My turban and white clothes had never felt so conspicuous and out of place. The only duty that remained would have to wait until that summer. My mother had requested that she be cremated, and that her ashes be spread in the New Meadows River. My siblings and I joined my father for that ceremony in July. A week later, after the kids had returned to their respective homes, I got a phone call from my brother Alex. "Did you hear the news?" he opened. "What news?" I asked. "About Pop." he continued, tantalizingly. "No, what?" I demanded. "He and Helen just got married."

I couldn't suppress my rage. It wasn't that I had anything against Helen. I barely knew her. It was the idea that she had been an illicit part of my father's life for nearly 15 years; that she had been the instrument of all those years of suffering and anxiety for my mother. It was the idea that he would now dignify that relationship by marrying her, and that he would do so only days after putting my mother's ashes to rest. How could he bring another woman into my mother's environment? How could he dishonor her memory this way? I was so angry I could barely speak. I commiserated with Alex for a few more minutes, then hung up the phone and for the first time since my mother's death gave in to my tears. But they were tears of rage.

The Golden Temple, known as "Harimandir Sahib," is the most sacred of all Sikh holy places.

CHAPTER FIFTEEN

First Trip to India

In the fall of 1973, I finally got a chance to go to India. It had been more than three years since I started taking Yoga classes. Ever since reading *Siddhartha* while in college, I had felt that going to India would represent an essential step in my spiritual development. Reading *Autobiography of a Yogi* had reconfirmed that conviction, and becoming a 3HO yoga student, then a teacher, then a Sikh, had turned it into an absolute necessity. India was the seat of Eastern wisdom, the source of spiritual knowledge, the wellspring of Ayurvedic medicine and the birthplace of the "eighteen forms" of yoga. It was the home of the Taj Mahal and the Golden Temple, and home to countless sadhus, yogis, wandering mystics, and holy men. It was a place of indescribable beauty and mystery, steeped in tradition, where seekers of truth could drink from the font of knowledge and find God.

After years of waiting, I was finally on my way, along with a group of American Sikhs, to touch the heart of the spiritual and cultural tradition I had adopted as my own. I joined Larry and Ganga, Yogiji, a couple of his secretaries, and 25 other Ashram members from around the county, to board an Air India flight in New York, bound for Delhi. Most of the entourage had paid a flat fee to cover airfare, hotel, transportation, and food while in India. But Larry had arranged it so that he, Ganga, and I were getting our expenses paid by the group in exchange for handling all the logistics.

Sat-Peter Kaur and my daughter, Amrit, stayed at home. I was too egotistical to appreciate how difficult this must have been for her.

Twenty-two hours after leaving New York, we arrived at Palam Airport on the outskirts of Delhi. I quickly realized that my fanciful ideas about India were somewhat off the mark. Stepping out the front gates of the airport, we were met with the fragrance of burning cow dung and rotting garbage. Clouds of exhaust fumes swirled around us, belching from the tailpipes of a dozen "three-wheeler" taxicabs, lined up, waiting for their fares. The authorities had done their best to keep the airport clear of beggars, but it was impossible to overlook the pathetic forms of street sweepers, coolies, and other lowly workers, dressed in nothing more than filthy burlap rags as they bent about their tasks. Some of them chewed on betel nut, which gave some narcotic relief from their misery while staining their lips and teeth a ghoulish red. All around on the sidewalk and curb were the signs of their addiction: splattered circular stains where ejaculated ruby-colored spittle had mixed with the dust.

Most of the street sweepers were old women. Some were bent over double to do their work, while others waddled around on their haunches armed not with any broom a westerner might imagine, but with short sheaves of straw bound together with string. I was told that they were lucky to have jobs, and to earn their street-sweeper's salary of five rupees per day while they broke their backs with these inhumane implements. The exchange rate at that time was about eight rupees to the dollar. The coolies got a better deal. After carrying out all our luggage, setting it on the sidewalk so that it could be counted, then loading it into the back of several taxicabs, they were paid 3 rupees each. At that rate, they were likely to earn 10-12 rupees per day. The $100 of American currency I had just exchanged inside the airport formed a bulging wad of rupee notes in my wallet, about which which I suddenly felt very self-conscious.

CHAPTER FIFTEEN: First Trip to India

Our taxis were all "Ambassadors," a four-cylinder, four-door sedan that was India's answer to the VW Bug. Although the car was, at best, a sub-compact by modern standards, and was licensed to carry no more that four passengers, it was not unusual—especially in outlying areas—to see six or seven people stuffed into the back seat alone. The driver of my taxi was an Indian Sikh with a maroon turban that looked as if it had been jammed on, rather than tied. Loose hairs protruded around the back of his neck and over his ears. He was wearing a faded blue pajama suit that had large grease stains on the sleeves and thighs. The interior of his taxi looked very much like his clothes, only more worn. Yellowing, plastic-coated pictures of the Sikh Gurus lined the dashboard, and the mantras *Sat Nam* and *Wahe Guru* in Gurmukhi script were painted in white letters on the visors. As we were loading our luggage, I noticed an old shoe hanging off the back bumper. Later I found out that it was a common practice among Hindus to "deface" their vehicles in this way so that the gods would not be jealous and cause them to have an accident.

Finally, after all our people and luggage were safely stowed into a line of taxis, we pulled away from the arrivals area. After a moment or two of feeble grinding my taxi's engine sputtered to life and, with a delicate maneuver that clearly came from our driver's intimate knowledge of the loose linkage in the gearbox and the sticky clutch, we lurched forward towards the main road, driving on the left-hand side. As we exited the airport, we pulled up behind an oxcart piled high with sugar cane. Our driver laid into the horn, which appeared to be the only piece of equipment on board that worked properly. Slowly the ox cart pulled to the left, and we went zooming past, our rear fender nearly catching the protruding hub of the ox-cart's massive wooden axle. In front of us, however, were two huge white Brahma Bulls, meandering along the road at their own relaxed pace.

We pulled up short and waited for them to pass. Brahma Bulls are considered sacred in India. They can go anywhere and do anything, and no one bothers them. There have been a few instances over the years since partition in 1947 when Muslims, just to spite the Hindus, have killed and eaten one, but generally the bulls and their female counterparts are safe, and "kings of the road" wherever they wander.

While we waited, I noticed to our right a ten-story building under construction. Erected around its perimeter, apparently for the purpose of applying stucco, was an amazing scaffolding constructed of bamboo and rope. It bent at crazy angles as it reached to the top floors. I wondered how anyone could work on it, for it seemed an engineering impossibility that it could even remain standing. I later learned it collapsed the next day, killing several workers.

After the bulls wandered off and we were under way again, we did not go more than 200 yards before pulling into a "BP" gas station. "Ten rupees, please," said our driver, looking at me with a smile and a peculiar sideways nod of his head. My quizzical frown elicited an explanation. "No petrol," he said, shrugging a little sheepishly. I pulled out a ten-rupee note and gave it to him. As he got out of the car he said, "Only five minutes, please." He exchanged a few words with the station attendant, then disappeared inside a concrete shed that appeared to serve as the station's office. The attendant pumped 3 liters of gas into our taxi, then went to join our driver inside. For several minutes we waited. Finally, I got out of the car to retrieve him. The "office" was an unbelievable mess. There was no counter, no register, no rack of items for sale, nothing that could be even remotely inviting to a motorist. It was just a windowless storage shed for oily rags and discarded automobile parts. But there in the middle of the room, sitting on a milk crate, was our driver, having a cup of tea with the attendant. When he saw me at the door, he quickly finished his tea, thanked the attendant and got back in the car.

On the road again we had a short stretch of light traffic. Our driver took advantage of the open space by accelerating to over 80 kilometers per hour. The car rattled and shook as the bald and out-of-balance tires bounced along the rutted pavement. The steering wheel shimmied in the driver's hands, threatening to pull hard to the left if he loosened his grip. Black smoke poured out the tailpipe, leaving a toxic cloud to our rear. Mercifully, within minutes we were inside Delhi and had to slow down when we encountered thick traffic again on the way to our hotel. The streets were jammed with bicycles, motor scooters, motorcycles, three wheeled bicycle rickshaws, ox carts, cattle, water buffalo, three-wheeled motorized rickshaw taxis, rickety diesel delivery trucks, gaudily painted dump trucks, worn out buses, pedestrians, wildly dressed Sikhs on horseback, beggars, stray dogs, and uncountable Ambassador automobiles, most with old shoes hanging off their back bumpers. Everything with a motor was belching black exhaust fumes. Everything with four legs was defecating on the street. Beggars with missing limbs or malnourished babes in arms were coming up to our car windows with hands outstretched in the most pathetic gestures. *Baksheesh*, they said, rubbing their bellies pitifully. *Kar Ja!* exclaimed our driver, shooing them away. I was as fascinated as I was unsettled by everything I saw.

Our hotel was located on the outer circle of Connaught Circus in the middle of New Delhi. It was a three-story concrete structure with granite tile floors and a blinking neon sign over the door proclaiming it to be a "luxury western style" hotel. Three bellboys appeared and helped get our luggage into the lobby. Larry was handling all the arrangements with the hotel. I was supposed to be in charge of the luggage. I sorted through everything, making sure each person had his or her bags, then stood around waiting as Larry got each person registered. Slowly the crowd in the lobby thinned out as one after another was assigned a room and given a key. I was sharing a room with my friend, Gurusher Singh, and was the last to get a room assignment. After getting settled in, we had the rest of the day to ourselves. Yogiji and his secretaries, who had taken rooms at the truly luxurious, "five-star" Oberoi Hotel, would join us the next morning to visit the historic Sis Ganj Gurdwara in Old Delhi. I had not slept in 36 hours, but I was far too restless to lie down for a nap. Instead, Gurusher and I washed up before taking a walking tour of downtown Delhi. Our flight had arrived at 8:00 AM, and it was not yet noon.

CHAPTER SIXTEEN

Getting Around Delhi

Our hotel's tiled floors ended with the lobby. Everywhere else was an ocean of polished, speckled concrete, hidden only occasionally in the bedrooms by a small section or two of oriental-looking carpet. The hallways were long and poorly lit, running lengthwise down the center of each floor with rooms on each side. Discolored fluorescent bulbs, mounted in bare industrial ceiling fixtures, emitted a garish, flickering light. There was no architectural beauty here. But at least it was clean, which was quite a contrast to everything we had seen since leaving the airport. The only accessory in our bedroom was a ceiling fan. No paintings hung on the wall, no lampshades softened the light from bare-bulbed fixtures, and there was no enclosure for the shower in the bathroom. Instead, located in the middle of the concrete bathroom floor, was a single drain. The whole place had a faint and oddly reassuring smell of disinfectant. The over-all impression was akin to the operating room of a veterinary hospital.

I was lucky to be the first to shower, for there was no preventing the entire bathroom from getting splattered with water. The toilet was an interesting affair. The tank was mounted high on the wall above. A thin chain with a wooden handle dangled within reach, but when I pulled it, the toilet did not flush. I pulled again, but only a trickle of water ran into the bowl. I tried again with the same results. Frustrated, I began yanking the chain rapidly up and down.

Each pull of the chain generated increasing signs of activity until, in a violent crescendo, the toilet roared to life. My education about Indian toilet facilities was only just beginning.

It was early afternoon when Gurusher and I walked out of the hotel for the first inspection of our surroundings. In spite of it being the middle of February, the weather in Delhi was balmy and pleasant, and we were lightly dressed in our white clothes and turbans. Connaught Circus is built on a grand scale and includes two concentric boulevards encompassing a large circular city park. The radial streets and avenues that bisect these boulevards, meeting at the central circle, create a confusing assortment of irregularly shaped blocks. Pedestrian walkways at the corners are treacherous zones, made more dangerous for us by the unexpected direction of the traffic. We had to learn quickly to look right for oncoming vehicles, instead of left. And we found that no rules of courtesy or safety applied to pedestrians. Vehicles of every variety had the right of way.

We were beset everywhere by beggars. It was impossible to ignore their misery. Each one looked more pathetic than the last. Many were disfigured, or were missing limbs. They hobbled around on canes and crutches. One man with no legs scooted about on a small square of wood that had wheels mounted at the corners. He was a pitiful sight, but lucky compared to another legless man who, with a block of wood gripped in each hand, used his arms as crutches, laboriously swinging his torso forward to land on burlap-covered stumps.

But the most heart-rending were the small children and the women carrying babies. Their pleading eyes seemed disembodied from their dark faces and filthy, tangled pitch-black hair. Their outstretched hands revealed bony arms that testified to their genuine poverty. These were not panhandlers. These were people for whom the next meal could mean the difference between life and death. I had been told not to give them money, but my compassion overcame the warning. One young girl carrying a baby approached me with eyes full of pain and sorrow. For a moment I thought the baby was her little sister, but it occurred to me with a shock that she must be her daughter. Flies buzzed around the baby's face, landing in her eyes and lips. I reached in my pocket and dropped a 20 paise coin into the mother's open hand. Instantly, Gurusher and I were surrounded by a dozen other beggars, pleading, demanding, reaching out, touching our sleeves. Some had angry faces and raised their voices aggressively as they intoned the beggars' mantra, "*Backsheesh! Backsheesh, Sardarji.*" ("A gift! A gift, please, Mr. Sikh Gentleman").

With each second, more beggars joined the outer edges of the crowd around us. Gurusher and I turned and fled, walking at an Olympic pace towards the corner. Many of the beggars followed us, calling out for Backsheesh. One was saying "Please, mister, please, mister." We did not look back, but could tell that they were dropping off behind us. Fortunately, the traffic light was in our favor when we reached the corner and we hastened across, leaving the last of them in our wake. A traffic cop in an ill-fitting olive wool uniform gave us a scornful look as we reached the far curb. The misery and the sheer numbers of beggars presented a considerable moral dilemma for me. How could I ignore them? Yet if I gave even the slightest hint of mercy, I would be swarmed, or even attacked. I immediately resolved to limit my giving of Backsheesh to those occasions when I encountered just one or two beggars at a time, thinking that in this way I would be safe. But even then, it was difficult, for some of them were not satisfied with a single coin, but sensing my weakness would pursue me, demanding more.

Gurusher and I soon found ourselves at the inner circle of Connaught Place. Buildings here lined only the outer edge of the boulevard, curving around in a vast arc, facing the expansive circular park in the center. All the buildings had a colonial appearance, with stone facades and elegant, pillared verandahs two stories high stretching over broad sidewalks. In rainy weather one could remain under cover while proceeding from building to building, or remain in the shade during the heat of summer. Some of the buildings housed offices and banks, but most had storefronts at the street level. It was a 19th century British version of a shopping mall. These were some of India's better retail establishments. There were fine jewelers selling exquisite 24 karat gold rings and ornaments, cloth merchants selling silk saris of the most beautiful designs, sellers of hand-woven oriental rugs, a musical instrument shop whose logo appears on half the exotic Indian instruments imported into America, perfumers selling oils of pure sandalwood, musk, and patchouli, and hundreds of different varieties of incense, men's and women's clothing stores selling western and Indian fashions, restaurants, travel agents, and dozens of other businesses designed to cater to tourists and wealthy Indians alike. On the sidewalks and between the pillars in front of these shops, street merchants were hawking all manner of hand-made toys and trinkets, as well as candy, snacks, and Indian sweets piled high on circular trays. An occasional snake charmer, tethered monkey, or scantily clad *Saddhu* complete with brass begging bowl, added yet more color to this overwhelming visual barrage.

 Gurusher and I dodged into the "Punjab Palace" restaurant to have a bite of lunch. The place was reasonably clean, though the decor was tacky in bright plastic and cheap wood veneer. But the food was delicious. We had *subzi* (vegetables), *sag paneer* (spinach with home-made cheese), *Dal* (spicy lentils), *Aloo Muttar* (potatoes and peas), *Raita* (yogurt with cucumbers and onions), *Chaval* (rice), and *Chapatis* (flat bread). Already over-stuffed, we ordered hot, fresh *gulab jamuns* for dessert. These lightly cooked balls of condensed milk solids, soaked in rose water and honey, were so sweet and delicious that we foolishly ordered a second, and then a third round of them. By the time we left the restaurant, we could barely walk. We managed to find our way back to the hotel, passing starving beggars at every corner, and finally collapsed on our beds for an afternoon nap from which we awoke the next morning.

Inside Gurdwara Sis Ganj, in the heart of Old Delhi.

CHAPTER SEVENTEEN

Welcomed by Punjabi Sikhs

GURDWARA SIS GANJ is located in the center of Old Delhi in the midst of one of the busiest bazaars in the world. From our hotel we hired taxis and proceeded through the wide, tree-lined boulevards of New Delhi past the Lal Qila, the famous Red Fort of Mughal days, where we turned left into the heart of Old Delhi. Connaught place had seemed sparsely populated compared to the crush of humanity we encountered here. Most of the streets in this section of Old Delhi were wide enough only for one car. It is one of the few places in India where pedestrians, by their sheer numbers, force all motorized vehicles to yield. We eventually dismounted from our taxis and found ourselves in front of an unimposing, but engaging structure of white marble, sandwiched between innumerable tiny storefronts. The entrance was a wide portal that opened directly to a set of ascending marble stairs. We removed our shoes and socks, leaving them in cubbies to the side of the entrance and, after washing our feet in a shallow trough, climbed the stairs to the interior.

There were over 30 of us, including Yogiji, his secretaries, and a number of Indian Sikh friends who were accompanying him. All of us were dressed in white, and all of us, including the women, were wearing turbans. To the gawking onlookers, we were quite a sight. Indians of the lower economic strata are unabashed about staring open-jawed at foreigners. We quickly got used to being the objects of such attention. As we climbed the stairs, leaving the noise and bustle of the street behind, we entered directly into the main part of the temple. The Guru Granth Sahib was situated to our right in the center of the room. It sat amidst richly embroidered vestments on a gilded bed. Behind it sat a somber-looking Sikh in dark blue pajamas and turban. At his side hung an enormous kirpan, the ceremonial dagger worn by all Sikhs. He tried to look neither right nor left, but his curiosity at our appearance overcame the assumed dignity of his role as the guardian of the Sikhs' holiest scriptures. To the side of the Guru Granth sat three Sikh musicians, or Ragis, two playing harmoniums, one on tablas. Their music reverberated through the lofty marble arches around us, amplified by crackling loudspeakers mounted on the four main columns.

One by one we bowed our foreheads to the ground in front of the Guru Granth Sahib, left a small donation of cash, and took seats on the floor—men to the left, women to the right. I sat for some time listening to the music. It was incredibly beautiful. The voices of the Ragis, in unison with their harmoniums, dipped and climbed in exotic melodies, accompanied by the complex and pulsing rhythms of the tabla. There was something truly mystical and unique about this place. Three hundred years earlier, during one of the most brutal regimes of the Mughal empire, Emperor Aurangzeb had confronted Guru Teg Bahadur, the ninth of the Sikh Gurus, demanding that he perform a miracle. Teg Bahadur had come to plead with the emperor on behalf of the Hindus who were being forced to convert to Islam, losing their property or their lives if they refused. Aurangzeb had taken literally a line from the Koran stating that any head that did not bow to Mecca should be severed from its body.

But Guru Teg Bahadur refused to perform a miracle for the amusement of the Emperor, to which Aurangzeb responded by threatening to have him beheaded if he did not comply. According to legend, Teg Bahadur replied that the only miracle the emperor would see was that a Guru of the Sikhs was willing to lay down his life for the protection of the Hindus. Eventually, the infuriated Aurangzeb carried out his threat. But, according to legend, as soon as Teg Bahadur's head rolled from his body a dust storm came up, concealing the scene; and when it cleared, both the body and the head had disappeared. Gurdwara Sis Ganj commemorates the spot where the execution took place. It is considered one of the holiest of the historic Gurdwaras in India, and the reading from the Guru Granth Sahib or the singing of Gurbani Kirtan—the holy hymns of the Sikh Gurus—never stops. One of the highest aspirations for any Ragi, perhaps second only to performing at the Golden Temple in Amritsar, is to perform Gurbani Kirtan in Gurdwara Sis Ganj.

For some time, the Kirtan continued, while the Gurdwara gradually filled with Sikhs. Many had come as part of an afternoon ritual just to bow to Guru Granth Sahib, but stayed due to their curiosity on seeing all the Americans. We were definitely an oddity. In five hundred years of Sikh history, nothing like this had ever happened. Westerners had never converted to Sikhism, nor bothered to learn the language. But here we were, thirty of us in the company of Yogiji, sitting in the heart of one of India's holiest shrines. By the time the Ardas, or traditional prayer, was performed, followed by the Hookum, or reading from the Guru Granth Sahib, the Gurdwara was completely packed with Sikhs. After the Hookum a couple of *sevadars* distributed *prasad*, a sweet bread pudding that we received with upheld palms. While this was going on one of the temple priests stood and addressed the congregation in Punjabi. He went on and on, occasionally eliciting nods and approving mutters from the congregation. It was easy to see that he was talking about us. From time to time we would hear the phrase *Amrikan Singhan*, or *Harbhajan Singh Ji Yogi*. For more than ten minutes he continued. Finally, in response to something the priest had said, Yogiji stood up and with head bowed and palms folded approached the priest. After a few more words, the priest unfolded a long piece of bright orange silk and placed it loosely over Yogiji's bowed neck. He called it a *Saropa*, which is a special kind of honor bestowed in the presence of Guru Granth Sahib.

Then, one after another, we were also called forward to receive our own saropas. As each of us approached, Yogiji told the priest our names, which the priest repeated for the benefit of the *Sadh Sangat* (congregation) as he placed the cloth around our necks. The assembled Sikhs were delighted. Some of our names, like Ganga's, inspired special signs of approval, while others, such as mine, made them smile. All in all, the Indian Sikhs were treated to quite a show, and by the time the last of us had received a saropa the enthusiasm and excitement was tangible. Someone in the back yelled out, *BOLAY SONI HAL*. To which the entire Sangat responded, *SAT SIRI AKAL*. This traditional battle cry of the Sikhs, passed down from Guru Gobind Singh's time, is now universally used to show approval and enthusiasm. Again and again the cry went up, each time eliciting a louder response.

The Indian Sikhs gathered there saw in Yogiji and his American converts a renaissance of the Sikh faith. Years of assimilation into the dominant culture, the fading of traditions, loss of identity and political power, the intermarriage of their children into Hindu and Muslim families, and the encroaching values of the western world had left the Sikh Dharma in India staggering. In us they saw the fresh faces of a reborn faith and the honoring of old traditions. Some of them stood up and unrolled beards, which for years they had kept tucked into a tidy and unobtrusive knot. Seeing our men with white turbans and flowing beards (all except me) gave them the inspiration and strength to more fully embrace their identity as

"Gursikhs," the true heirs of the heritage of Guru Gobind Singh. As we left the Gurdwara we were mobbed by a happy crowd of those who had been inside. Each one wanted us to come visit his house. "Please, you will just come and have one cup of tea?" they suggested innocently. They all wanted to speak with Yogiji, and many of them got their chance while our taxis, which had been waiting, tried to negotiate through the crowd to pick us up.

Yogiji had arranged a luncheon for us at the house of a prominent Sikh who lived in a residential area of Old Delhi. After lunch we were scheduled to have tea at someone else's house, and later on, a dinner in one of the wealthier neighborhoods of New Delhi. There was no shortage of enthusiastic Sikhs who wanted the privilege of entertaining and feeding us. We were herded here and there, fawned over, stuffed to the gills, subjected to hours of conversation and speeches in Punjabi—none of which we could understand—and finally released at 11:00 PM to return to our hotel for a few hours of sleep. The next day we would board the early train at the station in Old Delhi for an eight-hour ride to Amritsar. We would be spending the next ten days at the Golden Temple.

Photo courtesy of James Billingham

CHAPTER EIGHTEEN

The Train from Delhi to Amritsar

THE TRAIN STATION in Old Delhi had been built in English colonial times. There was an architectural majesty to its cast-iron trusses and vaulted ceiling, though one had to look past the filth, the trash, the beggars, porters and sweepers, bustling passengers, and perhaps most of all, the intense assault of aromas. Mixed with the smell of rotting vegetable matter and human excrement was the acrid stench of burning coal, emanating in billows from the smokestacks of waiting steam engines. I was amazed and thrilled that these antiques were still in commercial use. Back in U.S., steam engines had been relegated long ago to the role of specialty tourist attractions, replaced by modern diesel and electric engines. But India, in most ways, was still living in the nineteenth century, and these old engines, as well as the ancient passenger and freight cars they pulled, still formed an essential part of the country's transportation infrastructure.

My job, as "luggage sevadar" for the group, now suddenly took on a much more serious aspect. We had hired a truck to get everything from the hotel to the station, and I had to direct a team of coolies who were all eager to carry as many bags as quickly as possible in order to earn the greatest number of rupees. Whenever a train arrived or departed, the coolies swarmed to find work. They were all licensed, and each had a numbered medallion that authorized him to work in the station. Nonetheless, I didn't feel completely comfortable in letting these nameless minions work without close supervision, for if a bag or two were to end up missing between the truck and the platform, there would be no way to hold anyone responsible.

I enlisted the help of Gurusher and a couple of others from our retinue so that one American could accompany each group of coolies. After ten stressful minutes we got every piece of luggage, counted and intact, into a pile on the correct platform for the train to Amritsar, which had not yet pulled into the station. Meanwhile, Larry was purchasing our tickets with the help of Bahadur Singh, a young friend of Yogiji's, without whose ongoing assistance during our trip through India we would have been helpless. Tickets alone, however, are not enough on an Indian train. One must also purchase seat reservations unless traveling "bench class," an experience to be avoided if possible, and for which we were certainly not yet deemed ready.

Soon the Amritsar train came huffing and puffing into the station. Clouds of black smoke and bursts of steam billowed from the engine, sending a rain of cinders and ashes down on our heads as it pulled past. As the train came to a stop and the doors opened, complete pandemonium broke loose. Arriving passengers rushed to be first off the train, while coolies pushed their way through the crowd to find work, or having found it, struggled with their burdens among the press of humanity. Simultaneously, all the departing passengers rushed to be the first on the train, followed by coolies carrying their bags. Conductors tried to check seat assignments while tea sellers with trays of biscuits and sloshing teacups tried to find customers both on the platform and in the aisles and doorways of the train. Bahadur Singh raced up and down the platform trying to find the car with our seats, arguing in Hindi with conductors, fending off the tea sellers, dodging the coolies. The Americans stood around our pile of luggage, looking bewildered, and trying to fend off any beggars who had slipped past the station attendants.

Finally, Bahadur Singh, who was so short that he disappeared from view every time he dove into the crowd, reappeared at the doorway of a car 150 feet down the platform. He was hanging by one hand over the platform and waving at us with his free arm. Larry led the group through the sea of humanity that separated us from our seats, while I recruited every spare coolie I could find in order to get our luggage safely on board. Gradually, as arriving and departing passengers disentangled themselves and we reached the relative sanctuary of the car where our seats were located, a sense of order returned. After the luggage was safely counted and stowed away, I sighed with relief and collapsed into my seat.

I was sharing a compartment with Larry, Ganga, Gurusher, Bahadur, and two others from our group. Yogiji and his secretaries would be taking an airplane the next day and meet us in Amritsar. Our compartment contained two eight-foot-long vinyl-cushioned bench seats facing each other with an aisle in between. Folded into the wall above were two more benches that could be opened up to turn the compartment into a four-person sleeper. A sliding door separated the compartment from a hallway running the length of the car. "Air conditioned" class was not available on this train (nor was bench class), so the only ventilation was through the windows, which could be slid open about six inches. Small fans located strategically throughout the compartment were meant to circulate the air. Walls and ceilings were painted light green and gray, but the paint was chipped or worn through in many places and showed dozens of coats underneath dating back over sixty years.

Within a few minutes the conductors up and down the length

of the train called out the Hindi equivalent of "All Aboard," and slammed the doors shut. The engine's whistle sounded several long blasts, and with a jerk we were underway. Slowly we pulled away from the platform, accelerating gradually past the coolies and tea-sellers, past beggars and stacks of burlap-wrapped packages awaiting shipment, past drably dressed station attendants until, startlingly, we emerged from the gloomy twilight of the station into the bright morning sunlight. Along the tracks on both sides of us, inside the fence that separated the tracks from the rest of Old Delhi, were cardboard shanties. Their dark-skinned residents, clad only in rags, were going about the business of the morning, picking through the trash at the track's edge, looking for something to eat. I wondered, was it like this everywhere?

Slowly the train gathered speed. Clickety-clack went the wheels, ever faster on the uneven tracks. Gusts of sulfurous black smoke and an occasional live cinder flew in through our open windows, depositing a layer of ash on the small steel table under the windowsill. We conversed excitedly as the train slipped past neighborhoods of concrete, flat-roofed houses, past commercial sectors of garage-sized retail businesses, their proprietors just opening vertical sliding doors to the morning sun and setting out their goods for display on the street. We gathered speed past industrial areas of warehouses and one-room "factories," vacant lots with wrecked and dismembered motor vehicles, then past open spaces and pastures where farm boys herded their goats and dairy cows. Soon we were going full tilt through waving fields of yellow mustard and vast stands of sugar cane. Gradually the scenery became a homogenous mix of rural Indian life, and I turned my attention to the animated discussion in our compartment about what we had seen in Delhi and what we would soon be seeing in Amritsar.

CHAPTER NINETEEN

The Golden Temple

HALFWAY FROM DELHI TO AMRITSAR the signs indicating the names of rural train stations, most of which we rattled past without stopping, changed from Hindi to Punjabi, as did the appearance of those waiting on the platforms for local trains. Instead of the clean-shaven Hindu men and sari-wearing women who were prevalent to the south, we now saw mostly Sikhs, the men with their long beards and turbans, the women in traditional *salwar chemise*, a loose-fitting pajama suit with baggy pants and a long shirt-like dress. Most of the women wore their hair in a braid down the back, with a *chunni*, a 6-foot, delicately flowing scarf, worn over the shoulders and around the neck.

When we finally pulled into the station at Amritsar in the late afternoon we were met by a large crowd of Sikhs, led by a contingent of officials and administrators from the Shiromani Gurdwara Prabandak Committee (SGPC), which had its main offices inside the Golden Temple compound. Cheers of *Bolay Soni Hal* were raised as we stepped off the train, and each of us was given a necklace of bright orange calendula flowers. Sikh sevadars rushed to do the work normally done by coolies, cheerfully loading our bags onto the back of a large flatbed truck brought there for the purpose. The coolies were angry as they watched thirty rupees' worth of work evaporating before their eyes, but one of the Sikh officials appeased them with a small cash settlement. Amid continuing cheers and a sea of smiling faces, we were ushered into taxis and chauffeured through the narrow streets of Amritsar. As we approached the Golden Temple compound, the streets were lined with cheering and curious Sikhs of all ages. A sevadar threw open the gates, and we drove down a pedestrian courtyard straight to Guru Nanak Nivas, a "modern" four-story guest house, two floors of which the SGPC had made available for our exclusive use.

Everything was being done for us. Payment for the taxis was handled discreetly by one official, while another explained that the sevadars would unload and watch the luggage for us so that we could immediately go pay our respects to Guru Granth Sahib inside the Golden Temple. The sweet sound of Gurbani Kirtan echoed gently throughout the compound. Leaving our shoes at the doorstep of Guru Nanak Nivas, we walked barefoot across the courtyard and through a majestic arched gateway. Here the cobblestones of the courtyard gave way to an expansive walkway of intricately patterned marble tile in brown, amber, black, and white. We proceeded as a group down one or two steps, across which flowed a stream of fresh water to wash our feet. Through another arch we entered onto the *Prakarma*, a broad walkway tiled in marble with geometric, repeating patterns even more intricate than the one we had just crossed. One look at what lay beyond stopped us all in our tracks.

The Prakarma surrounds a man-made lake, which the Sikhs call *Amrit Sarovar,* or "Lake of Nectar." It is some five hundred feet square, and in the very center, as if floating lightly on the surface, is a small temple sheathed in pure gold and bright white marble. Everything about the Golden Temple is ornate and delicate, from the shape of the windows to the golden parapets, pillared turrets, and gilded central dome. The impression is magnified by the temple's glittering reflection on the surface of the Sarovar. Spontaneously, most of the Americans went to their knees and bowed their foreheads to the cold marble. I had never seen anything so beautiful, or sensed such a deep connection and profound reverence. This place, made by man, seemed to contain a tangible part of God. It was a place of extraordinary tranquility, even with dozens of sevadars, pilgrims, and visitors coming and going all around us. For several moments we stood in awe, drinking in the scene, while the sound of Gurbani Kirtan filled the air. No wonder the Sikhs call this place *Harimandar Sahib*, the Temple of God.

Slowly, we began proceeding clockwise along the Prakarma so that we could access the narrow walkway on the far side that would take us out to the temple itself. To our left, and all around the outer perimeter of the Prakarma, were two- and three-story buildings whose marble facades contained arched, cloistered walkways and ornate portals. At the far end loomed the Akal Takhat, five magnificent stories of intricately arched windows, portals, balconies, and gilded turrets. The Akal Takhat ("Immortal Throne") is the seat of the Sikh's highest religious authority. From its stately front steps are proclaimed from time to time the *Hookamnamas,* or guiding edicts of the Sikh faith. In front of the Akal Takhat the Prakarma widens to accommodate large gatherings. Directly across from the stairs is a small marble gatehouse with gilded doors. Through its arched doorway we proceeded onto a long, tiled walkway with elegant marble railings that stretched to the middle of the sarovar, ending at the diminutive front portal of the Golden Temple.

Amidst all this magnificence and splendor, the Golden Temple had been designed to embody humility before God. The doorway into the temple is quite small, and no one walks through it upright. The raised marble doorstep has been worn smooth from the lips of countless pilgrims who for hundreds of years have bowed and kissed it before entering this holiest of all Sikh shrines. We followed the example of millions of pilgrims before us. As we entered, there in front of us, in the very center of the small temple, was the Guru Granth Sahib on a raised platform, surrounded by the most opulent raiments imaginable. Encircling the platform and the whole central part of the temple was a short, brass railing. Just inside it sat two sevadars. One of them served prasad to each pilgrim after he or she had bowed and left the traditional cash offering. The other sevadar gave special presents to those who made offerings of more than one rupee. Despite the air of sanctity and wonder, I carefully watched those in front of me, and had the system pretty well figured out by the time it was my turn to bow. Any offering of one to five rupees earned a sugar biscuit, a light-as-air three-inch wafer of puffed white sugar. An offering of six to ten rupees earned a folded saropa of orange silk. Anything over ten rupees earned the saropa with two sugar biscuits folded inside. I quickly took eleven rupees out of my wallet, and after bowing, walked away with a saropa and two sugar biscuits.

I found a place to sit on the floor just behind the Ragis, on the left side by the railings surrounding the Guru Granth Sahib (all the women sat on the other side). There I watched the tabla player and tried to follow the amazingly intricate rhythms elicited from his primitive-looking instrument. I had grown up in a family of classical musicians, had started piano lessons at four, and prided myself on my own musical ability. But I couldn't figure out most of what the tabla player was doing. Some of it was in 4/4 time, but most of it left me bewildered. Later I found out that 5/8, 7/8, 10/8, 14/8, and even more obscure rhythms—like 15/8—are commonly used in classical Gurbani Kirtan.

As I sat listening to the Kirtan, I looked around at my surroundings. The main floor of the Golden Temple was about fifty by seventy feet, but it was broken into smaller areas by four massive internal pillars, which reduced the central floor area to about thirty by forty feet. Much of this was taken up by the Guru Granth Sahib's fenced enclosure, leaving room for perhaps a hundred people on the entire first floor. The central area, however, was open through to the second floor, where a mezzanine allowed another thirty or forty people to look down on the proceedings below. Surrounding the outer wall of this mezzanine were arched windows with broad sills, upon which pilgrims and worshipers could often be found sitting, reciting their prayers. At one corner was a circular stair that led to the roof. In good weather, the roof also offered many ideal spots for the private recitation of prayers. From where I sat on the first floor, arched portals opened to the Sarovar on all four sides. Guru Arjun, the 5th of the Sikh Gurus and the designer of the Golden Temple, intended to signify that it was open to people of all faiths.

After twenty minutes, sufficient time to show our devotion and take in some of the wonders of the place, we were led back out of the temple, down the walkway, the rest of the way around the Prakarma (it is traditional to walk only clockwise), and back to Guru Nanak Nivas where we reclaimed our shoes and our luggage. We were then assigned rooms, shown the facilities, and served a delicious snack of tea and biscuits. I was by now completely enamored of this place and felt I could be happy here for the rest of my life.

Music, prayer, and recitation of scriptures goes on 24-hours a day at the Golden Temple complex.

CHAPTER TWENTY

The Magic of the Place

That night, I could barely sleep. For hours I lay in bed listening to the soft echoes of people chanting in the distance, "*Sat Nam Wahe Guru, Sat Nam Wahe Guru.*" My bedroom was on the third floor in an open hallway directly over the courtyard with the Golden Temple beyond. Activities inside the Golden Temple compound continued 24 hours a day. From 3:00 AM until 11:30 at night everything going on inside the temple was broadcast over loudspeakers. Each evening just before midnight the outer gate was closed for a few hours while sevadars and volunteers went through the entire temple, cleaning it meticulously from top to bottom. During this time only *Amrit Dhari* men—those who had been formally baptized into the Khalsa—were allowed inside the temple. Outside, on the Prakarma, both men and women worked on their hands and knees using damp rags to scrub every inch of the marble walkway, chanting softly while they worked. Yogiji had told us many times how before coming to America he found liberation while performing the midnight *Seva* of washing the floors of the Hari Mandir Sahib. I dreamed of doing the same, but I was not yet an Amrit Dhari Sikh.

Shortly before 3:00 AM Larry knocked lightly on my door and said that we should get up and shower, for the whole group was going to the Golden Temple for meditation. In the chilly night air, the open hallways and shared cold water shower facilities of Guru

Nanak Nivas provided a strong incentive to bathe and dress quickly (or stay in bed). Back in my room, after showering, I was shivering while trying to wrap my turban. I was just finishing when there was another knock on the door. It was a sevadar with a tray full of stainless-steel cups, brimming with hot Chai. What a welcome sight! A few minutes later, wrapped in a heavy shawl, I joined Larry and several others of our group in the courtyard and proceeded barefoot into the Golden Temple compound. The marble underfoot was frigid, and my toes were numb before we had gone even halfway around the *Prakarma*. The door of the gatehouse was still closed, and for a few minutes we stood around in the dark trying to stay warm. Dozens of other pilgrims were arriving, and soon there was a substantial crowd gathered, waiting for the gates to open.

Then, with a rattle of ancient latches, a tiny door that was set into the gate opened and a sevadar signaled for us to come in. One by one we stooped and entered. There was a great rush as we proceeded down the walkway, for everyone—especially the older Sikh women from the villages—seemed desperate to be the first inside the temple. Upon entering, I was surprised to see that the Guru Granth Sahib was not yet installed on its platform. Nonetheless we all bowed and left our donations, receiving our respective saropas according to the level of our generosity. I sat in the same place I had the previous afternoon, wrapped myself in my shawl, closed my eyes and tried to meditate while warming my toes. All around me people were mumbling their prayers from memory or reading from their *Nit Nem*, the standard prayer book of the Sikhs. I couldn't meditate, however, for I was so enthralled with my surroundings. Every surface inside the Golden Temple is decorated in rich detail. The walls and pillars are inlaid with intricate mosaics of marble and semiprecious stones. Lapis, carnelian, turquoise, agate and others combine to depict peacocks and palaces, or geometric patterns more stunning and intricate even than those on the Prakarma.

Soon, the Ragis came in, carrying their instruments wrapped in blue cloth. One of them was blind, and was led by the tabla player to his place directly in front of me. Without further assistance he sat and unwrapped his harmonium. Within a few moments they began to sing, but it was nothing like the shabads I had heard before. Rather, it was a strange recitative, with some lines accompanied by harmonium, others sung a cappella, some verses sung by the main Ragis, others by the tabla player. From time to time the music would stop entirely and an old and venerable Sikh would stand up somewhere in the congregation and recite a few verses. Most of the time the tabla player hammered out a sparse, asymmetrical beat, or played nothing at all. Occasionally he would burst into a powerful, pulsing rhythm that would quickly crescendo to a syncopated climax before dropping out entirely once again. This was the musical form of the *Asa di Var*, one of the traditional morning prayers of the Sikhs. It lasted for more than an hour, lulling me into a sleepy, meditative state.

Suddenly, I was jolted awake by a loud, deep-throated horn sounding in the distance, its single bass note echoing and reverberating around the Prakarma. Instantly the mood inside the temple changed, though the music continued as before. Everyone was now attentive, and the air was taut with expectation. Again, the horn sounded, this time a little closer. By the third blast, it was evident that the horn was proceeding down the walkway towards the temple. Voices could also be heard, chanting or exclaiming "*Sat Nam, Wahe Guru*," slowly drawing closer. The horn sounded again and again, growing impossibly loud until, with a final blast, the doors were thrown open and the Guru Granth Sahib, resting in a heavy golden palanquin on the shoulders of eight or ten Sikhs, was brought into the temple. Everyone inside jumped to their feet, and for the next fifteen minutes stood attentively while the Guru Granth Sahib was ceremoniously placed on its platform, unwrapped from its elaborate raiment and opened at random for the first *hookam* (word, or command of the Guru) of the day, which followed a recitation of Ardas, the traditional prayer of the Sikh fath.

After the Hookam, the Ragis started up again, singing shabads while several sevadars meandered through the congregation, distributing prasad from large steel bowls. The mood was sublime and happy. When one of the sevadars drew near, I held my hands out, palms cupped right over left to receive the prasad. He looked at me and smiled, scooping up an enormous handful of the hot bread pudding and dumping it into my hands. The prasad was sweet and buttery and left my hands covered with grease. Without a napkin I didn't know what to do to clean it off. All around me the Sikh men rubbed their hands into their beards. But I had no beard, so I surreptitiously rubbed the excess onto my bare feet. Later, I was told that this was not a good thing to do, for touching one's own feet in the presence of the Guru is considered very bad form.

The music continued for another hour until dawn, when there was another Ardas and Hookam. Then a second group of Ragis came in to take over the music. I got up, stiff-kneed and tired, to head back to Guru Nanak Nivas for a nap before breakfast. I had gotten warm and comfortable while sitting amidst the crush of Sikhs inside, but when I walked out of the temple, the air felt quite cold, and the marble under my feet even colder. As I walked around the Prakarma, a number of Sikh men were ceremoniously immersing themselves in the cold water of the Sarovar. We were told that the water had healing qualities. The site had been chosen for the Golden Temple by Guru Ram Das, the fourth of the Sikh Gurus, especially for that reason. Legend has it that hundreds of years earlier a woman had been wandering in the forest with her deformed and crippled husband and had left him sitting by a stream while she went looking for food. As he sat there, he was surprised to see a black bird dive into the water and come out a brilliant white. Taking it as a sign, he dragged himself over and immersed himself in the stream, and was instantly healed. This was the spot that Guru Ram Das chose for the *Amrit Sarovar*, and it is still marked by a large tree, one of only two growing inside the Prakarma. Hundreds of thousands of Sikhs come from all over the world to bathe in the healing waters under this tree, not only as a treatment for their physical ailments, but especially for the healing of their souls.

When my daughters visited Amritsar many years after I was there, they stopped in to say hello to my tailor, Karnail Singh, who remembered me well and sent his greetings. He must have been well over 90 at the time, and still using a hand-operated sewing machine.

CHAPTER TWENTY-ONE

New Clothes

BREAKFAST WAS SERVED to our group of Americans in one of the hallways of Guru Nanak Nivas. We sat on the floor in long rows facing each other "Langar style," while sevadars ran up and down distributing stainless steel plates and spoons, then rice, dal, *subzi* (vegetables), *dahi* (yogurt), and *chapatis*. This "Langar style" proved to be a very efficient way to get a meal served. But Langar has a deeper meaning and significance. It is a tradition, hundreds of years old, by which every Gurdwara maintains a free kitchen. In most Gurdwaras meals are served only at the completion of a service. However, in many of the historic Gurdwaras throughout Punjab and northern India the Langar is open 24 hours a day to anyone of any religion who shows up. The Sikh Gurus saw that not only was Langar an important component in building community, it was also an "equalizer" in their fight against the caste system. No one in the Langar hall is seated high or low, or given any preferential sign or status. Everyone simply sits on the floor. There were times, as well, when the community's survival depended upon sharing resources. No one who lived in proximity to a Gurdwara would ever starve to death.

In the early days of the religion, almost every Sikh was a convert from either Hinduism or Islam. The Gurus drew from both these traditions, but they knew that in order to create a unified community, the Sikhs would have to share not only a form of worship, but also a uniform set of traditions, values, and lifestyles. It certainly wouldn't do to have converts from Islam arguing with converts from Hinduism over such issues as whether or not to eat meat, whether to pray five times per day or seven, whether to bow to the east or before idols and statues, whether to wear a turban or shave one's head, how to conduct marriages, the role of women in society, and many other details of daily life in which the traditions of Hindus and Muslims differed. When Yogiji had first started teaching us about Sikhism he had called it a "way of life," rather than a religion. Now I realized that it was a way of life not *instead*, but in *addition* to being a religion, for in Sikhism virtually every aspect of daily life has a tradition, method, prohibition, rule, or guideline attached.

The SGPC was giving our group of Americans special treatment that some fundamentalists might have frowned upon. Not only were they serving us in the privacy of Guru Nanak Nivas—a special hall dedicated to the serving of Langar was located just across the courtyard—they were also serving us special food, not available across the way. The "Guru's Langar," as it is often called, is supported by donations, left by worshipers when they bow before Guru Granth Sahib. In rural India it is not uncommon for a Sikh to bring a bag of rice or lentils as an offering instead of cash. In the historic Gurdwaras, which are managed by the SGPC, the administration determines how the Langar will be run and what food will be served. In the Langar at the Golden Temple we later discovered the food was quite a bit plainer than what we were being served at Guru Nanak Nivas. It was a minor point, however. We were grateful that the food was always excellent, and the special accommodations made things much easier for us.

Yogiji was to arrive later that afternoon, so I took the opportunity of some free time after breakfast to explore the town of Amritsar and look for a tailor. I wanted to have some *Kurtas (shirts)* and

Chudidas (jodhpurs) made that would fit me properly. Until that time I had only "off the rack" type of Indian shirts that were available at import stores in the states. I wanted something that looked more traditional, and the prices were so good that even with only a few hundred rupees I knew I could get a complete wardrobe to my liking. I did not have to go far. I walked out of the courtyard straight into a bustling bazaar. It was very much like a low-cost version of Old Delhi, except there were no beggars to speak of. The street may have been paved, but there was so much dirt and dust that it was impossible to tell for sure. Just outside, and to the right of the courtyard gate, was a line of tiny shops. They were the size of small storage lockers and had the same lack of amenities, except that they were all elevated three feet above street level. Most of them had their wares displayed on the doorsill, waist high for shoppers.

The first shop sold Sikh religious items: *karas, kangas, kirpans, Nit Nems*, and posters depicting the 10 Sikh Gurus. I immediately bought several items paying, I'm sure, the highest price in Amritsar. My total out of pocket was about 25 rupees, or $3.00 US. Next was a sweets shop. Other than *gulab jamuns*, I never did get used to the sweets that are popular in India. Deep-fried sugar pretzels and sugary doughballs just didn't appeal to me, nor did things with day-glow food coloring, nor hand-rolled delicacies called *Ladoos* sitting on trays in open markets sharing airspace with flies and dust. The next shop sold shoes and sandals, most of them made of cheap plastic—nothing there for me. But the fourth shop was just what I was looking for. On one side of the doorframe was a woman's brazier made with great skill but considerable lack of understanding about anatomy. But on the other side, on a hangar, was a simple white kurta. Clearly, this was a tailor who made up for his lack of understanding about a woman's body by his obvious skill at sewing kurtas for Sikh men.

I approached the shop and peered into the unlit gloom past the doorway. There, sitting on a milk crate near the back of the shop, operating a manual sewing machine, was an old "Baba," a portly octogenarian in wrinkled white clothes and a sloppy white turban. "*Sardarji*", I called to him. He looked up at me with utter amazement but a welcoming smile. "*Hanji*," he replied, followed by a bunch of Punjabi I didn't understand. "*Meh kurta chanda han*," I said, exhausting most of my Punjabi vocabulary explaining that I wanted a kurta. "*Hanji*," he said, nodding his understanding and obviously flattered that I attempted to speak his language. "*Idder ah*," he said, still flapping his downturned hand. Seeing that I wasn't understanding, he smoothed a place next to him on some fabric, indicating that I should come sit down. Then I understood. In India, the common hand motion for "come here" is upside down from what we are accustomed to in America. "Amrikan Singh?" he asked as I climbed up into his shop. "*Hanji*," I responded. "*Tera nan ki heh*?" he asked. Then, seeing he had lost me again said in halting English, "Your Name what is?" "Sat-Peter Singh," I replied as he held a cloth tape measure across my shoulders. "*Mera nam Karnail Singh*," he said, jotting down some unintelligible figures in a dog-eared composition notebook. "*Hanji*," I replied.

Karnail Singh quickly took the rest of my measurements, using a combination of sign language, Punjabi, and facial expressions to find out how long I wanted the hem, and whether I wanted Chudidas, too. One page of his notebook was now filled with chicken scratches. Next, we had to choose the fabric. He had five or six bolts of white cotton sitting on a shelf against the back wall. They all looked the same to me, but he insisted on pulling them out and showing each one. "*Cha Pio*", he said, looking over my shoulder at the doorway. I turned to see a street urchin holding a tray with earthenware cups and a teapot. Karnail Singh sidled past me, gave the boy a small coin and took the tray. There was no refusing the proffered cup when he had filled it and held it out towards me. The tea was delicious, and for a few moments we sat sipping and trying to carry on a conversation, which, of course, was impossible. Whenever Karnail Singh took a sip of tea, it got all over his white mustache and dripped down his long white beard. He used the hem of his kurta to wipe it off.

Eventually we got back to choosing material. He showed me the corner of one bolt, saying simply, "Best." "*Kittenay paisa*?" I enquired about the price. I couldn't understand what he said, but nodded my assent. Apparently, our business was done. "You coming just tomorrow." Karnail Singh smiled. He was not much better at English than I was at Punjabi, but there was a genuine friendliness and goodwill between us that overcame the language barrier. I took out my wallet as if to pay him, but he only shook his head and waved his hands back and forth. He would not take any money from me—at least not yet. The next day when I returned, the ill-shapen bra still hung outside the door, but the shop was closed, the rolling metal gate secured by an ancient brass padlock. The shoe seller in the adjoining stall saw me, and with a look of recognition said, 'Tomorrow. Karnail Singh Ji say tomorrow."

When I walked into the bazaar the next day, Karnail Singh was in his shop. He waved (upside-down) to call me over and smiled as if we were the oldest of friends. "Kurta ready," he beamed. I climbed up into his shop and looked on with anticipation as he unwrapped a bundle of white cloth. Instead of a kurta, it was all the pieces needed to make one, pinned together at the shoulders. Karnail Singh slipped the pieces over my arms, used a piece of blue chalk to make some marks, took it off, wrapped it back into a bundle, and said, "Tomorrow coming." Then, as if it was an afterthought, he took a measurement from the top of my foot around to the back of my heel and wrote it in his notebook. "*Cha Pio*?" he asked. "Tomorrow," I said. The next morning, I returned again and found to my surprise that Karnail Singh had completed three beautiful kurtas and three pairs of Chudidas. I tried on a set. The kurta was perfect, as were the Chudidas, my ankles just barely fitting through the tight calves. I was immensely pleased. Karnail Singh waved at the tea urchin on the other side of the street and within a few moments we were sharing a cup of tea together, practicing on each other our limited but growing vocabularies.

Eventually, I asked again, "*Kittenay paisa?*" pulling out my wallet in case my pronunciation left any doubt about my intentions. Karnail Singh said something that I didn't understand, so I started shelling out 50-rupee notes, looking at him inquisitively. When I got to the sixth note he stopped me, took the 300 rupees, and handed me 5 singles. He had charged me 295 rupees—only $36, or $12 per full set of clothes. We beamed at each other and tried to outdo one another in our profusions of thanks. This old man had such a genuine, friendly nature that I wanted to spend more time with him. But with our conversation so limited by the paucity of our respective vocabularies, I did what I thought would be the next best thing. I told my friends about him, and every time I returned to Amritsar, I had him make me more clothes. The last time I was there, in 1984, he was still sitting in his shop, still smiling, and still making kurtas from the same white cotton. He must have been well over ninety.

CHAPTER TWENTY-TWO

Another New Identity

WHEN YOGIJI ARRIVED at the airport in Amritsar that afternoon, we were there to greet him, along with all the leadership of the SGPC, half the staff of sevadars from the Golden Temple complex, and a couple hundred local Sikhs. There were a lot of flowers and saropas presented when Yogiji and his secretaries stepped out of the plane. Round after round of *Bolay Soni Hal—Sat Siri Aka*l went up from the enthusiastic crowd. Gurcharan Singh Tohra, President of the SGPC and one of the most politically powerful Sikhs in India, addressed Yogiji as a hero, then turned and gave a short speech in Punjabi to the welcoming crowd. More cheers erupted at key points in his brief talk. Then Yogiji spoke for a few minutes, thanking Tohra Sahib and the SGPC for the warm welcome and the hospitality that was being extended to all of us. After piling back into the buses, taxis and official SGPC vehicles that had brought us all out to the airport, we caravanned back to the Golden Temple complex where, in a large and animated crowd, we accompanied Yogiji as he paid his respects to Guru Granth Sahib inside the Golden Temple.

Later that evening I found out that Yogiji had arranged with the SGPC and the priests of the Akal Takhat for a special ceremony the next day so that all the Americans who wanted to could be baptized as Amrit Dhari Sikhs. This would allow us, at least the men among us, the privilege of serving as sevadars in the midnight cleaning of the Golden Temple. But even more exciting for me, I learned that he had arranged private lessons for me with one of the tabla masters of the Golden Temple. For this I clearly had Larry to thank, for I had told him earlier that I would really like to study tablas while in Amritsar. He had gone to bat for me, asking Yogiji on my behalf to set it up, and Yogiji had wasted no time doing it. It was incredible. I was going to be studying with one of the world's best Sikh tabla players. The next afternoon, one of the officers of the SGPC would be bringing my teacher to meet me so that he and I could make our own arrangements for lessons. First, however, would be the Amrit ceremony.

At 11:00 AM the following day about 20 of us were accompanied by Yogiji to the front steps of the Akal Takhat where we were met by five of the head priests of the Sikh Dharma. These were some very serious looking men. They were dressed in dark blue, knee-length kurtas under which they wore only *kacheras*, a traditional Sikh military underwear that hugs the thighs just above the knees and blooms out into a great mass of fabric at the waist, pulled tight with a drawstring. All five priests had long gray or white beards and dark blue turbans. Massive kirpans hung at their sides. They looked us over with inscrutable severity while one of them exchanged some words with Yogiji in Punjabi, gesturing towards us from time to time. We had been properly prepared for the ceremony, and were dressed in the same attire as the priests, except we were all in white. Kirpans hung at our sides, and karas made of stainless steel circled the wrists on our right arms. One of the priests went from one to the next of us, checking to see if we were wearing kacheras (we all were), and if we had a *kanga* (a small wooden comb) in our hair. He then separated a fold or two in our turbans, exposing a small area at the tops of our heads. We were told to stand at attention with our palms together at our chests while the five priests began the ritual.

CHAPTER TWENTY-TWO: Another New Identity

They all kneeled, sitting on one heel around a large steel bowl containing a gallon or two of water. One of them started reciting *Japji Sahib*, the first prayer that Sikhs are supposed to recite each morning, while another stirred the water with a long double-edged sword. This went on for about fifteen minutes. When Japji was finished, another priest began reciting *Jap Sahib*, the second of the *banis* or daily prayers of the Sikhs. It was a highly rhythmical poem composed by Guru Gobind Singh. We still stood at attention. For the next hour-and-a-quarter the priests took turns reciting all five of the daily prayers while stirring the holy water with the sword. Finally, the prayers were completed. For an hour-and-a-half we had been standing at attention. I couldn't imagine how the priests knelt on the cold marble the entire time. The head priest then addressed us in Punjabi, telling us the commandments of Guru Gobind Singh. We couldn't understand the words, but we had a pretty good idea what he was saying. *"Cigret, sharab nehi pindi"* (don't smoke cigarettes or drink alcohol), abstain from extra-marital sex; keep hair uncut, always wear the "five K's," recite all five Banis each day. I knew I would have trouble with this last one. I couldn't read or speak Punjabi—or *Gurmukhi,* as it is called in its religious context ("from the mouth of the Guru")—and it would be a couple of years before I would be able to recite the banis.

The Amrit ceremony of the Sikhs was first performed by Guru Gobind Singh in 1699 when Sikhs throughout northern India were being persecuted by the Mughal Empire. Gobind Singh put out a general call that all Sikhs should join him during the month of Baisakhi (March/April) in a remote village of Punjab, now known as Anandpur Sahib (place of bliss). He sent instructions that all should come wearing turbans (another blow to the caste system of the Hindus, which allowed only the noblest members of society to wear turbans). Many thousands of Sikhs attended. One morning, when all had gathered to hear their Guru speak, Gobind Singh surprised them by demanding that one of his Sikhs should offer him his head. The Guru's unsheathed sword added a literal interpretation that left the crowd unsettled. Amidst the confused silence one Sikh finally stepped forward saying, "I have already given you my life; what matter if I give my head as well."

Legends, myths, and historical accounts become blurred at this point. Gobind Singh led the volunteer into a tent, emerging alone after a moment, his upheld sword dripping with fresh blood while the stunned Sikhs looked on in horror. The Guru, now in an impassioned state, called out for another volunteer to give his head. Many of the Sikhs, now convinced of his literal and deadly intent, moved away from the front. Murmurs went through the crowd as those in the back, unable to see for themselves, learned of the Guru's activities. Amidst the confusion, another brave Sikh stepped forward to offer his head. Again, Gobind Singh led him into the tent, emerging with freshly bloodied sword held high for all to see. "Another head!!" he shouted above the restless shifting of the crowd. Many of those in the back, convinced that their Guru had gone crazy, began leaving. By Gobind Singh's fifth call for a head, the crowd was thinning rapidly as thousands of disillusioned, frightened, and discouraged Sikhs left to prepare for their long journeys home.

After taking the fifth volunteer into his tent, Guru Gobind Singh remained inside for some time. Only the bravest and most curious of the Sikhs remained for the miraculous spectacle to which they would next be witness. The Guru finally emerged from his tent, leading all five of his victims. Each was now dressed in brilliant blue raiments, and each held in his own hands his own severed head. With this miracle, Guru Gobind Singh changed forever the identity of the Sikh community. Unparalleled courage, commitment, and blind devotion to the Guru had been demonstrated as the highest virtues. The five brave volunteers were now glorified by the Guru. He called them his *Panj Piare,* his five beloved ones, and after restoring their severed heads to their bodies, showed them to his fledgling nation as the example of "true Sikhs." He then called the crowd back together to take part in a new baptism that would infuse them with courage, devotion, and humility before God and Guru.

Bringing forth a large steel bowl partly filled with water, Guru Gobind Singh began stirring it with his sword while reciting one after another of the Banis. He explained to the reassembled crowd that the water was being infused with the spirit of courage and righteousness. As if to prove the point, a sparrow is said to have alighted on the bowl and sipped from the water, after which it flew up and attacked a hawk that was flying overhead. Seeing this, one of Guru Gobind Singh's wives (the fact of his multiple wives always raised questions in my mind, which I ignored) stepped forward and crumbled some sugar into the bowl, saying that the sweetness was to prevent the Sikhs from turning their martial spirit upon each other. Rather, they should live in the sweet spirit of brotherhood. Guru Gobind Singh endorsed this addition to the baptismal nectar and proceeded with the ceremony by kneeling before the Five Beloved Ones and having them baptize him first.

The five head priests of the Akal Takhat now took that same role in baptizing the twenty Americans gathered before hundreds of onlookers in the bright morning sunlight. After the recitation of all the Banis, we were commanded to kneel while the holy water was sprinkled on our heads and into our eyes and faces. At the conclusion of the ceremony, the massive bowl was carried to each of us in turn, so that we could drink the sweetened water that remained. There was a lot to drink, and the bowl made the rounds several times before all the sugary liquid was gone. We were then told to stand, and amidst cheers of *"Bolay Soni Hal—Sat Siri Akal!"* we

Larry and I studied Punjabi together as we became more closely connected to the Sikh religion.

were welcomed into the fold of the Khalsa, the pure ones: Guru Gobind Singh's own soldiers of righteousness. We were told that our greeting from then on would be "*Wahe Guruji Ka Khalsa,*" to which the reply was "*Wahe Guruji Ki Fateh!*" (God of the Pure Ones; Victory to God!). This was a big step up from the simple "Sat Nam" that Yogiji had taught us back in America, or the "*Sat Siri Akal*" that most Indian Sikhs use as a greeting. But we had come a long way, too. In three short years I had gone from being a hippie rock musician to a baptized, turban-wearing, kirpan-wielding member of the Khalsa. And this was only the beginning.

CHAPTER TWENTY-THREE

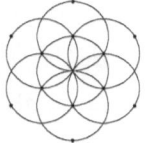

I Get a Tabla Teacher

LATE THAT AFTERNOON, towards the end of an early dinner in the hallway of Guru Nanak Nivas, Giani Mohinder Singh, one of the top administrators of the SGPC, came in asking for me. Mohinder Singh, or Gianiji, as he was usually called with both affection and respect, was a singular character. He was in his late sixties, but his pure white beard and mustache seemed at odds with the youthful look in his eyes, his mirthful and outgoing personality, and the spring still evident in his step. He was not more than five feet six inches tall, and weighed probably 115 pounds. But from this elf-like frame issued forth the most extraordinary voice. He would have been a basso profundo, but his vocal cords had been damaged earlier in life, and every word out of his mouth now sounded like the growling of a great bear. He seemed to be Yogiji's closest friend among the leadership of the SGPC and was chiefly responsible for the extraordinary treatment that we being given while in Amritsar.

Accompanying Gianiji was someone I immediately recognized. It was the tabla player who had assisted the blind Ragi at the Golden Temple the previous morning. I jumped to my feet in excitement as the two of them approached. "Sat-Peter Singh Khalsa?" growled Gianiji. "Hanji," I responded. "Wahe Guruji Ka Khalsa..." he said in exaggerated and expectant tones, dwelling on the last syllable to invite my response. "Wahe Guruji Ki Fateh!" I answered with a smile and equally exaggerated tones. He was clearly delighted with the exchange. "This man Gurbax Singh," continued Gianiji, nodding his head in his companion's direction, "Tabla master. You study. Tabla master becoming. *Oh day nal entizzam ker deo*," he ended, giving up on English. I understood only the word "entizzam," which means "arrangements," so the meaning of the rest of the sentence was pretty clear. I looked at Gurbax Singh and we shook hands, smiling. Having completed his introduction, Gianiji now turned and left us to figure out for ourselves not only when and where we would study together, but how we would communicate at all.

Gurbax could speak barely a word of English, and my Punjabi was equally limited. But what we lacked in the tools of language we more than made up for in our natural and spontaneous friendship and our shared enthusiasm, not only for the tablas themselves and the challenge of turning me into a respectable player, but also for the honor accorded both of us by our mutual assignment: for me to study with one of the masters of the Golden Temple, and for Gurbax to been chosen by the SGPC as the first ever to teach an American. Gurbax and I smiled at each other for some time, shaking hands and not knowing quite how to start. I struggled to put a polite sentence together. "*Mei kush...*" I stammered, trying to say, "I'm happy to meet you." But I had forgotten how to complete the phrase. Gurbax understood immediately, however, and returned with a glowing smile, "You...my house...coming." The sign language that accompanied these words would have been sufficient to convey his meaning. "Right now?" I asked. It was clear he didn't understand. I searched for the word in Punjabi. "*Hunay?*" I attempted. "*Hanji!*" he replied enthusiastically.

Gurbax Singh's house was actually a small apartment in a bleak two-story concrete compound facing an empty lot at the far side of the Golden Temple Complex. To get there, we walked out the main gate, turned left in the bazaar and twisted our way through a maze of

CHAPTER TWENTY-THREE: I Get a Tabla Teacher

narrow alleys and walkways, dodging three-wheeled delivery vans, ox-carts, delivery men carrying heavy loads, and a variety of domestic animals wandering freely in the streets. Gurbax introduced me to his wife, his two-year-old son, Prince, and his infant daughter in her mother's arms. "*Bettoh*," he said, after the formalities were over, indicating that I should sit on a mat in the center of his minimal living room. I looked around the apartment while he retrieved his tablas from a built-in concrete shelf next to the front door. The place was tiny, consisting of a living room, perhaps 10' by 12', an adjoining kitchen and a small bedroom in the back. The kitchen had only a cold-water sink, a concrete counter, a 2-burner kerosene stove and a small wooden cabinet that served as a kind of pantry. Gurbax's wife, like most Indians at the time, bought her food fresh each day in the nearby bazaar.

The living room walls were devoid of decoration. They were painted with a watery greenish whitewash that came off in a chalky smudge wherever it was touched. For furnishings there were two wood-framed armchairs, a low coffee table, and a flimsy, oriental-style throw rug in the middle of the room upon which I was sitting. It was so thin that it offered no protection for my ankles as I sat cross-legged on the concrete floor. The room had only one window. It was in the front wall, but had no glass panes. Instead, it had vertical steel bars built into the concrete window frame. A screen stretched across the outside and a pair of shutters opened to the inside. Hanging from a thin wire at the center of the living room ceiling was a single naked electric bulb. A small electric heater in the corner promised little relief from a cold winter's night.

The apartment had no bathroom, but shared a communal washroom and toilet with the four other second-floor apartments in the building. The toilet, however, wasn't anything a Westerner might expect. It was merely a hole in the floor with concrete footpads on each side. There was nothing to sit on, which actually seemed like a good idea to me. I had seen the same arrangement on the train from Delhi, and also at Guru Nanak Nivas. In fact, most bathrooms throughout India at the time offered the same basic accommodations. There was also no toilet paper. Instead, there was a small faucet protruding from the wall and a tin cup on the floor, which, when combined with a dexterous left hand, provided all the hygiene one could expect or hope for. It is for this reason, I quickly discovered, that no one in India eats or shakes hands with the left hand. Although I was distressed at first, I soon learned that these facilities were relatively civilized. In outlying areas, it was not unusual to find only a brick hut with no accommodation other than a pail of water, a tin cup, and a hole in the wall at one corner. The "flushing mechanism" would be a sevadar, who from time to time would throw buckets full of water across the floor, washing everything in its path out the hole into an open ditch. It is no small wonder that cholera, dysentery, and other diseases were so common.

Gurbax's wife was gracious, but very shy. She was dressed in a pale-yellow salwar chemise, the traditional dress of Punjabi women. After being introduced to me, she retreated to the back of the house where she divided her time between the tiny kitchen and her bedroom, attending to the needs of her infant daughter. Prince, in a pair of bottomless trousers—rural India's answer to disposable diapers—spent most of his time on the narrow front balcony playing with the children from neighboring apartments.

After unwrapping his tablas from the blue cloth that served as their carrying case, Gurbax placed them in front of me and sat down with the tablas between us. Gurbax was young, perhaps 27, relatively tall at 5 foot 10 inches, and robust. In fact, he was shaped like a Buddha. He was a man who clearly enjoyed eating, and his zest for life was apparent in everything he did, especially in playing the tablas. For an hour we sat together while he taught me the basics of how to strike each of the two unusual drums that, as a pair, comprise the instrument. The drum under my right hand, from which the instrument gets its name, was called the *tabla*. It could make a high-pitched ringing tone if struck correctly. The margin for error, however, was extremely thin, and for some time I could coax from it only a dull thunk. The *bayan* sits under the left hand and is played with a completely different technique. Its deep tone can be manipulated by the pressure or position of the wrist, which rests on the surface of the head. A skillful player can tap out a kind of bass line, wholly integrated with the combined rhythms of both drums. When played this way, the tablas become much more than just a rhythm instrument. Though they could hardly be called melodic, they do have, in the hands of an expert player, a compelling and exciting voice.

Gurbax also taught me the "language" of the tablas. Each sound—each way of striking either one drum or both together—has a special name. "Ta" is a clear ringing tone created by striking the head of the tabla with the first joint of the first finger of the right hand. "Ge" is created by striking the bayan with the tips of the middle two fingers of the left hand (but it can be created many other ways too) to produce a low, open bass note. If played simultaneously, "Ta" plus "Ge" creates a new sound called "Da." With multiple sounds available on each drum, the number of permutations and combinations of sounds is extensive. Added to the sounds themselves are the complicating factors of rhythm, pulse, pitch, and ornamentation.

Following the Indian musical tradition, the first rhythm Gurbax taught me was "Tin Tal," a sixteen beat "Tal" (rhythm) that is the foundation of most classical Indian music. Its basic beats are relatively easy to hammer out: *Da Din Din Da, Da Din Din Da, Ta Tin*

My tabla teacher at the Golden Temple, Gurbax Singh and his family, in 1973.

Tin Ta, Ta Din Din Da. I quickly found out, however, that there seemed to be no rule about where a piece of music might start within the 16 beats. Most often, a composition would start on beat 9, but sometimes it might be beat 5, or 13. To help identify the "pulse" within these 16 beats, Gurbax had me practice simply saying them out loud without playing the drums, clapping my hands together on the primary pulse, or pulses, and spreading them far apart (creating the sound of silence) on the secondary pulses. Later, while visiting a music school in Delhi, I found 4-year-old children practicing in the same way.

The initial simplicity of Tin Tal, however, was very deceptive. One can certainly pound out the same 16 *matras* (beats) from beginning to the end of a composition, serving only as a metronome for the singers and instrumentalists, and this is all I was able to do for the first several weeks. But the language and creativity within Tin Tal is remarkably expansive. Gurbax showed me some variations: "Dage Dage Dina Gina, Dage Terekete Tikata_ Terekete, Take Take Tina Kina, Terekete Da_tere Keteda_ Terekete, DA" (where the last beat is actually the first beat of the next phrase). In reading or writing this language, each word represents what in western music would be a quarter note. If the word has two syllables, therefore, each syllable is an eighth note; if it has four syllables, each is a 16th, and so on. Gurbax wrote down the matras (beats) in Gurmukhi script, which I was just learning how to read, but I wrote them in transliterated English, and quickly developed my own way of indicating rests and mixed phrases of quarter, eighth and 16th notes.

I found Tin Tal a very challenging exercise for my intellect and hand coordination, but I was never satisfied with it. To me it sounded flat, somehow: too square, too "heady." I also didn't have the patience to learn the hundreds of standard variations. What turned me on was *Tal Kehrva*, a simple 4/4 played with a hint of swing. This is the basic driving beat of Punjabi folk music. It exudes a kind of life and joy that is irresistible, adding excitement and urgency to the music. It makes you want to dance! But it, too, is deceptively complex. Gurbax showed me the basic Da Tin Take Din, but it would be two years before I figured out how to translate these four matras into something that felt exciting. It's all in the left hand: the way the pitch of the bayan is manipulated to add emphasis to certain beats. For now, I had to struggle along, like every beginner, putting in great effort just to coax any sound at all out of either drum.

After we had been working together for an hour Gurbax's wife brought us tea and cookies, which she called "biscuits". While we relaxed and tried to chat together, I managed to explain that I wanted to buy a set of tablas so that I could practice. Gurbax jumped right up, put on his sandals and signaled for me to follow him. Minutes later we were walking together in a back alley of the bazaar. All the buildings here were concrete bunkers with vertical rolling metal doors. Most of them were closed, for it was already early evening. But one had its door open and was illuminated by a single low-wattage bulb. In the center of the shop, sitting cross-legged on the floor in ragged, dirty gray clothes and sloppy turban, was a skinny young man absorbed in his work. He was struggling with a tabla, threading the long strands of camel or goat hide that hold the drumhead in place. He looked up and smiled when he saw Gurbax, and the two of them exchanged friendly words in a torrent of Punjabi, punctuated occasionally by the words "Amrikan Singh."

Gurbax's friend pulled out several headless tablas and bayans that Gurbax examined carefully one at a time. Finally, he selected one bayan and one tabla. The bayan he handed to me. "Two Kilos," he said jubilantly. "Best quality." I looked the bayan over. It was just an empty brass kettle with a chrome finish on the outside. Inside were bits of dirt and twigs, as if it had been sitting around for a long time. I had no way of knowing whether it was a piece of junk or a masterpiece, but Gurbax's expertise was not to be questioned. "*Hanji,*" I said. "*Kittenay paisa*?" After a quick consultation with Gurbax, during which the shopkeeper looked me up and down several times, they arrived at a price. "*Doh Saw Rupian,*" said the shopkeeper. Two hundred rupees. At the exchange rate of the time that was $25. Again, I had no idea whether this was a good price or if I was getting ripped off. "*Teek heh,*" I agreed. Gurbax exchanged a few more words with his friend, then turned to me and said, "Tomorrow, coming. Ready." He then said goodbye to his friend and walked with me through the darkening alleys, through the bazaar, and back to Guru Nanak Nivas. We had been together little more than an hour, but Gurbax already felt like a good friend. In fact, he was more like a big brother.

CHAPTER TWENTY-THREE: I Get a Tabla Teacher

That evening, and for the rest of the time I was in Amritsar, I would join ten or twelve of my traveling companions as the first group of Westerners ever to perform the midnight seva, the cleaning of the Golden Temple, which could only be done by *Amrit Dhari* Sikh men. After ten days we left Amritsar to accompany Yogiji on a tour of many of the major towns and villages of Punjab. We were treated as celebrities everywhere we went, offered unlimited quantities of delicious Indian food and sweets (which it was bad manners to refuse), and subjected to endless hours of speeches in Punjabi that we did not understand.

By the time we left India, three weeks after arriving at New Delhi, I was thoroughly enamored with Indian culture. More importantly, I finally felt secure in my newly baptized identity as a living embodiment of the spirit of Guru Gobind Singh. I was now an Amrit Dhari Sikh, and upon my return to America would be regarded as a leader—one of Yogiji's most deeply committed students. My identity crisis, at least for the time being, had apparently come to an end.

There was one more significant event before I left India. Yogiji asked me to accompany his children to a boarding school in Mussoorie in which they were enrolled. I recruited Gurusher to assist me on the long journey from Delhi to Rishikesh and from there up into the mountains where the Guru Nanak Fifth Centenary School was located in a former "hill station" of the British Raj. The trip itself was uneventful, other than the close relationships I developed with Yogiji's children, but it opened the door to an extremely important chapter in the history of the American Sikhs.

When I asked Yogiji why his children were staying at a boarding school in India instead of coming to live in America, he told me that American culture was fundamentally corrupt and that children would do better in the spiritually grounded environment offered by the remote boarding school. Further, he said, children would in general do better if they were not subjected to the constraining environment of their parents' own issues, but were instead free to grow into their own spiritual identity. I became an early advocate of this philosophy, and nine years later, in 1983, sent my 10-year-old daughter Amrit with one of the first groups of American Sikh children to attend the same boarding school.

One year later, Sat-Peter Kaur and I took our five-year-old, Sat Hari, to join her sister. I had no idea how abusive the environment there would be for her, for Amrit seemed to be thriving and enjoying it. The head of the school was an aging Sikh whose generous and courteous demeanor was not shared by all his staff, and we did not know that the housemother, or *Aya,* with whom we entrusted Sat Hari, was a poor and uneducated Hindu who, I discovered nearly 20 years later, daily slapped and used other physical punishments in vain attempts to discipline my young daughter. If I had even an inkling of these abuses, I would have made very different decisions, but I trusted Yogiji and honestly felt that my children would better off away from their parents, whose relationship was anything but healthy.

Yogi Bhajan convinced us that our 5-year-old, Sat Hari, would be better off with her sister in boarding school in India than at home with her parents.

CHAPTER TWENTY-FOUR

Key Relationships

BY THIS TIME, MY LIFE was completely absorbed into the Sikh community and what I saw as Yogi Bhajan's mission to save the world through the teachings of Kundalini Yoga, meditation, and Sikh Dharma. I lived and breathed, ate and slept, dressed, and even used the toilet according to the teachings of Yogiji and the Sikh Gurus. All my friends were Sikhs or yoga students. I read nothing that wasn't written by a Sikh, for Yogiji taught that intellectual pursuits were a useless waste of time. I didn't listen to any popular, or even classical music. For the most part, I ate only food that was prepared by Sikhs or according to Yogiji's teachings. In spite of this cultural isolation, I felt deeply rewarded in the aspects of life that were most important to me. Perhaps it would be more accurate to say that the strength of my religious and ideological convictions eclipsed any thought that my life was lacking in some way. If it weren't for my unhappy marriage, which I refused to acknowledge as important, I believed I had everything I wanted.

I had deep and growing friendships, all of which were predicated upon our shared beliefs. My closest friends were Ganga, Livtar, who headed the Ashram in Atlanta (and had married Sat-Peter Kaur's former roommate, Rose) and Gurushabad, a fellow Scorpio guitarist who ran the Ashram in Amherst, Massachusetts. I had lots of other friends as well, including several of my yoga students. But it was with Ganga that I had the closest and most meaningful conversations. Ganga's "stream of consciousness" raps were legendary. She had an uncanny ability to explore any subject from a variety of spiritual viewpoints, integrating multiple layers of ideas into a seamless, logical, and aesthetically inspiring exposition of Truth. Ganga seemed completely sure of herself, and her eyes glowed with passion and conviction when she spoke. We often talked together about the evolution of human consciousness, especially as it applied to, or manifested in our own lives and relationships. She was able to expound on the 300-year-old teachings of the Sikh Gurus in terms that seemed completely relevant to our contemporary experience.

Ganga and I were as intimate as friends could be, but we never crossed the line. For, no matter what may have been transpiring at an instinctual or emotional level, we were both far too wrapped up in the fear of betraying our ideological commitments to do anything even remotely improper. No words were ever exchanged between us that might acknowledge in any way the underlying attraction that pulled us together. The safety of this rigid and unspoken boundary actually allowed for an ever-deepening exchange of ideas and platonic love. We depended upon each other as the closest of friends, and before we had opened the Golden Temple Conscious Cookery, when Ganga took a job in 1971 as the chef at *YES!*, a local vegetarian restaurant and health food store, she quickly arranged for me to be hired as her assistant, and I soon took over as manager. Yet there were constant reminders that we were not equals. In the hierarchical structure that Yogiji had created within the 3HO organization, Larry and Ganga were my superiors. And though we socialized together regularly, Larry always maintained an aloof distance, and the exclusion of Sat-Peter Kaur from our circle reinforced the reality that not only was I not equal as an individual, but as a couple we were even further from the honored status enjoyed by Larry and Ganga.

Fortunately, my friendships with Livtar and Gurushabad were

on a more equal footing. Although they were both directors of ashrams in their own right, they also came under Larry's jurisdiction, for Larry was the Regional Director. And as "second in charge" of a Regional Center, I had more or less equal status with other Ashram directors in the region. In any event, rank and status did not interfere with the musical and social camaraderie that I shared with my two best friends. Our musical collaborations were egalitarian and richly rewarding. Gurushabad, like me, had been trained in classical guitar and was quite a bit better than me in technical proficiency and the extent of his repertoire. However, unlike me, he was not able to improvise. Our partnership developed effortlessly, therefore, as he played compositions and songs from memory with predictable precision, while I added colorful and dynamic lead lines with unfettered abandon. The result was nearly always good, and sometimes it was extraordinary.

Our friendship evolved as effortlessly as our musical partnership, and soon we were finding every excuse possible to get together—no easy task considering that we lived nearly 500 miles apart. But we managed. Every time Yogiji taught a course in a city within the Eastern Region, we would both make a special effort to attend. This happened every two or three months. And Gurushabad was able to use his job to create other opportunities. He had a Doctorate in Education and had integrated Kundalini Yoga and Meditation into a one-week course on "altered states of consciousness," which he was contracted to teach at various colleges. Whenever he was teaching within a few hours' drive of Washington, he would invite me to join him, adding our "musical meditations" as a means for achieving altered states. These meetings were musically and socially liberating for both of us. Gurushabad, as an Ashram director, also kept a self-imposed social distance from his Ashram students that I sensed left him longing for a peer group as much as I was. We quickly

Gurushabad (now Stephen Josephs), me, and Livtar Singh in 1972, conspiring together to form the Khalsa String Band.

developed an intuitive sensitivity to each other that seemed to make up for the lack of time and opportunity we had for practicing.

I shared a similar musical and personal intimacy with Livtar, whose guitar playing was modest, but whose song-writing talents were prodigious. After the three of us had played together only a few times, we were ignited with a passion to create something of lasting significance. At the summer solstice of 1972 we hatched a plan to put together a recording in answer to a poorly produced cassette tape of mantras and songs entitled *Sat Nam West*, created by some of our musical counterparts from Ashrams in California and Arizona. By the late fall we got together in Amherst, where a friend of Gurushabad's, who was an engineer at a local radio station, had offered the use of the station's two track recording studio. We assembled a group of musicians and recorded live in stereo, writing songs, practicing, and working out harmonies and instrumental arrangements as we went. We called the group "Sat Nam East" and named the tape *Jewels from the East*. The production was rough in places—by today's standards little better than a garage recording—but over-all the sound quality was acceptable, and some of the music exceptional. We were all thrilled, and the 3HO family responded favorably. The first run of one hundred cassettes nearly sold out at the Winter Solstice in Florida. Perhaps most importantly, the mix of spiritual songs and traditional mantras set to new tunes provided a unifying musical theme for more than 100 3HO Ashrams throughout the US, Canada, and abroad.

In early 1973 we got together again in Amherst to record a second album. We called this effort *Music of Life*. It followed the same "songs and mantras" format, but marked a turning point for us in that we could not suppress the gleefully good time we were all having together. Gurushabad had a wonderful sense of humor that insinuated itself into his lyrics and the musical styles in which he wrote his songs. Along with soaring, richly textured choral arrangements of mantras, and lullingly peaceful devotional songs, we included rollicking ditties like "No Time for Hangin' Around in the Bliss" with scatting, percussive spoons, and barnyard vocals. The recording quality was awful, but we were still pleased with the end product. It spanned the spectrum from the sublime to the raucously profane and was fairly bursting with energy.

Within a few months we recorded a third album that we called *Winds of Change*. By now we were starting to look at ourselves as a band. In addition to Livtar, Gurushabad, and me, we were joined by three women who sang back-up and sometimes lead vocals. Our material was now covering an even broader spectrum of musical styles, from repetitive, trance-like choral arrangements of mantras, to Livtar's doo-wop take-off on "What's your Name," and Gurushabad's irreverent "Long Tall Yogi," complete with screaming guitar lines utterly unsuitable for yoga classes and other meditative exercises. The friendships of all those involved in the recording were cementing fast and we were beginning to see ourselves as a kind of sub-group of "spiritual music anarchists" within the staid and self-righteous 3HO family.

In the fall of 1973, we undertook our most ambitious project to date, the recording of a real vinyl LP album, cut on 16 tracks at the National Recording Studios in New York City. We arranged for all the best musicians in the 3HO family to join us, including Guru Singh and Krishna Kaur from Los Angeles, Sat Nam Singh and Singh Kaur from Arizona, Gurudass Singh from Puerto Rico, Marty from Ohio, as well as Amar Singh and his wife, Sahib Amar Kaur—by far the best musicians in the lot. Both were classically trained: Sahib Amar on viola, and Amar on clarinet, flute and keyboards. For some of the numbers we hired a local drummer to fill out the sound. The resulting nine songs were pressed into a vinyl album that we named *Spiritual Nation*. We called our group *The Khalsa String Band*, putting our own twist on the name of the *Incredible String Band*, whose "A Very Cellular Song" remains to this day the universal ending for every 3HO gathering.

The *Spiritual Nation* album was a serious project and had none of the raucousness that marked our earlier cassette albums. In part this was due to the sobering influence of our West Coast and Arizona friends who were for the most part a great deal "holier" than we were. Bowing to their travel schedules, we recorded their material first, allowing them most of the artistic direction for the album. After a few days, however, they all left, except for Krishna, a charismatic Afro-American woman and former television personality who, like us, enjoyed having fun at least as much as she enjoyed meditating. The pressures of endless and often tedious hours in the studio now gave way to almost drunken orgies of giddiness and bingeing on foods we normally avoided. One evening as we left the studio with seven of us piled into a car, all of us singing, joking, and laughing, we were stopped at an intersection by a New York traffic cop who yelled at Marty, our driver, "Turn your lights on Buddy, you can see better that way!" The natural rhythm and cadence of these words struck us all simultaneously. For the next 30 minutes, as we wended our way to the Ashram on Bergen Street in Brooklyn where we were staying, we yelled, stomped our feet, rocked the car from side to side, huzzahed, cheered, whistled, and chanted as if it were our new mantra, "Turn your lights on Buddy, you can see better that way!"

When we reached the Ashram we went storming in, laughing and racing up the stairs like a bunch of happy kids. But we had gone too far. Our hostess, the Ashram director's wife, complained to him that we were acting like ruffians and that our energy was disturbing the shrine-like peace and quiet of the place. Later that evening he came and scolded us for our indiscretion. We feigned sincere remorse, promising to behave in a more dignified way in the future. But we knew from each other's glances that we didn't really believe it. We had tasted the freedom of joyous abandon. Our experiences together had broken the shell of sanctimonious piety by which we and so many of our spiritual brothers and sisters had been constrained. In a few months we would turn both our music and the good times we enjoyed together into a kind of mission as we took the Khalsa Sting Band on a tour of nearly every Ashram in the country. We were going to show everyone that it was OK to have fun.

Playing with the Khalsa String Band at Summer Solstice celebrations was one of the highlights of my time with the American Sikh community.

CHAPTER TWENTY-FIVE

The Khalsa String Band

THROUGHOUT 1973 the Golden Temple Restaurant at Dupont Circle roared along, dragging all the Ashram members with it. The place's popularity was wonderful, but the burden on the staff was almost unbearable. On our second day I calculated that the minimum crew we needed to run all the operations, from dishwashing and maintenance to hosting and ordering, was 36 people, each working a single eight-hour shift. But there were only 18 of us living in the Ashram at that point, two of whom had a brand-new baby. As a result, we all worked double shifts. In spite of our exhaustion, our spirits remained high. We approached our work with a missionary zeal evident in a song I wrote at the end of one particularly trying day. In retrospect the lyrics look lame, but they were well-served by the music, a hard-driving cross between Chuck Berry and Led Zeppelin.

> Working at the Golden Temple, working all night and day,
> Working at the Golden Temple, working all our karmas away,
> We've been working, we've been working so hard…
> *Ek Ong Kar, Sat Nam, Siri Wha Guru*, guide us on our way.

The song immediately became a standard in the repertoire of music we performed each evening after closing, sometimes to customers' delight, just as often to their irritation. "Working at the Golden Temple" was pure rock and roll: a floor-shaking, guitar string-breaking, full-force assault. Wait staff would start dancing. Kitchen staff in food-smeared aprons would bang out rhythms on tabletops with serving utensils. The dishwasher, with his turban askew, would peel off his big black gloves and emerge from the kitchen in galoshes and black rubber apron, banging on a 40-quart stainless-steel pot with a wooden spoon. We were all nuts, driven by a sense of relief that the workday was almost over, and supercharged by our youthful energy and shared destiny.

Most of the Ashram members were under 23, many of them only 17 or 18. Larry and Ganga were among the oldest at 27. The youngest was my daughter, Amrit, who spent many lunch hours napping in a playpen on the second floor of the restaurant while both her parents slaved away downstairs. For several weeks when we first opened, Amrit got more attention during the day from customers who came upstairs to use the bathroom than from her own mother and father. Sat-Peter Kaur and I were both tortured by a sense of neglect, but there was nothing we could do about it until reinforcements arrived.

As time went on Larry, did a lot of recruiting, especially at the solstice celebrations. Yogiji also helped a lot, regularly sending new students and newly married couples to Washington to "study" with Larry and Ganga. Soon we had enough people living at the Ashram and working at the Golden Temple that Larry was able to graduate from the kitchen to "office work." I quickly moved through each position in the restaurant, learning every task so that I could take over the management and free Larry and Ganga to accompany Yogiji on trips to India. I learned about ordering, food prep, juicing, dishwashing, cooking, salad and sandwich making, kitchen management, bussing, waiting, hosting, cashiering, menu layout, printing, and front floor management. Within a few months I knew everything about running the restaurant except the accounting, which Larry handled exclusively.

CHAPTER TWENTY-FIVE: The Khalsa String Band

In early 1974 I, too, graduated to an office job, handling most of the restaurant management from a desk in a second-floor office I shared with Larry. I also handled publicity and PR for our yoga classes and for the special courses that Yogiji continued to teach in Washington, once every four or five months. But I had much higher ambitions than working in an office under Larry's supervision. I had been quietly scheming to get all my musician friends together again to go on tour. We had been talking about it for some time, and had already recruited the people we would need to fill out the band. Livtar, Gurushabad, and I would be on guitars, Gurudass on bass, and Livtar's friend, Jerry, on drums. Gurushabad lined up three of his students: Marty on keyboards, Amar Singh on flute and keyboards, and Sahib Amar Kaur on viola. In addition, we had two female back-up singers, GuruVir Kaur and Sat Kartar Kaur. Livtar borrowed enough money from one of his students to buy a sound system and equipment truck. We were ready to go. But Larry was not about to let me walk out on all my responsibilities with the restaurant and Ashram. My leaving would chain him to his desk and deny him the freedom to travel with Yogiji.

It did not take me long to work out a solution. My friend, Bob, from the Claude Jones days, had followed a path similar to mine and was serving as the head of the 3HO Ashram in St. Louis. Bob had been a successful drug dealer and anti-war activist with Students for a Democratic Society. Shortly after he and I started taking Yoga classes together in 1970, he was sentenced to a year in jail by a Pennsylvania court for—in his own words—breaking into the US Army's War College in Shippensburg and photographing plans for military operations in Viet Nam. It was a great story, but no more noble a cause for which to go to jail (in our eyes) than the real reason. Apparently he had been busted in 1969 with several hundred hits of LSD. Bob's affiliation with 3HO served him well, for he was able to negotiate a work-release program, allowing him to spend his days running a yoga-based drug rehab program in Columbia, Maryland, while returning to spend each night in a Pennsylvania jail.

Bob—now Kamal Singh—was a very capable organizer, a fact Larry noticed and rewarded by sending him to open an Ashram in St. Louis as soon as his jail sentence was completed. But St. Louis was not a hotbed of alternative lifestyles or spiritual thought, and the Ashram did not do well. I knew that Kamal's talents were being wasted there, and that if I could find a reasonably competent substitute to take his place, I could free him up to take *my* place in DC. Livtar had the perfect guy, a young student who was super-devoted, modestly ambitious, and readily available.

Within a few weeks the switch had been arranged. With my DC responsibilities firmly in Kamal's capable hands, I was free to pursue my dreams and my destiny. Little was I aware, however, of the stakes, nor how significant the choice I had made in Kamal. I assumed that my position as second in charge in DC was still intact, that Kamal was only a temporary replacement, and that should the Khalsa String Band not turn into the huge success I envisioned, I could always step back into my former role. But Kamal was a great deal more ambitious and resourceful than I had given him credit for. If I had thought about it at the time, I would have had to admit that I viewed him as a pawn in my own grand scheme. But almost immediately upon my departure, Kamal used his considerable abilities to consolidate power and entrench himself solidly in the position I had handed him.

At the beginning of May, all ten members of the band assembled at an Ashram in the suburbs of Detroit for two weeks of rehearsals before the first concert of our tour. We were full of hope and bursting with talent and creativity. Our rehearsals in the Ashram attic went well. The vocal blends were rich, the harmonic arrangements snappy and powerful. Occasionally, an instrumental break in the middle of a song would transform into a spontaneous, improvised jam. In these joyous moments we would beam at each other with surprised glances and satisfied smiles, recognizing how good we really were. Our shells of piety and restraint, carefully crafted from years of austerity and chanting mantras, melted away as the rock & roll burst from our souls.

Our first concert was a triumph. Guru Marka, the Ashram director, had done a great job of organizing and promoting it: nearly 150 people, mostly yoga students, gathered to hear us in the basement auditorium of a local church. We played exceptionally well, and each song was greeted by enthusiastic applause. I had brought along hundreds of copies of albums and tapes for sale—material we had recorded in the previous years—and they sold well. By the end of the night, we had collected more than $700 in ticket and album sales. It was, in our view, an auspicious start, and we were full of confidence. The next day we packed our equipment into the truck, and our luggage into our three cars, and caravanned our way down to St. Louis to prepare for our second concert.

Livtar had organized our tour schedule. He had called the heads of most of the Ashrams from Michigan to Arizona and assigned them dates for our appearances stretching over a two-month period, ending with the Summer Solstice celebration in New Mexico. Each Ashram director along the way had agreed to host the band and to organize and promote a concert for us. The venues were usually church auditoriums or community centers. We were not under any great delusions about the significance or appeal of these concert venues. But with even modest receipts from ticket and album sales, and with the ashrams providing room and board, we could, in theory, go on for a long time, and we intended to make full use of the experience to hone our act for the larger venues and growing

The Khalsa String Band went on tour in the spring of 1974, performing in cities from Detroit to Vancouver. The tour ended with recording sessions in San Francisco, resulting in the "Sons of the Tenth Guru" album.

popularity we envisioned for our future.

The trip to St. Louis was uneventful enough, considering the condition of a couple of our vehicles—especially the 1964 Volvo 122S station wagon I owned at the time. As we drove through East St. Louis in a drizzling rain, I was struck by the endless grayness and depressing desolation of the place. The Ashram was on a "private street" in the western section of the city, but its separation from nearby slums was merely nominal. We decided it would be a bad idea to leave the truck unattended overnight, so Livtar volunteered to sleep in it for the three nights we were there. Our concert the next evening was a disaster. Livtar's student, Teja Singh, who had replaced Kamal as the Ashram director only a few weeks before, had not had sufficient time to organize and promote it properly, and he had a meager pool of yoga students to draw from. He was not as surprised as we were, therefore, when an audience of only twelve people greeted us in silence as we took the stage.

Further, the beginner's luck that had graced our first concert with a near-perfect performance deserted us. We stumbled through songs we had played flawlessly dozens of times. Our vocals and on-stage repartee were flat. By the third song, every sour note or missed cue resulted in accusing glances. By the end of the first set, we all wore glowering expressions. We sold only one album. Our total income for the night, including ticket sales, was $27.00. And to top it off, at 3:15 AM the next morning, just before everyone in the Ashram got up for morning meditation, a young black guy tried to steal our truck with all the equipment and Livtar in it.

The resourceful thief had jimmied the door, hot-wired the ignition, started the engine, and was just beginning to drive away when Livtar woke up. The bed Livtar had arranged for himself was perched on top of the P.A. speakers just behind the driver's seat, accessible only by the pass-through opening connecting the passenger compartment to the back of the truck. Looking up, or rather down from his perch, and seeing only the back of an Afro, Livtar yelled out in alarm. The thief, even more alarmed than Livtar, opened the driver's door and, without stopping the truck, jumped out and ran away. The now driverless truck continued to roll slowly down the street, and before Livtar could extricate himself from his sleeping bag, came to a jolting halt against the curb, burying Livtar in an avalanche of guitar cases, microphone stands, and speaker wires from which he struggled to free himself for more than ten minutes while the engine idled on unattended. When Livtar finally emerged, the street was empty.

Our meditation time that morning was somewhat less than contemplative, taken up, as it was, with the recounting of Livtar's adventure. We spent a lot of time speculating and planning how to protect ourselves against it happening again. Over breakfast I devised a clever counter-measure for any future thief. I mounted a series of five unmarked toggle switches on the dashboard and ran the ignition wiring through them all. Some were mounted with the "on" position up, some with it down, so that unless the driver knew the exact combination, the truck would not start. With 32 possible combinations, we felt pretty secure. We joked that any thief who could figure out the binomial code deserved to take the truck anyway. The brilliance of the concept, however, was tarnished slightly by my sloppy installation. A couple of weeks later the wiring shorted out and the dashboard caught fire on Route 10 just outside Tucson.

When the band performed at the Summer Solstice celebration in 1974, three of my friends from Ahimsa Ashram in DC joined us on stage, threw off their turbans, and danced around like go-go girls. Apparently, this unfettered display of joy did not sit well with Yogi Bhajan.

CHAPTER TWENTY-SIX

Rise and Fall of the Band

OVER THE NEXT SEVERAL WEEKS we played concerts successively in Madison, Chicago, Kansas City, Oklahoma City, Colorado Springs, Tucson, Phoenix, Salt Lake City, and Denver. Some of these were wonderful events with appreciative audiences; some were almost as bad as St. Louis. We arrived in Phoenix to find that the Ashram director had forgotten we were coming, and had made no arrangements at all. Overall, we were improving quickly, writing and learning new material as we went, and starting to think about recording another album together. But we were getting tired, and everyone's nerves were wearing thin from being constantly on the road. Our concert in Denver went poorly, and the next morning I found myself confronted with a mutiny. I was accused of driving the band too hard, of being insensitive to everyone's needs, of not organizing things properly, and worst of all, of being arrogant. Even Gurushabd, my best friend, was upset. I had offended him on stage the previous evening by pretending to snore through a long and (I thought) tedious introduction he was giving for one of our songs.

My heart sank as I looked around at the sea of angry faces. My apologies seemed to do no good. Could it all come crashing down right here, I wondered? Then Livtar spoke up. "You know," he drawled "Yogiji put Sat-Peter in charge of this band, and as far as I'm concerned, I think he knew what he was doing. Nobody's perfect, but if Yogiji tells me to follow Sat-Peter, right or wrong, I'm going to do it." There was a long silence. I knew that Yogiji had nothing to do with putting the band or the tour together, and I was pretty sure Livtar knew it, too. But nobody else did. The prospect of potentially angering Yogiji slowly sank in. After a few minutes, Gurushabd offered that he'd stick it out if I promised never to embarrass him on stage again. One by one, the rest of the band fell in line, each exacting from me a promise and a second apology for whatever I had done to offend them. I looked at Livtar in awe. I had never felt so grateful to anyone in my life.

The following week we played a concert for the entire 3HO family—over 1000 strong—at the summer solstice celebration in New Mexico. Our musical skills were now well-honed and we were received like heroes. Until that time, mantras, chants, and a little bit of Indian Kirtan had provided the organization's only musical expression. Our English lyrics, amplified instruments, and polished performance provided a new sense of identity that the community embraced with both gratitude and joy. Soon, our tapes and albums were being played in every Ashram, used in yoga classes, and were even aired from time to time on local radio stations. Our tour had also done a lot to loosen up the 3HO family, with the exception of those who clung desperately to their sanctimonious personas. Yogiji, who until that time had never heard us play live, immediately annexed us into his summer tour, arranging for us accompany him at a "Holy Man Jam" in Boulder, and at a series of speaking and teaching engagements up and down the West Coast from Los Angeles to Vancouver Island.

We were excited to be associated so closely with Yogiji, but traveling with him was even more grueling than what we had already been through. His sponsorship and constant proximity, however, kept everyone in line. We hadn't gone more than a couple of days before Yogiji saw how the land lay with some of the band's

CHAPTER TWENTY-SIX: Rise and Fall of the Band

During the summer of 1973 I spent several weeks commuting between Espanola and Corales, NM to do a ground-up restoration of Yogiji's Model A at my friend Bill Klenck's repair shop. Sadly, the car's cooling system was no match for New Mexico's high desert highways, and I was apparently the only person who could deal with the car's other eccentricities. A couple of years later I was disappointed to learn that Yogiji traded it for a battered WW II jeep.

interpersonal relationships. He intervened by marrying Jerry to Guru Vir Kaur. This was a great disappointment to me. Guru Vir Kaur was a good friend and quite beautiful, and I didn't think much of the match with Jerry: it was so obviously a mere expedient for appearances. My assessment proved correct, for the marriage lasted less than a year. A day or two later we experienced Yogiji's wrath when our performance in Boulder failed to ignite the crowd. We were struggling against an unfamiliar sound system with unbalanced monitors, borrowed drums and amplifiers, and a soundman who had never heard us play before. It was no small wonder that we sounded terrible. But Yogiji showed no mercy and no understanding of the technical difficulties. His rage on this occasion was one of the first cracks I had seen in his spiritual armor.

When we got to Los Angeles on our way to Vancouver, Yogiji decided he wanted me to chauffeur him for the trip north in his mint-condition 1961 Cadillac sedan. It was only one of many classic and vintage cars he owned, from a 1930 Model A Ford that I had restored for him in New Mexico, to a fleet of Mercedes. I was surprised at his decision. It was, after all, a round trip of more than 2,000 miles. But I was excited and honored by the prospect of spending so much time in his presence, and was not too worried about potential mechanical problems. I was pretty handy with cars.

Most of Yogiji's speaking engagements, it turned out, were with the Indian Sikh community, so we had little opportunity to play as a band. Mostly, he would have us bring in a guitar or two and show us off to his Indian friends for 5 or 10 minutes—always ending with "Song of the Khalsa" whose last verse was in praise of Yogiji, himself—before launching into hours of heated discussions in Punjabi. With so little to look forward to in the way of live performances, and no touring future in sight, our enthusiasm for the band flagged. We soon determined that if we couldn't make a go of it as a touring band at least we should record an album in San Francisco on our way south from Vancouver.

Livtar lined up a recording studio through our friend Sat Santokh Singh, who had formerly managed the Grateful Dead. We made arrangements to stay at the "Banana-Ananda" Ashram (so named by Yogiji) in San Rafael while we laid down the tracks. This part of our journey was delightful. Steve, our engineer, had a small, four-track studio in the heart of San Francisco that he managed with great skill. By a laborious process of laying down tracks, over-dubbing, mixing down to a second tape, then adding more tracks, we created a complex and sophisticated, multi-track musical fabric. We spent several weeks planning and laying down parts, enjoying the idyllic

Yogi Bhajan attracted many celebrities into the fold, including the former Vic Briggs, lead guitarist of The Animals. He and I became good friends and often played together. Years later, after we were both out of the cult's clutches, we did a musical tour of New Zealand together.

Autumn weather, and wearing thin our welcome at the Ashram.

For ten days in the middle of these sessions I was able to have my daughter, Amrit, who was now just over two years old, come and stay with me. Leaving Amrit with her mother had been one of the only things about which I felt remorse when I left DC in April. My relationship with Sat-Peter Kaur was marked mainly by long-suffering endurance on both our parts. We had so little in common, and her nearly constant emotional turmoil and gnawing insecurity gave our relationship about as much joy as driving a car with four flat tires. Ganga once noted that Sat-Peter Kaur's role in life appeared to be to keep me sufficiently deflated that I wouldn't explode from my own energy. It was not a comforting thought, but the metaphor played out again and again in negative ways, often in public.

During the two weeks of rehearsals at the beginning of our tour, I had caved in to Sat-Peter Kaur's entreaties and invited her to come spend a weekend with me in Detroit. On the first day she was

My daughter, Amrit, visited me in San Raphael while the band was recording our "Sons of the 10th Guru" album in San Francisco.

there, just as the band was warming up to one of our spontaneous, high-spirited jams, she came charging into our attic rehearsal hall. We all stopped in alarm, thinking something terrible must have happened downstairs. She stood in the doorway and yelled that we were too loud and that what we were playing sounded "just like rock and roll." The entire band was aghast, and I was mortified at the audacity of her intrusion.

I knew I had myself to blame for much of the misery that marked our relationship. It was true that I had not done a great job of providing financial "abundance," and I was only too glad to leave her out of most of my social activities. But worst of all was the impact of my lack of interest in her, compounded by my overt interest in so many of the other women we knew. The whole thing was a setup for disaster and unhappiness. Yet, as much as I resented my marriage, I clung to the institution and simply tried to minimize the pain.

My relationship with Amrit was a different story. She was a darling little bundle of blonde curls and affection, and was as trouble-free and agreeable as any child could be. I welcomed the chance to spend time alone with her, away from the corrosive influence of her parents' unhappy relationship. Amrit was so adorable that she captivated the entire Banana-Ananda Ashram family, and I had no trouble finding people who were willing to spend time with her during my recording sessions. The Ashram was a huge old Victorian mansion with dozens of rooms and a swimming pool out back. More than 30 people lived there full time. The band brought it to over 40, so there was constant activity and high energy. Amrit thrived in the attention and stimulating environment, and we spent many happy hours together.

Our recording sessions were going well. But after all the instrumental and vocal overdubs had been completed, most of the band members departed for their respective homes on the East Coast. Jerry and Guru Vir Kaur drove the equipment truck back to Atlanta. Marty drove his car home to Ohio with Amar and Sahib Amar. Gurudass drove my station wagon back to DC with Gurushabad. Sat Kartar Kaur was flying to DC, so I arranged for Amrit to fly back with her. Suddenly, after months of traveling, living, and playing together as a 10-person band, only Livtar and I remained to oversee the final mixing of our new album.

Both my daughters were delightful children. Amrit, the oldest, came to visit with me when I was on tour in Los Angeles in 1974, when she was 2-years old. We are shown here at the "Guru Ram Das Estate" playing pattycake.

Mixing was a very tricky process and took us at least two more weeks. Using new DBX noise reduction equipment, we were able to retain remarkable sound fidelity, even after as many as 6 generations of overdubs. Livtar and I were extremely pleased with the results of our work, but we both felt a tremendous sense of loss that the band had dissolved. There was almost no chance we could ever put the group together again except for occasional unrehearsed performances at the Solstice gatherings. In spite of the fine quality of the album we knew that our dream was dead, and we both felt adrift. Neither of us had any idea what we would do next. Livtar would go back to Atlanta; I would go to DC, and we would try to pick up our lives. We didn't even have a way to get home.

When all our work was done, we caught a ride to Albuquerque with the studio's assistant engineer, where we found a "drive-away" company that needed a car delivered to Florida. From there we contracted to deliver a small truck to Philadelphia. I dropped Livtar off in Atlanta and continued on, alone, to DC. As I drew close to Washington driving north on Interstate 95 I had a disturbing Deja vu. I had been on the road for six months so it was natural that I should have some pangs of nostalgia. But what I experienced was more like a vision from some distant future. I sensed that I had been away from the Sikh community and my adopted religion for at least forty years. I had the distinct sensation that the mantras and prayers I was going over in my mind had been left unspoken for all that time. I descended into a feeling of tremendous loss, and sadness so intense that it brought tears to my eyes. The vision made no sense to me. I was the most devoted of students. The thought of leaving Yogi Bhajan or the Sikh way of life had never crossed my mind. It would take many more years of growing, and a lot more disillusionment before the idea of leaving would crop up as a real possibility.

CHAPTER TWENTY-SEVEN

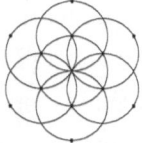

A Stranger Back at Home

THINGS HAD CHANGED SIGNIFICANTLY in DC while I was on tour with the Khalsa String Band. Kamal had so thoroughly taken over and secured my former role as second in charge that I did not have a position to come back to, either at the Golden Temple Restaurant or the Ashram administration. Further, the organization's entire social and economic fabric was changing. The Ashram now had more people living in it than could be productively put to work at the restaurant, and more than could be housed in the two townhouses that had comprised the Ashram community when I left. Already there were four houses. It still wasn't enough, and the profits from the restaurant could not support everyone. Larry and Kamal had been scrambling to get other businesses established to make use of the labor force and bring in additional income. In the works were a shoe manufacturing business, a landscaping business, and a retail "emporium" in Georgetown that would sell health foods, gifts, and Birkenstock Sandals. These ventures were already well underway and the only task still available for which I had both interest and skills was some advertising design and production work. I also took over teaching most of the yoga classes at the Ashram.

There were even bigger changes about to be set loose upon the community. Ever since the opening of the Golden Temple restaurant in the spring of 1972, the entire Ashram community had come together to work as a unit for the common good. The business paid for our rent and food, tips were divided equally among us to cover incidental expenses, and anyone with an extraordinary need could usually get it taken care of by asking Larry for extra money. A few Ashram members also had their own inherited money and they tended to be generous, so the entire community shared in the benefits. It was a tightly and beneficently managed central economy that took care of everyone's needs while asking only that each person contribute according to his or her abilities—a functional form of communalism very similar to what I had created with the Claude Jones family a few years earlier. But by the end of 1975, with an excess of under-utilized labor and increasing expenses, the system, according to Larry, was not working anymore.

The new system that Larry and Kamal imposed brought many unexpected changes to the character and focus of the Ashram community. Under the pragmatically named, but much resented "Rent and Wage" system, they established a schedule of wages for the various positions available in the Ashram businesses and announced that each person would be responsible for his or her own living expenses, including food and a portion of the rent. It did not take long for most people to figure out that they could not make ends meet under these conditions, and a nickname was quickly coined to describe the new economy: *the rent and RAGE system.*

One by one, people started taking jobs in the "real world," or started their own independent businesses. One couple opened a massage business at a local health spa. Another started a honey-sweetened natural soda business. Another started a used car dealership. Others went to work variously as accountants, private investigators, mortgage brokers, and teachers. I was at a loss what to do. Livtar, with whom I spoke often, was in a similar "real-life situation" crisis in Atlanta. He kept exploring new "opportunities," from chimney sweeping to delivering newspapers. One day he called,

The Golden Temple Conscious Cookery—Natural Foods Restaurant, located on Connecticut Avenue at Dupont Circle, was the first full service vegetarian restaurant in DC when it opened in 1972.

highly excited, to tell me about a new weight-loss program called "Slender Now." It was a multi-level marketing program that paid not only retail profits on whatever product a distributor could sell but also gave enormous commissions (kick-backs) for the wholesale purchases by any additional distributors a person could sign up to the organization.

On the way back from the Winter Solstice celebration in January of 1976, I stopped to visit with Livtar to learn about Slender Now at a massive marketing meeting that the parent company was sponsoring in Atlanta. The meeting took place in a huge banquet room of a fancy hotel and was attended by least 600 people, and the excitement was tangible. The room was full of "prospects" who had come to learn a foolproof way to get rich quick, and they were not disappointed by the presentations. First came a testimonial from one of the company's most successful distributors, a 27-year-old self-described "former beach bum." He stood at the podium in a $1000 Italian suit and recounted for the crowd his own personal journey from rags to riches. Most of the audience was in tears of empathy and excitement by the time he finished. The applause was thunderous.

Next came a presentation about the miracle product itself, with testimonials by many formerly obese people whose lives had been forever changed for the better by the "amazing amounts of ugly fat" they had shed with the help of Slender Now. A doctor then provided long-winded testimony about the health benefits and safety of the product's scientifically balanced formula of vitamins, minerals, and proteins. Just as the audience's attention and excitement was starting to wane, the subject shifted to the marketing plan. With a series of overhead slides and more testimonials, we were taught how to build our own "down-line" organizations of distributors. Each additional generation would multiply our personal profits exponentially. One slide showed a giant pyramid with larger and larger dollar amounts associated with the lower levels. It was easy to see that despite the nominal emphasis on retail sales, all we really had to do was sign up lots of distributors and get them to buy as much inventory as possible.

By the time I got back to Washington I had already made my list of prospects for up to three generations of distributors, balancing the breadth and depth of my future marketing organization in order to maximize kickbacks. Larry was quick to see the possibilities of the geometric marketing and kickback structure and immediately agreed to sign up with me as his "sponsor," provided I let him sign up most of the other ashram members. Within a week I had two other "first generation" distributors, and each of them had his or her own "down-line" organization, elevating me almost immediately to the level of "Senior Lead Distributor," and Livtar to the level of "Blue Diamond Lead Distributor." My first bonus check was almost $1,000 and I had not yet sold a single unit of retail product. The future looked bright! Even my oldest brother signed up, though his first "sure thing" sales pitch to an overweight aunt ended in disappointment (she wouldn't speak to him for more than 20 years.)

But there were two big problems with the program. First was the level of long-term personal commitment it would require from me, which I was not truly willing to make: mainly, that if I were to follow the formula outlined by the millionaire beach bum, I would have to live, breathe, and talk about Slender Now in virtually every social and business interaction. It would have to consume my life. The other problem was that I was only one of thousands, or perhaps tens of thousands of enthusiastic distributors demanding product and distributor start-up kits from a company that was under-capitalized and incapable of delivering on their exponentially increasing sales. The first several bonus checks arrived on time, but the seventh was late, and the eighth never came. Some of my down-line distributors at this point had garages full of product they had bought in order to elevate themselves instantly to "Lead Distributor" status with its promise of ever-larger bonus checks.

The demise of Slender Now was both sudden and brutal. Incredibly, however, neither I nor thousands of other distributors were greatly dismayed. We had tasted the potential of multi-level marketing and we had visions of instant wealth—if only we could position ourselves at the top of another successful multi-level sales pyramid. Even before Slender Now crashed into oblivion, Livtar had turned me on to another multi-level marketing opportunity: a company that was manufacturing see-through plastic drain traps equipped with a convenient snap-on/snap-off clean-out plug. The inventor, whom Livtar knew personally, was toying with multi-level marketing as a way to distribute the new product, but needed a little convincing. I tipped the scales for him by offering to design, for a very reasonable fee, a marketing plan and bonus structure, and even write the distributor's manual. I didn't have any particular expertise in this arena, but I was bold and self-confident. I also had the Slender Now manual as a template. I convinced the inventor over the telephone that I could get the job done. I did it, too. Within three weeks I delivered a complete manual with marketing plan and bonus structure. Further, I believed it was substantially better than the one Slender Now had offered, for it gave added incentives to sell the product rather than just build a distribution network.

But this company faced the same problem Slender Now had faced, with not enough capital or production capacity to meet the exponential growth that would inevitably occur. Fueled by a network of enthusiastic distributors, most of whom were already in place because of Slender Now, the company burned out within weeks. I got paid for my writing and production work, but never got a single bonus check. This time, however, I learned my lesson and was transformed into an eternal cynic about the get-rich-quick promises of multi-level marketing. I couldn't even be persuaded to work for "Skinny and Sexy," Yogi Bhajan's own multi-level marketing company, selling his direct rip-off of the Slender Now weight-loss formula. Besides, I hated the sexist name.

CHAPTER TWENTY-EIGHT

Danger

IN THE SUMMER OF 1976 Yogi Bhajan's staff managed to get him included on the list of speakers of the annual convention of the American Vegetarian Society taking place in Bangor, Maine. Yogiji asked me to put the Khalsa String Band together again to accompany him, with a promise that Larry would cover all our expenses. I was thrilled and flattered, but was able to assemble only six of us, including Ellen, a former yoga student of mine who was unhappily married to one of my 3HO friends. With no drummer, no bass player and almost no rehearsal time, we settled on an acoustic set of old stand-bys that nearly everyone in 3HO knew by heart. Our performance, therefore, was competent, but uninspired and uneventful.

What was memorable for me, however, was the realization, as we saw Yogiji off at the airport afterwards, that everyone else in the band was going home separately, and I was about to be left alone with Ellen 600 miles from home. Further, we were only a few miles from my family's summer home on the Casco Bay, the most romantic spot on earth, as far as I was concerned. "Be good," said Yogiji with a wink as he waved goodbye. "I will," I lied. As soon as his back was turned, I reached for Ellen's hand. She responded by warmly gripping mine as we headed to my car.

Two hours later, we pulled off the Interstate and started wending our way through the back roads that led to my grandfather's log cabin on a peninsula in the Casco Bay, inconveniently occupied at the time by my oldest brother and his wife and children. Our arrival was a complete surprise, and my brother's and sister-in-law's pleasure at seeing me was clearly tempered by their confusion about my companion. After sitting through an uncomfortable dinner and making hasty and transparent arrangements for the use of the basement room with its two single beds, I escorted Ellen down the wooded path to the waterfront for a moonlit sail in my mother's sloop, the *Royal Tern*.

The tide was near its flood and the sea and salt air were exquisite, but there was no moon and barely a hint of wind. From the dock we could just make out the *Royal Tern* at her mooring thirty yards away. We climbed into the skiff and I paddled out quietly. We said nothing, but occasionally motioned to each other. Ellen was also a sailor and needed no special instructions. When we reached the *Royal Tern*, she climbed on board and held the skiff for me while I followed.

The *Royal Tern* was a lovely 21' wooden sloop with a gaff-rigged mainsail and a small bowsprit. She had been built specially for my mother by a local boat builder, Charlie Gomes, in 1956. Charlie had designed the boat with classic, graceful lines and had given her a spacious cockpit designed to accommodate our entire family of seven. She was a "daysailer," meaning she had no cabin, so it was easy to move about fore and aft to handle the sheets and halyards. Although she had old-fashioned fittings for the jib and main sheets and no winches to lighten the work of trimming the sails in a strong wind, I had learned to sail her single-handed at an early age. She was a delightful boat and nothing could seem more romantic to me than sailing her at night with a willing companion. It was clear that Ellen felt the same way, and after I raised the sails and cast off from the mooring, we snuggled closely while coasting gently out of the cove.

CHAPTER TWENTY-EIGHT: Danger

The night was so still that our sails hung limply. I was surprised that we could gain any headway at all, but slowly we eased out of the cove and coasted along the pitch-black shore, leaving the faintest phosphorescent ripples in our wake. After an hour we had gone no more than a mile. We talked in whispers and snuggled closer against the growing chill of the evening. But I was uneasy about where this was heading. It could have stayed completely innocent, though neither of us wanted it to. But I was unsure of myself, and it was quite a while before I found the courage to kiss her. Ellen responded willingly, and for some time I left the tiller and sails unattended while we embraced, lying together on the floorboards.

We did nothing more than kiss. But the enormity of our peril weighed heavily on me. I sensed that Ellen was willing, even eager to throw restraint to the wind, but I could not bring myself to do it. I was also concerned about letting the boat drift at will. I could envision us running aground, or being carried out to sea on the outgoing tide. But mostly I did not know where this growing intimacy would lead, and I was afraid of the possibilities. Ellen and I were unhappy in our respective marriages and we were both desperate for love, affection, and validation. But I did not know what expectations, emotions, and responsibilities might be attached to our intimacy. All I knew for sure was that I was unwilling to consider ending my marriage. I had too much invested in appearances and the religious ideology I had embraced. I called it faith, but it was really a combination of ego and fear. I considered myself a pillar of the community and I was terrified at the prospect of having my stature tarnished, of being labeled a backslider, or of disappointing Yogiji. I was also afraid of setting loose the flood of passions I sensed welling up in Ellen. So, I did nothing and for the next hour we drifted slowly back to the mooring.

Even after we had moored the boat, returned to the cabin to say

Members of the Khalsa String Band in New Mexico, June 1974.

our guilty goodnights to my brother, and gotten into our separate beds in the basement room, I did nothing. I lay awake for hours pretending to sleep while I struggled with my thoughts. It was not until just before dawn that I finally crawled into her welcoming bed. As we drove home later that day, I knew I was in the most dangerous of territories. I sensed that Ellen's delicate emotions and fragile self-esteem were now invested for my safe-keeping, and though I did not shrink from the responsibility, I did not want to encourage the relationship at the expense of our respective marriages and our positions in the community. Back in Washington, we used our musical collaboration as an excuse to meet together as often as we could without causing suspicion. But I diligently avoided any circumstance or environment that might provide cover for renewed intimacy.

CHAPTER TWENTY-NINE

Conflict in India

IN THE FALL OF 1976, I was part of a large delegation of American Sikhs who accompanied Yogiji on a speaking tour of the historic Gurdwaras of Punjab and New Delhi. I had two main duties on this trip: to be the tabla player for a Gurbani Kirtan group (comprised of Ganga, Ellen, and two other women), and to provide additional security for Yogiji. We were to serve as missionaries, to inspire the Indian Sikh community with a renewed sense of their historical religious identity. But Yogiji's agenda clearly had political implications as well. He seemed anxious to solidify support and increase his prestige among the Sikhs of India, especially with the SGPC and the national political leaders of both the Congress and Akali Dal parties.

However, the rivalry between Yogiji and his former teacher, Virsa Singh, had never been resolved. Virsa Singh's followers attended and tried to disrupt nearly every event. Usually, it was harmless enough, with one or two people standing up in the middle of a congregation to yell out some defamatory accusation in Punjabi. But feelings in the Virsa Singh camp ran so high that Yogiji had received death threats, and our own security detail was on full alert all the time. At one event in Ludhiana there were over 100,000 people crowded into an outdoor amphitheater. It was an awesome experience for us and it was evidently an emotionally charged one for Yogiji. I was sitting only a few feet from him as he stood addressing the crowd, and I could see that his knees were trembling, and could hear the anxiety in his voice.

In the middle of his talk, a number of Virsa Singh's people stood up in different parts of the congregation yelling insults and threats. Most of the crowd was unsympathetic to these disruptions and there was a great deal of commotion while the demonstrators were encouraged or forced to sit down, or were escorted out by the SGPC security detail. Progressively these demonstrations had become more threatening, and they finally boiled over into violence a week later in Gurdwara Bangla Sahib in the heart of Delhi. Delhi was the center of Virsa Singh's operation and there were scores of his people in and around the Gurdwara.

Gurdwara Bangla Sahib is not very large. Several hundred people were packed in so tightly that we were completely locked in place when we managed to reach the stage. Our music was enthusiastically received, but when Yogiji stood up to talk, demonstrations immediately broke out. It started with a woman who stood up and announced that she had been "roughly handled by Yogiji's people" the week before at Ludhiana (this was translated for me by an Indian friend sitting next to me). Suddenly, dozens of other people jumped up yelling and gesticulating threateningly in our direction. The SGPC security detail advised us that we should immediately follow them out of the Gurdwara. We formed a close knot around Yogiji, with me just ahead on his right. The crowd gave way slowly and closed behind us like quicksand. We had not gone ten feet when I sensed a commotion to the right. As I turned to get a better look, a shabbily dressed Sikh pushed his way through the crowd and brought a sheathed sword crashing down on the top of Yogiji's head.

The attacker's stroke was weakened by having to reach over the head of one of Yogiji's secretaries, but the force was great enough to shatter the wooden sheath exposing a three-foot stainless-steel blade. Without thinking, I turned and lunged, grasping the blade with my right hand and pulling it down behind the assailant's back. As I did so, I unintentionally twisted the sword, trapping the assailant's hand in the hilt and immobilizing him. With my left fist I beat repeatedly on his face, bloodying my knuckles and losing my turban in the process. This all lasted perhaps two or three seconds before the now-helpless man was grappled by several Indian Sikh men and dragged away. Later I heard he had been stabbed multiple times and was in the hospital.

At this point, the entire congregation was in an uproar. Two other attackers on Yogiji's left side had been stymied before they could inflict their blows. I stood in front of Yogiji, crouching like an enraged lion, with my long hair flying in all directions. I was like a wild man, physically and verbally threatening anyone I did not recognize who stepped within six feet of us. The SGPC security detail quickly cleared a path through the crowd and led most of our group to a narrow stairway that accessed a small upstairs room. With my back to the rest of the group, I was unaware that they were moving, and one of Yogiji's Indian friends had to come back to get me. I was still holding at bay a couple of dozen Indians who looked on in astonishment. Yogiji's friend begged me to calm down now that the trouble was over and handed me the crumpled mass of white cloth that had been my turban, indicating that I should at least cover my head since I was still in the Gurdwara. He then led me up the stairs to join the rest of the group. Yogiji was there, retying his own turban. He had been protected from a direct strike of the sword by a pair of Kangas (traditional Sikh wooden combs) that he wore in his hair.

Later, back in Yogiji's hotel room, a huge crowd of friends and admirers gathered to congratulate him on his narrow escape and to hear the episode recounted again and again from each person's

The American "Ragi Jatha," with me on tabla, performing in front of the Akal Takht at the Golden Temple in Amritsar.

perspective. Several people remarked on my bravery, but I felt more ashamed than brave. I knew that my reactions and subsequent defensive posturing had been rooted in fear and pent-up rage, not courage. But in the heat of the moment, most people probably didn't know the difference. Yogiji held animated conversations in Punjabi with his friends and supporters, handing out 100-rupee notes to the men who had played a role in disarming the assailants.

A week later Yogiji and many of the Americans went back to the United States while a smaller group of us went on to the Golden Temple in the heart of Punjab. The SGPC provided us rooms at Guru Nanak Nivas, and for several days we were to enjoy the peace of the temple and its surrounding sacred pool. I could take up studying the tablas again, and all of us who had taken the Amrit ceremony could take part in the midnight Seva.

Throughout the trip so far, Ellen and I had spent very little time together except playing music. The second night we were in Amritsar, however, she offered to massage my feet, which I readily accepted. I was sharing a room with Hari Singh, a friend from New Mexico, and thought nothing of having Ellen come into our room while Hari Singh was there. I lay down while she sat at the foot of my bed, armed with a towel and almond oil, and began the massage. Hari Singh sat on his bed reading. It was all innocent and safe. But after a few minutes Hari Singh announced that he was going over to the Golden Temple to meditate for a while and to do the midnight Seva.

With the departure of our unsuspecting chaperone, the normal boundaries of a foot massage soon gave way. Things were about to get really serious when the door burst open and Hari Singh reappeared. Ellen's reactions were quick, and she managed to reposition herself at the foot of the bed before the door was fully open. I pretended to wake up as Hari Singh entered. He explained that he had felt a little ill and wasn't up to doing midnight Seva, after all. With no further explanation and without remarking in any way upon the scene into which he had intruded, he got in bed and turned on his side facing the wall.

For a few minutes Ellen made a perfunctory show of finishing up the foot massage. We exchanged a few innocuous sounding pleasantries, said goodnight, and she departed, leaving me to lie awake ruminating for most of the night. Hari Singh's timely return had saved me from what I believed would have been a huge mistake, and for that I was grateful. It was several days before Ellen and I had a chance to even exchange private words. After all the months I had spent being protective and considerate of her emotions, I was now tactless and harsh. In the two or three minutes we had to ourselves I told her it was over, that we could never again be alone together, and that I was committed to making my own marriage work. I didn't talk with her again, and a week later we all left India.

I knew I had sounded judgmental and self-righteous, leaving

Ellen with the impression that I blamed her. I made no attempt for many months afterwards to change that impression. I simply avoided her in order to protect myself.

Several months later, Yogiji was visiting again in Washington, DC. I went to pay my respects and found him on his bed reclining against the wall, receiving a foot massage from Premka. Larry was sitting to one side in attendance. As I walked into the room Yogiji looked at me through half-closed eyes, raised his arm lazily, pointing vaguely at my crotch and asked, "How's that thing doing?" "It still works," I replied, smiling smugly at the cleverness of my comeback while hiding my astonishment at the question. "So I've heard!" he said, the words dripping with innuendo. "What do you mean?" I stammered, imagining he could see all sorts of possibilities in my aura. "Do you want me to be specific?" he retorted mockingly, "Shall we talk about a moonlight sail in Maine?"

So, Ellen had shared our secret, and now Yogiji was using it against me. I was angry and ashamed. It was bad enough that the fact of the affair had been revealed, but for Ellen to have confessed the circumstances, especially the details of our sail, was a crushing blow. The two hours that she and I had spent together in the sailboat were much more meaningful to me than anything else that had occurred between us, and I still treasured that memory. Yogiji, with this one question, had intruded and despoiled it, even while Larry and Premka looked on in condescending satisfaction. I fought down my anger. I resented Ellen for being so weak, but for the first time I also began to resent Yogiji for stripping me this way of both my privacy and my dignity, and doing it publicly. "OK," said Yogiji as if he were pronouncing my sentence, "Don't let it happen again."

For several years after this incident, I struggled to tame my behavior towards women. Despite renewed efforts at being chaste, the affair with Ellen and its aftermath had created a breach in the fortress of my faith. As much as I was grateful for the relatively light way in which Yogiji had dealt with me, the very casualness of the exchange affected me deeply. It was as if he were saying that my only fault was in not being discreet enough. He was not angry about my having an affair, only that it had been revealed. "Fake it and you can make it," he was fond of saying in his classes.

I had very few reasons in the past to question the perfection of Yogiji's wisdom, but the implication that appearances were more important than fact was troubling to me. It was also dawning on me that Yogiji's sense of ethics was situational. While we were on tour together in Vancouver in 1974, I had been horrified to watch him try to intimidate a ferryboat captain into giving our four vehicles precedence over others that were ahead of us in line. His anger and the insulting way he treated the ferryman impressed me poorly. Apparently, he sensed that many of us were uncomfortable with this display, for he made a point of explaining that such tactics were justified by the importance of our timely appearance at the Gurdwara to which we were headed. I was not convinced. In fact, it was my first hint of what I later realized to be a fundamental flaw in Yogiji's character. In his world view, the end justified the means.

The offices of the "Secretariate of Sikh Dharma of the Western Hemisphere" occupied a nondescript building on Robertson Boulevard in Los Angeles. The amount of authority Yogi Bhajan invested in his "secretaries," many of whom had no other qualification than his sponsorship, created a backlash among some Ashram directors, one of whom coined the term "acid reign" to express his resentment.

CHAPTER THIRTY

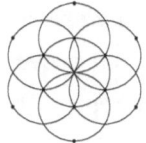

Cracks Appear

By 1976 the 3HO Community was a well-developed organization with established, though dysfunctional, social and administrative structures, and a deeply engrained religious culture—most of it focused on Yogiji. At the nominal apex of the religious hierarchy was the Siri Guru Granth Sahib, the holy book of the Sikhs, and the sacred memory of the ten Sikh Gurus who had lived through the 16th and 17th centuries. For most of the people in 3HO, however, Yogiji served as the ultimate temporal and spiritual authority. Next in line was the "Secretariat" of Sikh Dharma, which was made up entirely of Yogiji's secretaries, whom he appointed or removed at will, and to whom he dictated virtually all policy and administrative details.

Next was the Khalsa Council, made up of Yogiji's appointees, all of whom held impressive religious titles bestowed by Yogiji, and most of whom, besides me, were directors of ashrams. The Khalsa Council was supposed to work in an advisory capacity, but it had absolutely no authority to make decisions about policy, no access to the organization's budget or books, and no authority to make financial decisions. Khalsa Council meetings, therefore, were little more than giant encounter groups.

Another layer of the organization's administration was the five geographical regions and their respective regional directors, all longtime students, or couples like Larry and Ganga. The exception was the Los Angeles area, which was over-loaded with so many long-time students, most of whom were endowed with enormous egos and considerable ambition, that power struggles and conflict were inevitable. The Los Angeles region, therefore, was under Yogiji's direct supervision.

Finally, came the administrative structure of the individual ashrams. Generally, the ashram directors followed the authoritarian model demonstrated by Yogiji. In fact, it seemed to be every director's greatest aspiration to be a cloned replica of Yogiji. Many of them even imitated his Indian accent and mannerisms. The authority of the ashram directors over their own students was absolute, as long as no one appealed directly to Yogiji. When that happened, which it did with increasing frequency as time went on, even the strongest ashram director might find his power and influence eroded. Eventually, Yogiji initiated a weekly *Peoples' Problem Project* (PPP) meeting, to be held in every ashram. The idea was to give the rank-and-file members a way of voicing their concerns and suggestions. This steam-releasing mechanism helped preserve the authority of the ashram directors, but Yogiji would intervene if the peoples' problems could not be solved.

Very few people questioned the absolute authority that Yogiji exercised over the organization and over our personal lives. In fact, an alarming number of people subjected themselves even further by seeking his guidance for their most intimate or mundane personal and business decisions. Anyone bold enough to question Yogiji's authority or his way of running things was sure to be ostracized. Once ostracized, it was hard for the detractor to recover, and it was nearly inevitable that he or she would soon leave the organization under a barrage of abuse and threats. When this happened, it was not just a matter of excommunication. It was much worse. Yogiji would often give shocking public commentaries about the defector's perverted sexual practices, corrupt motives, or emotional instability. Virtually every person who left the organization was, according to Yogiji, a deviant or a delusional sociopath. Most of us were inclined to believe him, for those who left were often so upset that they unleashed what sounded like hysterical accusations, usually including allegations about Yogiji having illicit sexual relations with his secretaries and other female students. Yogiji always denied these charges, of course. Eventually, however, allegations started coming from some of his former secretaries. His denials and counter-accusations then became increasingly strident and improbable. At one point, when rumors and rumblings had reached an uncomfortable pitch, Yogiji interrupted the Khalsa Council in the middle of one of its pointless meetings and demanded that anyone who had questions or doubts about his integrity should address them to his face, then and there. It was a gamble on his part, but a masterful stroke, for no one took up the challenge and Yogiji was vindicated by our silence.

I was not swayed by the accusations that surfaced from time to time. I did, however, begin to rationalize away the negatives in Yogiji's character. It was a terrible shock to realize that he was not perfect in every way. Not only was my concept of a liberated "master" shattered—expectations based on reading *Autobiography of a Yogi*—it meant that I had to take increasing responsibility for my own decisions and my own failures. Until 1976 I had been perfectly happy to "take orders" from Yogiji, and simply do my best to carry them out. My success or failure would not then be the result of my own faulty initiative. There were some significant exceptions to this tendency, such as my decision to take the Khalsa String Band on tour, but in general it was easy to give Yogiji the responsibility for significant life decisions.

The disillusionment I was beginning to experience, and the knowledge that I could no longer trust Yogiji unconditionally, occurred at the same time that the "Rent and Wage" system was forcing me to take fuller responsibility for my own financial well-being. It was a trying time, but I still did not question my involvement

Premka, Ganga, Larry, Krishna, and I were sent by Yogiji to represent Sikh Dharma at the inauguration of President Jimmy Carter in January, 1977. At an event in front of the Lincoln Memorial we met with Coretta Scott King, widow of Martin Luther King, Jr.

with the organization. I had so much invested at this point that to leave and admit I had made a mistake was unthinkable. Instead, I found new ways to explain the inconsistencies and lapses of integrity I saw in Yogiji and the organization. "Even if the rumors about his sexual activities are true," I rationalized, "It's not for me to judge. The only thing that is relevant is how his role as my spiritual teacher helps me progress towards my liberation."

Since the demise of the Khalsa String Band, I had been like a ship with neither a rudder nor a port. I needed to be meaningfully engaged in something that I cared about. But without music, and no role in the ashram, I was facing a crisis. It was with relief and joy, therefore, that I accepted Yogiji's request that I take another trip to India in the fall of 1977. I was still one of the only people in 3HO who was proficient on the tablas and could speak some Punjabi. Larry would again cover all expenses, and I could do what I loved, accompanying a Gurbani Kirtan jatha with my tabla playing while touring throughout Punjab. Once again, however, my family would be left at home.

I was lucky to be the first person in 3HO to study tabla. Here I am performing with Amarjit Kaur and Vikram Singh, formerly Vic Briggs of The Animals.

CHAPTER THIRTY-ONE

A New Life in India

BEFORE I DEPARTED for India in the fall of 1977, we learned that Sat-Peter Kaur was pregnant again. She was unhappy about it, and we discussed the options at length. Although I had no ideological objection to abortion, I felt very strongly that we should have this baby. Amrit, now five, was in most respects a dream child and would be able to help with the new baby in a year or two.

Already the burdens of parenthood were fairly light. Amrit had been going to Montessori school since the age of two, and our large ashram community, with more than a dozen children, provided abundant opportunities for shared childcare. We had even organized a summer camp for the children on a rented Maryland farm about an hour south of Washington, DC. Under these circumstances, I felt that having a second child was not an unreasonable thing to do. I even promised to take primary responsibility for her, including changing diapers. By the societal norms of the time, especially in the patriarchal culture Yogiji had created within the American Sikh community, that was an unusual offer.

It was understandable, given the stresses and dysfunction in our relationship, that Sat-Peter Kaur would be hesitant about bringing another child into the world, but eventually she resigned herself to it, a decision that raised her greatly in my esteem and resulted for a short time in some genuine feelings of affection on my part. A few weeks later, I was on my way to India for a six-week tour. But the six weeks stretched into five months.

For the first several weeks of our tour we followed what was by now a standard agenda: a few days in New Delhi, a week or two at the Golden Temple in Amritsar, and a few weeks of touring the historical Gurdwaras throughout Punjab. Initially, there were about fifty of us. However, neither Yogiji nor Larry came on this trip. Instead, Yogiji had sent his wife Bibiji to be the principal speaker at our appearances, and Ram Das Singh to be the tour's administrative leader. Ram Das' wife, Ram Das Kaur, was one of the *raginis*, or singers in our Gurbani Kirtan Jatha, along with Ganga and another friend, Sat Kirpal Kaur.

This was by far the most rewarding of my trips to India. Without the suppressive, authoritarian influences of either Yogiji or Larry, we were a lot freer to enjoy ourselves, and we approached our missionary work with a lightness of heart that sometimes bordered on giddiness. The four members of our musical group, in particular, had a lot of fun together. Each had a good sense of humor, and the oddities of Indian culture—as well as the personality quirks of the people we met and with whom we traveled—provided us a lot of material for entertainment. The tedium of having to sit through endless hours of speeches in Punjabi also provided a backdrop against which any opportunity for levity was greatly amplified. It was not unusual to find us on stage with tears in our eyes from trying to suppress our laughter at some little joke or observation we discretely pointed out or whispered amongst ourselves.

Typical of our appearances, except for the size of the event, was an educational conference in Kanpur celebrating the 300th anniversary of the birth of Guru Gobind Singh. All of Sikh academia from Punjab and beyond was represented: thousands of educators, writers, politicians, and government administrators. The event took place on a soccer field under a huge open-air tent. Since nearly everyone attending this event spoke English, Bibiji decided to have both Ram Das Singh and Ram Das Kaur address the group. I had never been much impressed with Ram Das Singh, He seemed to hide behind the title and authority bestowed on him by Yogiji, but at his core I sensed that he was quite insecure. However, on this occasion he did quite well. His very appearance at the microphone elicited gasps of appreciation, for he was endowed with an enormous salt and pepper beard that flowed like a banner in the breeze. Dressed in brilliant white kurta and chudidas with a massive kirpan hanging over his shoulder he cut quite an impressive figure.

Most of the Indian Sikhs in the congregation were wearing western clothes and had their beards rolled up compactly under their chins. This unattractive style had originated with the military under British rule and had been widely adopted by the better-educated and professional classes. Ram Das Singh spoke passionately, if somewhat self-righteously, about being proud of the Sikh heritage, of boldly wearing the five "K's" given by Guru Gobind Singh, and of unabashedly displaying his beard as a sign of faith. His talk elicited many cheers from the audience. Several of the conference organizers, caught up in the spirit of the moment, joined Ram Das at the microphone and publicly affirmed their faith and pride in the Sikh tradition by unrolling their beards on the spot. Their example was followed by hundreds in the audience, each one jumping to his feet and calling out the traditional battle cry *"Bolay Soni Hal—Sat Siri Akal,"* as his beard waved free for probably the first time in his life. It was an inspiring and emotional scene, and Ram Das Singh's speech ended in thunderous applause and full-throated battle cries that continued for several gratifying minutes.

Next on the agenda was a talk by Ram Das Kaur about the historical significance of the five "K's." The purpose of this talk was not to educate the group (they were as familiar with this material as Americans are with the Pledge of Allegiance) but to demonstrate further what a wonderful job Yogiji had done in converting Americans to the Sikh religion. Ram Das Kaur got off to a good start, talking about the esoteric, religious, and practical significance of the uncut hair (*Keshas*), the steel bracelet (*Kara*), wooden comb (*Kanga*), and the dagger (*Kirpan*). But when she got to the fifth "K," *Kacheras*, the knee-length underwear, she faltered, a little unsure of how to explain it.

"Back in the old days," she began, "Everyone just wore *dhotis*, a long piece of cotton fabric wrapped Mahatma Gandhi-style around one's legs and waist. These were very inconvenient in battle, because with all the swords flying around and everything you never knew what might happen." Polite clearing of throats and some snickering could be heard from the audience. Ram Das was unable to recover from the direction her talk was taking, and her explanation got increasingly vivid. "Anyway," she concluded quickly, "That's why Guru Gobind Singh came up with Kacheras. *Wahe Guruji Ka Khalsa, Wahe Guruji Ki Fateh!*" Ram Das Kaur escaped to a smattering of applause while the Master of Ceremonies took the microphone. "Thank you, Mrs. Sardarni Ram Das Kaur, for that very interesting and informative talk about the Five "K's" of Guru Gobind Singh Ji. And now we will hear the Amrikan Ragi Jatha perform a shabad."

We were all in hysterics. Ram Das Kaur was unabashed and good-natured about her gaff. In the sexually repressed culture of India, any mention of intimate body parts was socially incorrect, to say the least, and even more so in a formal public setting like this one. Bibiji was blushing, but exchanged bemused and slightly conspiratorial glances with us as we prepared to play. Our Gurbani Kirtan came off extremely well. The audience again greeted us with stentorian battle cries. More people stood up to unfurl their rolled-up beards. Later, the Master of Ceremonies thanked us

I was very fond of Giani Mohinder Singh, one of the officials of the SGPC, the administrative body for the historic Gurdwaras of India. I was there to welcome him and several other officials when they visited Yogiji in New Mexico in 1974.

profusely for our wonderful performance and presentations. He took a fatherly approach with Ram Das Kaur, congratulating her for the informative talk and tactfully suggesting that the next time she might leave out some of the details about the kacheras.

After our impressive success in Kanpur, Bibiji telephoned Yogiji back in Los Angeles and convinced him that a small group of us should stay on in India after the rest of the Americans went home the following week. There would just be five of us: Bibiji, Ganga, Ram Das Kaur, Sat Kirpal Kaur, and me. We were to stay in Yogiji's house in the Nizzamudin East section of New Delhi and carry out an aggressive schedule of appearances in public and private venues throughout Delhi. I was amazed and happy that Yogiji agreed to this plan. As soon as we got settled in, I found a music school in a rustic Gurdwara only about a mile from Yogiji's house where I could study both tabla and sitar in a more formal setting. Nobody there spoke any English at all, but my facility with Punjabi had increased to the point that I could carry on a stilted conversation.

My tabla teacher was a young Sikh whose technical skills were far inferior to those of Gurbax Singh, my teacher at the Golden Temple. But he played expressively and was a master of the folk style, manipulating the tone of the Bayan, the bass drum, to create driving pulses that added a new level of excitement to the music. For six years I had been playing *at* the tablas, but within a few weeks, something shifted in my playing and I found myself able to use the instrument to add new shape and dimension to our Gurbani Kirtan.

My sitar teacher was a very old man named Baba Karnak Singh. He had been blind since birth. When we first met, he ran his hands over my face and upper body, stopping with surprise when he got to my chin. I was 27 years old, but still had almost no beard. "*Kesha nehi heh*?" He asked ("You have no beard?"). "*Mehn jeeva han,*" I replied ("I'm still young"). He smiled broadly and laughed. Babaji did not actually play the sitar. He played the *sarangi*, a small, fretted instrument that is bowed like a cello. By tuning my sitar to the same scale, I was able to learn from him by following note for note. We had a great time together and I would often go hear him play when he performed at Gurdwara Bangla Sahib. These were happy days for me. I loved learning, and immensely enjoyed the interactions with my two teachers, both of whom were blessed with warm-hearted natures and a rustic simplicity that was uncommon in Delhi.

After a few weeks in Delhi, Bibiji decided we should start teaching public yoga classes. We already had something of a captive audience in a group of young, well-educated Sikhs from wealthy Delhi families who were rediscovering their religious roots through the Institute for Gurmat Studies (IGS). IGS was started and operated by an impressive, big-hearted idealist named Captain Harbhajan Singh. Through a series of week-long youth camps held on the outskirts of Delhi he had provided scores of teens and young adults

On tour in India with Ganga, Ram Das Kaur and the American Ragi Jatha.

a way they could learn the prayers, music, and traditions of the Sikhs in the company of their peers. On several different trips to India some of the Americans had participated in these camps. Our extended stay in Delhi now allowed us to provide a more regular schedule of activities in which they could participate daily or weekly.

These young people had been exposed to all the perils of western youth culture, including rock & roll, drugs, and sex. Although Harbhajan Singh had some serious reservations about Yogiji, he was happy for the strategic alliance with us and greatly appreciated the fact that we had all "been there," had survived "youth culture," and had found refuge and meaning in Sikh Dharma. It was an example he wanted to share with the IGS youth.

I became very close friends with Harbhajan and his niece Jasjit. We spent long and happy hours talking together, often at the house they shared with his parents. Harbhajan, in his late thirties, had a charismatic personality and strong convictions, tempered by a progressive attitude and compassionate rapport with his wayward protégés. Jasjit was my age, intelligent, modern, well educated, exceptionally attractive, and quite elegant in both dress and bearing. I was far from home, lonely, and in extreme danger of making a fool of myself and bringing dishonor upon us all. Fortunately, that never happened, for I was protected at all times by the complete absence of privacy. Once, while saying goodbye at the top of the stairway, I took her hand firmly in mine as if to express the passion and admiration that was growing in me. Jasjit, her eyes full of understanding and kindness, just patted the top of my hand gently and withdrew her own. No other sign ever passed between us, and our love and respect for each other was never tarnished.

Not everybody in our group, however, was so lucky. All of us were unhappy in our arranged marriages, including Bibiji, and we had been too far from home for too long. Eventually, one of the IGS boys took a strong liking to Ganga, and she responded in kind. I was not aware of things getting out of control, but Bibiji discovered them one day in the storage room in a compromising situation. If it had gone no further, things would probably have worked out, but Bibiji felt compelled to tell Yogiji, and suddenly we had a serious international incident on our hands.

Yogiji made a huge stink about it. Larry was informed. Word got out to all of 3HO, and almost overnight Ganga's life was ruined. She not only lost most of her former prestige, but worse, she seemed to lose her self-confidence under the burden of guilt and judgment that was heaped upon her. And it did not stop there. Yogiji, intent on protecting at any cost his own reputation and that of the American Sikhs, made a public issue of blaming the IGS boy for whatever had happened. Accusations and counter accusations went flying back and forth, even after we had left India and returned home. It was an ugly end to an otherwise wonderful trip, and raised one more question in my mind about Yogiji's motivations and integrity.

CHAPTER THIRTY-TWO

Big Yellow Bus

MY SECOND DAUGHTER was born on June 30, 1978. I was five hours late for the birth, which like that of my first daughter took place at home amidst a crowd of softly chanting Ashram members, with a midwife attending, I had been gone for over two weeks, serving as the driver and mechanic of the Ashram's aging yellow school bus, which we used to transport members to and from the summer and winter solstice celebrations. Everyone contributed $125 to pay for the trip. I went for free in exchange for my services. Considering our numerous breakdowns and the work of replacing various water hoses, fan belts, the generator, water pump, three flat tires, and a fuel filter, the value of my services could have paid for my entire family and a few others to boot. But I didn't see it that way at the time. Rather, I felt ashamed that I was somehow taking advantage of my senior position at the Ashram, and that the arrangement I had made with Larry to gain free passage to solstice was more a reflection of my having no job and no money.

The news of my daughter's birth was relayed to me by CB radio as we approached the Potomac River. The school bus was one of six or seven vehicles that were traveling in caravan, all equipped with CB radios in order to coordinate our movements. The exercise of keeping that many vehicles together helped break the tedium of long-distance driving, as did the constant road chatter of passing truckers, and the other millions of CB radio nuts on the road in the late '70s.

Before cell phones, CB radios offered not only a great way to communicate while on the road, but with their open channels and 3 to 5 mile range they helped spawn an entire culture of people who assumed new personas and entered into friendly banter with complete strangers. The anonymity provided by the CB radio was especially valued by the turban wearing, white-clothed, and bearded American Sikhs, for in the visual vacuum of radio frequencies we could communicate easily with anyone—from redneck truck driver to Ivy League college student. As in so much of American culture, the lowest common denominator prevailed, so most people spoke in a southern accent, even if they were from Boston. For several years in the late 1970s, CB radios were so in vogue that we didn't limit our use of them to road trips. Almost everyone in the Ashram had one in their car and they went online with a turn of the ignition key.

As we neared Washington, DC, I went on the air: "Breaker, Breaker. This is White Eagle. Come back, anyone."

"Hey there White Eagle, this is the High Flyer. Do you read me? Come Back."

"Hello there, High Flyer, I read you loud and clear. We're headed North on the 95. What's your 10-20? Come back."

"I'm going south on 95, headed to Florida for some good times. What are you driving there, White Eagle? Come Back."

"We're in a big yellow school bus, headed to DC from New Mexico. What are you in? Come Back."

"Hey there White Eagle, are you that old school bus with the blue tarp on top near the 495? Come Back."

"That's us, High Flyer! 1500 miles behind us and only 5 more to go!"

"Breaker, Breaker. This is the Undertaker. I'm right behind you, White Eagle. About to pass on your left. Come back."

"Come on by, there, Undertaker. We'll make plenty of room for you. Hey there High Flyer, you have yourself a fine time down in Florida, OK? Come Back."

"OK, there, White Eagle. Welcome to DC. Y'all have fun now, Good Buddy. Over."

"Breaker Breaker. This is the Undertaker. Hey there, White Eagle, I'm that silver 18-wheeler that just passed you. I'll be shakin' the trees for ya for a while. Come Back."

"OK there Undertaker. We'll be rakin' the leaves. Where you headed? Come Back."

"I'll be in Toronto tonight. Got a long way to go. Come back."

"Well, you drive safe there, Good Buddy. We'll be wishin' you well. Over."

"Breaker, Breaker. This is the White Dove calling for the White Eagle. Do you read me, White Eagle? Come back."

"Hey there, White Dove, I read you loud and clear. What's your 10-20? Come back."

"I just left the Ashram where your wife gave birth to a ten-pound baby girl just four hours ago. Congratulations. Come Back."

"Oh my God! Hey there, White Dove, did everything go OK? Come back."

"Everything went fine. SPK went into labor about four AM and gave birth this morning at 8:40. So you've got yourself a little Cancer. Her name is Sat Hari Kaur Khalsa. Come Back."

"Hey there, White Dove. Where did that name come from? Come back."

"We called Yogiji as soon as she was born and reached one of his secretaries. She called us back a few minutes later with the name. What's your 10-20, Good Buddy? Come back."

"We're almost at the Memorial Bridge. We'll be home in about 15 minutes. Over."

"Breaker, breaker. This is the Undertaker. Hey there, White

Eagle, congratulations on that new baby girl of yours! Y'all git on home and take care of her, y'hear, Good Buddy? Come back."

"Thank you, Good Buddy. I'm a-gittin'. Over."

"Breaker, breaker. This is the King Bee callin' to the White Eagle. Couldn't help over-hearing that you're a new papa there, Good Buddy. Congratulations. Over."

"Breaker, breaker. This is the Motorman. 10-4, Good Buddy!"

"Breaker, breaker. This is the Morning Star. Hey there, White Eagle, is that you in the old school bus full of Q-Tips? Come back."

After dropping off passengers and luggage at three or four different houses that now comprised the Ashram community, it was nearly an hour before I was able to get back to my home and new baby. Seeing Sat Hari for the first time brought tears to my eyes. She was adorable, and Sat-Peter Kaur looked beautiful as she lay in bed with our baby snuggled at her side, eyes not yet open. Our first child, Amrit, now six years old, was in attendance, already seeming to relish her role as big sister. My heart was awash with love, and I was ready to let go of all our past difficulties. For a short while, I thought that it might work out for us to be a happy family, after all.

However, I was upset that the choice of a name for our new baby had been preempted by Yogiji, even though it was a beautiful name, meaning "True Princess of God." If I had arrived home a few hours earlier to take part in the birth, I would not have called Yogiji, and instead would have insisted that Sat-Peter Kaur and I choose a name. It seemed such a basic part of being a parent, and yet even that had now been taken away from us. Only later did I come to grips with the fact that denying our legitimacy and traditional role as parents was just one more way for Yogiji to manipulate and control his followers. I consoled myself that at least Amrit had the name we had chosen for her.

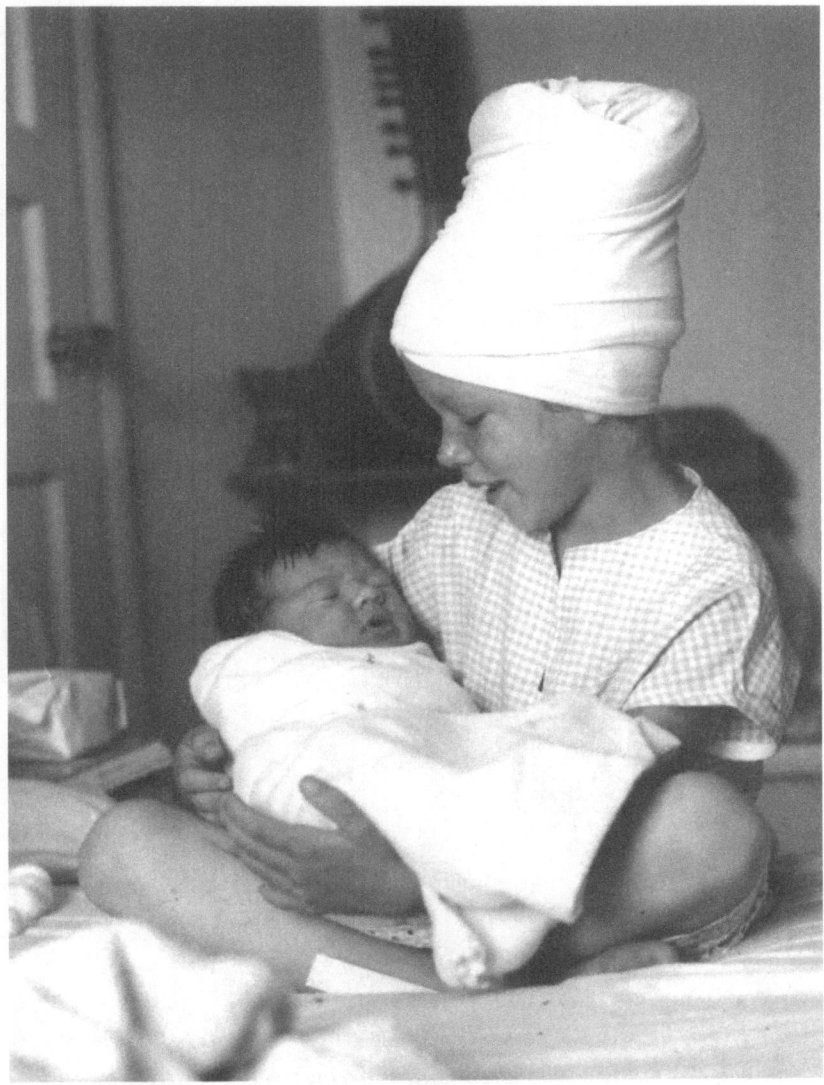
Our older daughter, Amrit, was delighted to have a baby sister.

In spite of the many challenges in our marriage, Sat-Peter Kaur and I gave our children a lot of love, which they returned in kind.

CHAPTER THIRTY-THREE

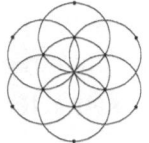

Making A Living

LIFE IN WASHINGTON, DC was getting increasingly difficult for me in the last years of the 1970s. I struggled to make money to support my family of four, and things were not going well. I tried to get work as a taxi driver, feeling confident that I knew my way around the city as well as anyone. I did fine on the written test, but was told that I would not be allowed to wear a turban, since it was against company policy. I was thunderstruck. I had plenty of experience with individual prejudice—people calling me an "Arab," or "raghead," or dozens of other epithets related to my white turban. But I had never before faced discrimination as an institution, as an official corporate policy.

Despite the blatant injustice, I was not yet ready to take on such battles, so I kept looking for other jobs. I applied for several teaching positions for which I had no credentials. I applied for a job with the Post Office, but was told I was over-qualified. I looked into telephone sales, but couldn't bring myself to tell people I was a paraplegic, seeking donations for the Crippled Children's Fund. I made a little money by teaching tabla courses in Ashrams wherever I could generate enough interest. I had developed a 3-day "weekend intensive" format by which I could teach a group of beginning students enough that they could provide basic accompaniment for Gurbani Kirtan. The system really did work, and I trained about forty students this way in ten cities from Boston to Los Angeles. But it was not enough income to maintain my family.

In an entrepreneurial effort to buy and sell valuable cars, I went into a loose partnership with Kamal for the purchase of a turquoise blue 1955 Thunderbird convertible. It was a beautiful-looking car and Kamal had convinced me we could sell it at a huge profit in Los Angeles. I had no cash, but I had recently opened a credit card that had a $4,000 cash advance. With stars in my eyes, I spent every penny of the cash advance as my contribution to the $9,000 purchase price. My other contribution, to make it an equal partnership, would be to drive the car to Los Angeles where Kamal had made arrangements with one of his friends, the director of the Ashram in Long Beach, to sell it for us. We were planning to list it for $18,000 in LA, so even after paying the commission we would make out quite well.

I recruited my friend, Gurudass (who had played bass in the Khalsa String Band), to make the cross-country drive with me. We left on a bright fall afternoon with the top down. What a sense of adventure! But when we got onto Interstate 70 in Pennsylvania, it began to rain and we had to stop by the side of the road to put the top up. The rain came harder as the sun went down, and soon we were in a torrential storm in total darkness. The low-slung Thunderbird felt pathetically small in company with the huge tractor-trailers that sped by at 80 mph, blinding us with their spray. It was terrifying, and we were looking for a place to pull off the highway when there was a loud clunk from the rear left wheel. I immediately pulled onto the shoulder, for I knew what must have happened. The fender skirt that covered the rear wheel had come loose and fallen off. I ran back a hundred yards in the pouring rain to find the part in the dark and came abreast of it just as a tractor trailer drove over it. I waited for a break in the traffic, watching helplessly as two more trucks ran it over, then dashed out and retrieved the battered piece of metal, got back in the car and drove on, soaking wet, cold, and much distressed..

It was heartbreaking to realize that the formerly perfect car was now cosmetically damaged. Several hours later when we pulled into Columbus, Ohio, I got a little encouragement from the head of the Ashram, who said one of his yoga students had a body shop and could fix it in the morning. Fix it he did, and only charged me $50, but the fender skirt would never be perfect again, though it looked OK from a distance. But our friendly auto body worker pointed out another defect. The entire front left fender was a replacement part made of fiberglass. Far from being in "original condition," as the smooth-talking guy who sold it to us had said, this car had been in a very bad accident. My heart sank as I came to grips with the reality that our Thunderbird was not worth anything close to $18,000. It probably wasn't even worth the $9,000 we paid for it. There was nothing to do about it, however, but to continue on to L.A. and try to unload the car for whatever it would bring.

Two days later, Gurudass and I made quite a sight as we drove with the top down to the front entrance of the Flamingo Casino in Las Vegas. The valets and bellboys, thinking we were rich sheiks rather than a pair of impoverished Sikhs, treated us like royalty. We basked in the attention. Once inside, we agreed to a limit of 20 quarters each for the slot machines. It was just a goof, anyway. But the $10 I won on the second quarter tempted me to keep trying, even after the machine had taken back all forty quarters plus the 20 I had started with. A look around at the rows and rows of hapless gamblers—mostly old men and women, cigarettes dangling from their lips, plugging quarters mindlessly into one-armed bandits—was sobering enough to convince us to cut our losses.

When we got to LA, we delivered the T-bird to Long Beach and caught a flight back to DC. The car, however, did not sell. It sat on the street in front of the Ashram gathering dirt, rust, and corrosion.

The Ashram was on the waterfront and the salty ocean air was no friend to antique cars. Back in DC, I tried to put it out of my mind, leaving to Kamal the task of selling the car. I had other things to worry about, including how to pay the monthly bill on my credit card, which was now maxed out and coming due. I briefly tried my hand at real estate. Finally, I answered an ad for a position as an advertising account rep:

> **"Seeking motivated individual for advertising sales. Excellent commission structure. Set your own hours. Qualified applicants only."**

I called the number and reached a man with a strong Brooklyn accent.

"Yeah?"

"Um…I'm calling about the ad in the paper for an advertising account representative…"

"Yeah?"

"Well, can you tell me a little bit about the job?"

"Sure. We're in the advertising business, and if you've got a car and some motivation, I can show you how to make a lot of money. Have you got a car?"

"Um…yeah…Can you tell me what I'd be doing?"

"Sure, kid. We serve some of the area's finest businesses. We're in the direct mail industry. Say, I like your phone voice. Why don't you come on out for an interview in person?"

"Um…OK. Where are you located?"

The voice, which belonged to Irving Goldstein, gave me directions to an address in rural Fairfax County. We agreed on a time later that afternoon. My car at this time was a 1955 Chevy "210" four-door Sedan. It was a fine car, given to me by an old lady in Bethesda who wanted it out of her backyard. It had a "straight six" engine and automatic ("slip-slide-omatic") transmission, got 20 miles per gallon and 250 miles per quart of oil, and could cruise along at 70 all day without overheating. Perhaps, most importantly, it qualified for GEICO's very affordable "antique" car insurance, provided I only drove it once or twice a month in parades and festivals. "That's exactly what I use it for," I had lied.

The address Mr. Goldstein gave was not a business, but a funky house in a rundown neighborhood. I parked my car and knocked on the door. "JUST A MINUTE," a voice called from inside. I waited for several minutes and was just about to get back in my car and go home when the door suddenly opened. A short, fat, balding man of 60 or 65 peered out at me in astonishment.

"Are you the guy who called?" he asked. Apparently, no one else had answered the ad.

"Yes," I answered solicitously. "I'm Peter. It's nice to meet you Sir."

"You can call me 'Irv'," he answered. "Come on in."

I followed Irv in through an entryway strewn with coats and old shoes and turned left into an office that looked like the city dump. Cardboard boxes, flyers, plastic sacks, and newspapers were strewn about ridiculously. A single desk was buried under papers and file folders. As we entered, the phone started ringing.

"Hello? Oh, Hello Sam! How are things going?...No, the mailer went out last week. You haven't gotten any coupons back? Well, sometimes the Post Office is a little slow. Let's give it a few days and see how things work out.

"OK, Sam. Well, don't worry about anything. Sometimes it just takes a little time. Take care now, let's talk next week."

Irving turned towards me and said, "You see, young fella, it's all about taking care of your customers. Now I'll tell you something: the only people who want to advertise are the people who are just getting started in business or the people who are about to go broke.

If you get them at the beginning, or near the end, you've got yourself a good customer...at least for a while. But the fortune tellers are different. They advertise all the time, and they're some of my best customers. They always pay in 100-dollar bills. The only problem is that a lot of folks don't like to be in the same envelope with fortune tellers..." Irving looked at me absently.

"What kind of business is this?" I asked.

"Well, this is the finest business opportunity in the world today," replied Mr. Goldstein. "We're in the Direct Mail business. Do you know about Direct Mail, Son?"

"No Sir, I don't. But I'm ready to learn."

"I like your attitude, young man," said Irv. He went on to explain that he sent envelopes full of printed coupons and ads to groups of 10,000 homes in a neighborhood, using mailing lists he procured from a local company. "Are you interested in making a lot of money?" he asked.

"Yes Sir," I answered. "I've got two kids now and a wife to support and I think I can do this!"

Irv looked at me intently, as if for the first time noticing that I was wearing a turban, but forcing himself to overlook it. "I like you, son," he said. "I think you can do well in this business."

"Thank you, Sir," I said. "When can I start?"

"Right now!" Irv proceeded to tell me all about the direct mail business, how to identify the kinds of businesses that were likely to advertise (dry cleaners, carpet cleaners, chimney sweepers, auto repair shops, oriental restaurants, window replacement and home repair contractors, and, of course, fortune tellers). He told me how to sell the 'sizzle' ("Just imagine the impact of getting your coupon into the hands of 10,000 of your local customers!"), how to handle the contract forms and the collection of deposit checks. It all seemed pretty simple to me. Our company would design and print 10,000 advertising coupons for each client, then send them out in a shared envelope to every homeowner in the area. There might be as many as 20 coupons per envelope. In fact, the more coupons the better. The company broke even at about 10 coupons and only made "good money" when there were more than 15 per envelope.

I was fascinated and somewhat uneasy at my exposure to the 'real world' of the advertising business. I liked Irv, probably because he displayed no prejudice towards me for my turban and white clothes. In fact, Irv seemed like a real human being, though I wasn't entirely comfortable with his taking advantage, by his own admission, of naive and desperate entrepreneurs. Irv's wife shuffled into the room while we were talking. She was wearing dirty slippers and had a cigarette dangling from her mouth as if it were glued to her lower lip. Her hair was a mess. She didn't seem to notice me.

"Mr. Kim keeps calling on the house phone," she started in a coarse and disrespectful tone. "He wants his money back. Says he doesn't believe the mailer went out yet and the dated offer is about to expire."

Irv looked a little nervous but overcame it. "Honey, this is Peter. He's going to be working with us. Peter, this is my wife, Mabel."

I stood up respectfully and said "Nice to meet you Mrs. Goldstein."

Mabel looked me once up and down and answered as if in passing, "Yeah." Then addressing Irv, "So are you going to call him back or what? I'm tired of dealing with it."

"I'll take care of it, Honey. I'll be over in his neighborhood a little later and I'll drop in on him. Don't worry about it."

Mabel turned and shuffled out without another word. Irv pulled out a map of the Washington metropolitan area and pointed to Bladensburg, MD, one of the poorest neighborhoods around. I couldn't help thinking that my wife was from there. "This is where I'd like you to get started. We need to build up a client base in Bladensburg. There's lots of potential there, and if you do a good job, you can make a lot of money. So, are you ready to get started?" I greedily accepted the job. There was no salary promised, and no benefits, no paid expenses, and no guaranteed income of any sort. Further, I would have to pay for my own gas and oil. If I was able to get at least ten clients from Bladensburg to advertise at a cost of $350 each, I could make a 15% commission, or $535. I was eager to get started and make a lot of money.

I worked for about four months, driving my 1955 Chevy for several thousand miles around the Washington Beltway. I put up with doors slammed in my face, rude comments of all kinds, and multiple automotive breakdowns, including a broken differential and cracked "third member." But I had gathered more than 15 clients for a special mailing to the Bladensburg area, and along the way I had helped each client design a coupon, which often included suggesting a special offer to "bring in the customers." Most of the time I used my imagination, but Irv went out of his way to give me tips about the business.

Irv was always fatherly and kind. "You're doing a fine job, Son," he said. "In fact, you've done so well that I'm going to give you a 20% commission instead of 15%. By the way," he added, "I'm going to be selling the business and thought you might be interested, though I do have another buyer already lined up. Mabel and I are going to be moving to Florida." In the four months I had been working for him, Irv had written me checks for slightly more than $1,000. But I owed more than $300 on my Exxon credit card just for gas and oil. At that rate, I was making a little more than $1.00 per hour. Twelve years earlier I had been making $2.73 per hour in a summer job as a sheet metal worker in my uncle's air conditioning business. It made no sense at all, but I got excited about the prospect of buying the business.

In preparation for the possibility of my taking over, Irv took me to meet his service providers, who included a graphic artist, a printer, and an envelope stuffer and mailing company. The graphic artist, a huge slovenly fellow named Fred, worked out of his home, a meandering suburban slum in Fairfax, Virginia. Upon entering, I was taken aback at the overpowering smell of urine and animal litter. But I was even more surprised at the numerous residents. Several deformed and blank-faced boys and girls (actually they were young adults) wandered in and out of the "office" where Fred created the graphic designs for the direct mail coupons upon which our clients pinned their hopes for survival. Irv explained to me later that Fred made extra money by taking care of several disabled and mentally-handicapped wards of the state. It didn't seem to me he was taking very good care of them.

On another day we went to visit Irv's printer. This gentleman lived on the outskirts of McLean, and had clearly lived there for many years—long enough, at least, that his house predated the affluence for which that DC suburb had been known for the past several decades. I had never seen, or even imagined that someone could live in such a mess. Not one square inch of floor or counter space was free of litter. In one corner of the kitchen was an old single-color printing press. Various colors of ink were spattered all about, even on the ceiling. Irv spoke with the printer in confidential tones, and eventually introduced me. I felt rather conspicuous in my turban and white clothes, but Irv's friend gave no indication that I was different in any way.

Bob, the printer, was overweight by at least 150 pounds. He told me that he had been a heavyweight wrestler when he was younger. He spent some time explaining to me about the wrestling business, including the news that all heavyweight wrestlers are members of the

Actors Guild, and all carry insurance. "The real action doesn't take place in the ring," he told me. "It takes place in the dressing rooms after the matches when the losers get even with the winners. Every match is scripted," he confided, "But if someone gets too carried away in the ring, he's sure to pay for it afterwards." Bob had a big scar running across his forehead. I didn't ask if it was the result of a locker room battle.

Bob and Irv were delighted that I took an active interest in the printing process. Bob spent some time showing me how the press worked, and explained the limitations and capabilities of the different kinds of printing presses. Irv was indulgently patient, offering his own pointers from time to time. Most of Irv's coupons were 1/3 of a page, so we printed them "three-up," or three to a page, then cut them into individual coupons. Irv also offered his clients half page and full-page coupons, which made the logistics of layout and printing somewhat complicated. But Irv enjoyed solving these little problems and took pride in telling me his strategies.

The envelope stuffing operation was critical to the success of Irv's business. The envelopes were pre-printed with a company logo, a bulk mail permit, and a catchy advertising line designed to ensure that each recipient opened it up before tossing it in the trash. "Free Coupons Worth $$$ Hundreds of Dollars Inside!" Each envelope had to bear a generic "Current Resident" address label, and needed to contain one of each coupon. Sometimes there were more than 20 different coupons in a mailer. Each mailing consisted of 10,000 envelopes, but Irv often had two or more mailings happening simultaneously. "It makes it easier to work out the printing logistics," he winked. But combining mailings this way seemed to have a big downside, too, often causing mailings to go out late. Mr. Kim was not the only client who wanted his money back. Quite a few of Irv's customers complained that their coupons were expired before they were even mailed out. "That's why you never want your customers to put an expiration date," Irv confided.

Irv introduced me to the owner of the company that did the envelope addressing and stuffing. He took me to the post office and showed me how to handle bulk mailings. He introduced me to the company that supplied the pre-printed address labels, and basically taught me everything he knew about the business. And he gave me tips about selling. "Just help them design the ad," he said. "You don't even ask if they want it or not; you just help them figure out what size they'll need. And always have your sales form ready. By the time you're done filling out the form they can't say no. But you've got to ask for that deposit check. You haven't really made the sale till you have the money in your hand.

"Let me tell you a story about selling. When I was 15, I went to work for my uncle in New York. He had a clothing shop. My first customer bought a suit off the rack. It was just what he wanted, and I was beaming from making my first sale. My uncle said, 'What are you all excited about? You call that SELLING? If that guy came in looking for a gray suit in size 40 and we didn't have one, and you got him to buy a green suit in size 38 that he didn't even like, THAT'S selling. What you did wasn't selling. It was just customer service.'" Irv ended his story with a triumphant gesture. I smiled weakly. I liked the idea of customer service a lot better than "selling," but I let it pass.

A few days later I showed up at Irv's office and found him with a visitor, a lanky guy about my age who had an aggressive, wolf-like look in his eye. I hated him at first sight. "Hello, Peter," said Irv a little nervously, "I'd like you to meet David Steinmetz. David is the fella I told you about who was buying my business, and as of yesterday afternoon he's taking over. I'm just going over with him some of our accounts so he can hit the ground running. And I'm glad you came in Peter, 'cause I've been wanting for the two of you to meet. I've been telling David what a great job you did for us in Bladensburg," Irv went on and on as if he were afraid of what might happen if he stopped talking. He could see that I didn't like David at all, but more importantly, he knew that I felt betrayed by his selling the business to David instead of to me.

"David has been running a similar kind of business," Irv continued desperately. "He and his dad, who you'll be meeting here shortly, do door hangers. They put the coupons in a plastic sack and leave them hanging on every door in the neighborhood. David, why don't you show Peter one of your door hangers."

David seemed reluctant, but reached into a large briefcase between his knees and pulled out a flat 9"x15" clear plastic bag. Six or eight coupons of varying heights were inserted in such a way that one line of copy on the top edge of each coupon showed through the front of the bag. "Isn't that clever?" Irv pointed out. "Every customer gets at least some 'front page' exposure. David, why don't you tell Peter a little bit about your business."

For the first time since my entering the room, David opened his mouth to speak. I wished that he hadn't. In fact, I wanted to be out of there as fast as possible. David was just starting to tell me how his plastic sacks were better than mailing envelopes "because the ads can be seen whether the recipient opens the bag or not" when his father showed up. David's father was a wiry little man of 70 with heavy-framed glasses and white hair. His clothes were frayed around the edges and his shoes were old, worn, and dirty. His name was George. He reminded me of a homeless version of George Burns.

George was on back slapping terms with Irv—he told me with a wink that they both attended the same Synagogue—and seemed to take an immediate interest in me. He was solicitous in his praise for the good work I had done in Bladensburg and the fine job I was

CHAPTER THIRTY-THREE: Making A Living

doing in Silver Spring. "Irv has told me all about you," he enthused. It was pretty clear that Irv had been talking me up in a big way, though David gave no indication he was impressed. It occurred to me later that the perceived value of my participation in Irv's business and the new customers I had already brought in the door probably impacted the purchase price. George made a great effort to make friends with me, but I felt that his overtures were insincere, as if he was practicing some ancient Dale Carnegie techniques on me.

By the time my visit concluded I had a sinking feeling that I was caught in a trap. I had invested so much time and energy learning about the business and developing new customers, many of whom would give me repeat business, that I couldn't follow my instinct to get out of there as fast as possible and never look back. Instead, I bit the bullet and agreed to come to a sales meeting the following Monday at George and David's office in Wheaton, MD. I said goodbye to Irv and Mabel and wished them well on their trip. Irv informed me they were leaving the next morning for Florida. I thanked Irv for all his help, but with George and David sitting right there, I couldn't say a lot of the things I wanted to. Irv looked really guilty and ashamed at having let me down, and seemed anxious for the goodbyes to be finished. I think he also wanted to get George and David out of there, and I couldn't help thinking that his sudden trip south had more the feeling of skipping town than "retiring" from his illustrious career in direct mail advertising.

As I drove back home to Washington, my mind was working a mile a minute. I knew that I could not last long working for David and George. Yet what were my options? Could I just start my own business and take with me the clients I had developed? I certainly knew most of the ropes. But there were other considerations. If I was going to start from scratch, I could do it just about anywhere. My attachment to Washington DC had been fading for several years and the situation at the Ashram was less and less pleasant. I had been unable to pay my monthly rental obligations, so Larry had been extending me credit. I already owed several thousand dollars and my prospects for getting paid up and on track seemed remote. But where could I go? Maybe I could move to Los Angeles. I had wanted to do that for years. And some of my musical friends lived there, among them Guru Singh and Krishna Kaur. Both of them had participated on the first Khalsa String Band Album.

At the Monday sales meeting in Wheaton I didn't give any hint of what I was planning, but I had already made up my mind that I was going to move to L.A. It was just a matter of time. The sales meeting went about as I expected it to, except that George and David both talked a great deal about all the bad things Irv had done. They had spent the previous four days contacting every client, and it turned out there were a lot of unhappy people among our customers. According to David, who spoke with real disdain for Irv, many customers had given deposit checks for which they had never seen an ad. Several complained of late mailings and expired coupon dates. Others had never seen or approved a copy of their ads before the printing and mailing had been completed. Quite a few claimed that Irv had promised them a free mailing because of some earlier mistake.

David was livid, but George tried to calm him down. "Remember, son, 'the buyer's the liar.' These people could all just be trying to take advantage of us. Especially the Gypsies! You just can't trust 'em."

"Dad," retorted David with an ugly snarl, "I'll run the business, if you don't mind. Now let's go over the new ground rules." David proceeded to outline how he expected the business to run. He talked about fixed deadlines, standardized processes, and firm prices. Irv had cut all kinds of special deals, ignoring his own rate card. David outlined a plan for integrating the direct mail program with his door hangers, strongly favoring the door hangers. He outlined the new commission structure that cut me back to 15% unless I got more than 20 customers per mailing area, in which case I would get a 3% bonus. He also took back a number of "company accounts" that Irv had generously let me service and collect commissions on. Further, no commissions would be paid until an account was paid in full. Irv had always paid me upon my collecting the deposit. All in all, I hated almost everything David said.

By the time I left the meeting I had substantially shortened my timeline for moving to L.A. I didn't think I could last much more than a week. I didn't mind George so much, other than the fact that he was dirty and smelled bad, but seeing that George had no real say in the business caused me to give up any hope of being able to put up with David. Earlier in the year, I had taken a short trip to Los Angeles to attend a meeting of the Khalsa Council. Balwant Singh, one of my friends there ran a telemarketing business selling office supplies and had told me I could work with him if I ever moved to the West Coast. He had reiterated the offer when I showed up with the T-Bird. I hadn't taken it seriously at the time, but now I had reason to check it out.

When I got home from the meeting with George and David, I discussed the situation with Sat-Peter Kaur, then called Balwant Singh. He was enthusiastic about the idea of my coming to L.A. and said I could work in the Telex paper supply division. "We've only got one other person working that division," he said, "And he's pulling in a thousand bucks a week! I've just got to OK it with my partner, but I'm sure he'll be excited to have you on board." That cinched it for me. We were going to Los Angeles just as quickly as I could get it organized. It would be a whole new start for me. I was going to get rich selling office supplies! I'd pay off all my debts and have money to get a nice place for my family. Life was going to be good. Goodbye DC. Hello happiness!

A week later I was on the road, driving cross-country in my '55 Chevy with a back seat full of musical instruments and a trunk full of luggage and tools. DC, with 30 years of my personal history, was in my rearview mirror and I wasn't looking back. I was traveling alone in order to get things lined up for the rest of my family. I would get an apartment, get settled into my work, get a little ahead, then bring my wife and kids to join me. I was positively elated. I would be arriving in Los Angeles on May 1, 1980.

CHAPTER THIRTY-FOUR

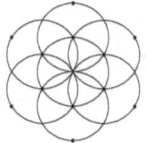

A New Life in Los Angeles

Moving to Los Angeles felt like liberation. It was to be a new life, free of the old entanglements of the 30 years I had spent in Washington DC. I sensed I would be able to re-invent myself, unfettered by the attitudes, expectations, and relationships that had shaped my life up to that point. The closer I got to L.A., the higher my spirits soared. Along the way I picked up my friend, Dayal Singh, in Espanola, New Mexico. By coincidence, he was also moving to Los Angeles and had been promised a job in the same Telex supply business where I would be working.

Dayal and I had much in common in our educational and cultural upbringing, and our connections were already quite deep. We had been collaborating for some time on an album of original songs. He would send lyrics from New Mexico and I would set them to music, recording them with simple guitar and vocal arrangements. By the time I left DC we had just completed an album's worth of songs. Strangely, our identical and simultaneous decisions to relocate to Los Angeles had been made independently and without knowledge of each other's plans, a fact that caused us much wonder and delight.

Like me, Dayal was in an arranged and unhappy marriage. He and his wife had lived for a short time in DC after their wedding, then spent several years trying to run an ashram in London. By the mid-1970s their relationship became so difficult that his wife returned to live in DC for several months. Eventually, with Yogi Bhajan's permission, they gave up on London, got back together and moved to Espanola with its large and vibrant Sikh community. But New Mexico was a difficult place to make a living and Dayal was unhappy there.

During the two days' drive from New Mexico to Los Angeles Dayal and I regaled each other with stories of our past hardships and shared our hopes for the future. But there was something I could not share with him: a guilty secret that festered in my heart. I did not know how to deal with this secret, and I just hoped that enough time had passed that even if it were revealed, it would not damage our friendship. But I was not willing to risk bringing it up. Not only did I fear hurting his feelings and ruining our friendship, which I highly valued, but I shrank from the exposure and shame I would feel if he were to discover that it was his wife who, five years earlier, had accompanied me on that fateful moonlit sail in Maine. As it turned out, honesty would have served me better. Dayal's relationship with his wife was so estranged that any damage would have been only to his pride, not his heart. My fear of telling him the truth and my lack of trust in his ability to handle it, eventually caused more damage than the facts themselves. As we neared L.A., however, this challenge to our friendship was not yet on the horizon.

When we pulled into Preuss Road in West Los Angeles we found a chance parking spot directly across the street from the Ashram. We knew that parking in this part of town was hard to find, so we saw this as a sign that things were going to go well for us here. But Dayal and I were both in for some unpleasant surprises.

Before I left Washington, Los Angeles had been described to me as a "con man's paradise" and the "Land of Sodom and Gomorrah." I did not give much weight to these characterizations, for my visits to L.A. had always been delightful. The Los Angeles of my experience included beautiful spring weather, tropical flowers, hummingbirds, and a friendly, vibrant social environment within the Sikh Community. As it turned out, there was truth to both of these opposing visions of the "City of Angels."

I was thrilled to be in Los Angeles. I would eventually come into my own there in music, business, and community life. But everywhere around me were subtle and not-so-subtle challenges to my integrity. Some of these I could identify and keep at arm's length. But many were so insidiously interwoven into the culture in which I found myself that I was only marginally aware of the moral and ethical erosion that was taking place in and around me. For example, every job and business opportunity was tainted with deceptive practices that seemed unavoidable if one was to make any money. "Sell the sizzle, not the steak," Irv had told me back in DC. As distasteful as such lingo seemed to me, I had hardened myself to the idea that a certain amount of "BS" was necessary in sales. But in Los Angeles I found that sales practices were guided by a different standard—that ethics and morality were simply incompatible with success. "Making the sale" was all-important, and any means was justified. My first job was like a boot camp in this twisted ideology.

I moved to Los Angeles on the promise of a high-paying job selling supplies for Telex machines. I was to be disillusioned on several counts. First, my friend Balwant Singh, who had promised me the job, had not checked with his senior business partner. The day after I arrived in L.A. he informed me that the position was no longer available. The reason, he explained, was that the salesman handling the "Telex Division" was moving such a large volume of merchandise that the company could not afford to finance the supplies, since all orders were sent out on a 30-day billing cycle. Balwant was apologetic, and as an alternative offered me a job in the "School Supplies Division." He also offered to find me a place to stay with one of his other employees until I could get my feet on the ground. Being completely out of money with no place to live and no prospects, I accepted my friend's offer with no questions asked. Dayal, who had come to Los Angeles with the same expectations, got the same treatment, and he also accepted Balwant's offer. Balwant told us the workday started at 5:00 AM when long distance rates were low and we could reach schools and businesses in the Eastern time zone where it was already 8:00 AM. He told us to come in first thing Monday.

Balwant's business was called "GRD" (for Guru Ram Das, the 4th of the Sikh Gurus). It was located in a 1960s vintage, two-story office building on Robertson Boulevard just across from the "House of Guru Ram Das," the main Ashram for the Los Angeles 3HO community. When Dayal and I showed up at 5:00 AM for our first day of work, we found the GRD offices already humming with activity. Balwant greeted us warmly and offered to show us around. There were about 12 people already hard at work in the complex of four or five sales offices. Even in the hallways their voices could be heard, melding into a cacophony of sound. Occasionally someone would ring a bell and call out a dollar figure. Balwant explained that this meant the person had just made a sale. If it was a big sale, people from adjoining offices would hoot and yell their approval and support. It was a high-energy environment and people seemed to be having fun.

Balwant suggested that Dayal and I should sit in and listen to one of the better salespeople. He introduced us to Ram Ravi Singh, then found us a couple of chairs and handed us packets with company policies, products, prices, "premiums," and phone scripts. "Just read through the scripts a few times, listen to Ram Ravi, and you'll get the idea," he said. "In thirty or forty minutes I'll set you up to get started yourselves."

Ram Ravi was working through a directory of elementary and

middle school principals in South Carolina. As soon as he got someone on the phone, he put on a Southern accent and a familiar, patronizing tone:

"Hello, is that you, Jim? Well, this is your old buddy Bob Thomas from Central Supply out in Los Angeles. How's everything going out there in God's country? Yeah? Well, a little rain's good for God's green earth, don't you think? Course we could use some of that out here in L.A., you know what I mean? Maybe you could send some of it our way (friendly laugh).

"Well, Jim, let me tell you why I'm callin' today. Have you got a pencil handy? I need you to take down an insurance number 'cause we're about to send you one of those brand new, credit card-sized pocket calculators, absolutely free, as a premium to go along with the second half of your order for school supplies. Are you ready? Good. That number is 8737539. Did you get that? OK, I'll repeat it for you: 8-7-3-7-5-3-9. Great, that's it! Now listen, Jim, it looks like we've got you down for 25 sets of liquid crayons, five dozen boxes of #2 pencils, seven reams of wide-lined, three holed paper in the handy 50 sheet packages, two dozen Donald Duck coloring books, and six of the Dunstan Company teacher's art handbooks for K through 6. Does that sound right?

"Great, Jim! Well, we've also just got in a new product that I thought you might want to try out, too, and it's on special. It's the Kaptain Kangaroo 'Counting is Easy' plastic calculator suitable for grades 1 through 3. Can I throw in a dozen of those for you? That's great Jim. Now let me just check and make sure we still have your correct shipping address. Is that 17 Rebel Road in Peaville, South Carolina, zip code 30112? Good, that's what I thought. Now Jim, I can't remember, do we need a purchase order number on this, or can we send it out on your verbal OK? Excellent. Well, the order will be arriving in about ten days. Oh, one more thing! Do you want me to send that credit card calculator along with the order, or would you prefer to have it sent directly to your home address? OK, that's a good idea. Let me get that down. OK, that's 34 Scrimshaw Terrace in Peaville; and it's the same zip code? OK, I'll get that right out to you, and you be sure to give me a call and tell me how you like it, OK? Well, alright! Well, Jim, it's been a pleasure talkin' with you. Now you be sure to look us up next time you're out in L.A., y'hear? All right then, well you have a fine day, now. Thanks for the order, Jim, and I'll be in touch soon."

Upon completing the call, Ram Ravi grabbed a little bell, started ringing it wildly, and called out "Seven Hundred Sixty-three Dollars!!" "Woohoo," came cheers of support from other salespeople. I did a little rough calculating and figured the products Ram Ravi had just sold to Jim had a retail value of maybe $75. Ram Ravi's commission alone would be nearly twice that. Dayal and I were simultaneously fascinated and appalled at this method of sales. We could see that the rapport Ram Ravi established with his client was smooth, fun, and upbeat, even if it was phony and condescending. I envisioned Jim as a pathetic, insecure, lonely, bored, and not-too-bright elementary school principal. No wonder he fell for Ram Ravi's pitch. Jim was taken in by the mystique of having a charismatic friend in Los Angeles and receiving a "premium" as a perk for placing the order. What did it matter that Ram Ravi used a phony name and gave Jim a meaningless insurance number? What did it matter that there was no first half of the order? What did it matter if Jim was paying ten times more for all this junk than he would pay at his local drug store? What did it matter if Jim was enticed into a little bit of dishonesty by accepting a personal gift as a reward for placing an absurdly overpriced order with us?

Actually, it did matter, and I knew it. But I was so desperate to start making money that I was willing to do even this. And so was Dayal. After all, many of our friends and peers were already doing it. Further, it looked easy, and even at the starting rate of a 15% commission it appeared like a good moneymaker. "It's just a numbers game," Ram Ravi explained to us. "You'll get four or five hang-ups for every sale you make. You just have to keep dialing for dollars." We listened to him deliver several more pitches over the next half hour, most of which ended in a "no" or a hang up. But he made two other sales during that time. At that rate we could see that Ram Ravi was going to clear about $100 per hour in commissions. That was pretty good money back in 1980.

Soon, Balwant set us up with our own phones and handed us a public-school directory, each for a different state. Dayal and I would be in separate rooms from here on out. We wished each other good luck and went to get started. I was put in a room with two other salespeople. I sat for a while listening to each of them deliver their pitches in turn. Neither of them was as skilled as Ram Ravi and most of their calls ended poorly. Once in a while one of them would make a sale and ring his bell. "Ninety dollars!" he would call out; or "Hundred twenty dollars!" Sales of over three hundred dollars appeared to be a rarity.

Everyone in the place was using "Bob Thomas" as his sales persona. When I asked Balwant about this he told me that it made things easier because school principals got called a lot, often by different salespeople. "We don't want to confuse them by making them think they're getting calls from a lot of different people from the same company." In effect, Balwant explained, we all benefited from whatever rapport a previous salesperson had established. "They usually don't know the difference, but I'll tell you a funny story," said Balwant. "One time we had a black guy working here, and he had a pretty thick accent. I was making calls to Alabama and reached a principle that this guy had just spoken to the previous week. The principle said, 'Well, Bob, I just got a call from a Bob Thomas last week, but he was a black man.' I was so flustered that I said, 'Oh, that was my cousin!'" Balwant laughed heartily at his joke.

I finally got up my nerve to try a call, working from a directory for a public school district in Oklahoma. After several calls to schools where the principle was unavailable, I eventually reached Fred, the principal of a middle school in a tiny Oklahoma town. I found myself imitating his accent. "Fred, this is Bob Thomas calling from out in beautiful Los Angeles. How are you doing today over there in God's country?" "Fine," replied Fred, "What can I do for you, Bob?" "Well Fred, I need to have you take down an insurance number. Have you got a pen or pencil handy?" "Sure, Bob. But what's this for?" "We're sending you, absolutely free, one of those new credit card size digital calculators to go along with the second half of your order." "But Bob," said Fred, "I never placed an order with you." I was not prepared for this turn of events. "You didn't?" I replied weakly. I had lost control of the conversation. "No, Bob, I didn't. Someone else named Bob Thomas called here two weeks ago, but I know it wasn't you. He had a different voice. And I told him we had already made all our purchases for the semester." "Oh, I'm sorry Fred," I said. "My mistake. When should I call you back?" "Well, Bob, I don't think you should call me. We do all our purchasing locally."

Fred was at least polite, which was much more than I deserved. The next call did not go so well. I reached Betty, an elementary school principal. She did not like my patronizing tone and told me so, "And besides," she said coldly, "I'm not the buyer. Hold on and I'll transfer you." Like an idiot I waited on hold for quite a long time. Eventually, a young black woman picked up the phone. "This is Frances, how can I help you?" she introduced herself. "Hi there, Frances. This is Bob Thomas out in Los Angeles. How are you doing out there in God's country?" Frances was not fooled for one second by my wooden delivery. She ended the call by saying that I was "full of shit" and hung up on me.

It took some time for me to get up the courage to make another call. Eventually I made a sale. Excited, I rang my bell and called out "Seventy-two dollars!" "Woohoo!" came the hoots from other salespeople. Balwant came in and congratulated me personally. "Now you've broken the ice," he said warmly. "You're going to do great. Just keep dialing away. It's a numbers game." I asked Balwant for advice on how to handle some of the more difficult situations I had already encountered on the phone. His suggestions seemed plausible. "Don't go feeling guilty," he continued. "You're providing a valuable service. A lot of these middle school principals don't have much going on in their lives. Talking with us is kind of a therapy for them. And remember, Yogiji says there's no karma on the telephone."

No Karma on the telephone! Now that was a stretcher if I ever heard one. I was willing to keep at this phone sales thing for a while, but there was no way I could accept the idea that lying and cheating on the telephone was free of karmic consequences. I *knew* that Yogiji was wrong about this. And yet I continued working at GRD. I tried writing my own scripts, more in keeping with my personal style and less dependent upon outright deception and manipulation. But I did not do well. Ram Ravi was pulling in close to $4,000 per month in commissions. My first paycheck, after two weeks of hard work, was $327.46. The problem wasn't solely with me, however. I soon discovered that I would get no benefit of repeat sales. As soon as I made a sale, Balwant or his senior partner Hari Singh would take the paperwork. Thus, they would always get the benefit of calling known "buyers," while I would be perpetually "cold calling."

I lasted only three weeks under this arrangement. But during those three weeks I learned more than I ever wanted to know about the unsavory side of Balwant's business. One morning I came in to find a number of salespeople working from stacks of used carbon paper. "What's this all about?" I asked. I took one of the carbons and held it up to the light where I could make out the impression that had been left on it. It was a sales slip from another business. There, clear as day, was the name and contact information for a middle school principal in Idaho, along with a list of all the items he had purchased the previous week, the price he was being charged, a purchase order number, and shipping address. "Where did this come from?" I asked. One of the other salespeople whispered that Mookta Singh had been "dumpster diving" that morning in an alley behind one of GRD's competitors in Culver City. I wondered aloud if there was no karma in dumpster diving. "Hey, don't worry about it," said my friend. "It's what we have to do to stay competitive."

While I was at GRD a steady stream of new sales recruits came through the door. Most of them were Sikhs or yoga students, many referred by Yogiji, himself. Making money in the real world was not easy for Americans wearing white robes and turbans. The anonymity of the telephone seemed like a perfect solution. I heard later that Yogiji regularly received hefty amounts of money from Balwant and Hari. I was never quite sure what the arrangement was, but if it was true, it looked an awful lot like a conflict of interest to me, especially the bit about no Karma on the telephone.

After the third week, I approached Balwant Singh with a proposal. Since the job he had originally promised me had not worked out, and since I was not making enough money selling school supplies, I proposed to start a direct mail advertising service. I knew every aspect of the business, I promised, and it could make a lot of money. I suggested that we do it as a partnership since I needed a space to work from and had no working capital or credit. GRD would provide phones and office space as well as a financial "umbrella" in exchange for 50% of the profits. I outlined the potential profits and showed him a pro forma based on optimistic projections. He liked the idea and suggested we run it by his partner. Hari reluctantly agreed, but said he would only do it if each of us was an equal partner, including Yogiji's son-in-law. This would leave me only 25% of the profits. Although this seemed quite unfair to me, it was not a great surprise, for I had seen enough of how these guys operated to expect they would screw me as much as they could. I was planning on making most of my money from commissions, anyway, so I accepted their terms. I even got them to agree to let Dayal and one other salesperson, Siri Seva Kaur, work with me. None of us had been making any money selling school supplies.

Within a few days I lined up everything I needed to make the business viable: a good printing company, a graphics person, a mailing house that could supply address labels and assemble the materials, a US Postage bulk mail permit, sales forms, a price sheet, and sample mailers that we could use as a sales tool. Working with the mailing house I identified twelve areas of 10,000 homes each in West Los Angeles and Santa Monica. I planned to mail to three areas every six weeks or so. This should give enough time for each of the three salespeople (myself included) to recruit at least 10 customers for each mailing, the minimum needed for the business to break even. I would be able to make about $1,200 per month just on commissions, so I didn't care that much if the business didn't make a lot of profit. In fact, I rather relished the thought of getting back at my greedy partners by operating the business close to the break-even point so we could make money while they didn't.

We identified potential advertisers by looking in the yellow pages, by driving up and down commercial streets, and by looking at ads in local magazines and newspapers. Usually, we would call the prospect first in order to establish some rapport. Cold calling in person in our Sikh regalia did not usually create a good first impression; but if we had already developed a relationship over the phone, it was harder for a customer to say no to us based solely on our appearance. Even so, we had prospective customers who would take one look at us when we showed up for an appointment and say, "I'm not interested." Those occurrences, fortunately, were rare.

Initially, the business did fairly well. By the end of July, we got mailers out to our first three areas: two neighborhoods in West L.A. and one in Santa Monica. All three were profitable to the company and provided ample commissions for the salespeople. Balwant and Hari were satisfied with our good start and my two friends and I were enthusiastic and greatly relieved to be out of the school supply business. I even had another salesperson ask to join me, so now there were four of us.

We were all happy to be in Los Angeles as a family again. Sat Hari enjoyed bathing in the kitchen sink.

More importantly, I was finally making a little money. By the middle of June I had enough from commissions to rent a small two-bedroom apartment that came available on Preuss Road, just one block from the ashram. I then made arrangements for Sat-Peter Kaur and my two daughters to join me from Washington. In spite of a few setbacks, things seemed to be going pretty well.

CHAPTER THIRTY-FIVE

Closer to the Master

THE FIRST EVENING that I spent in Los Angeles I attended a lecture by Yogiji at the ashram on Preuss Road. It was heartwarming, the way I was welcomed by the community of Sikhs and yoga students as I entered the ashram. Nearly everyone knew me because of my travels with the Khalsa String Band, my tabla playing and teaching, and my regular musical contributions at the Summer and Winter Solstice celebrations. My friend, Guru Singh, who had written and performed some of the songs on the Khalsa String Band album with me six years earlier, was a big cheese in L.A. He had many responsibilities around the ashram, including providing music and chanting at the start each of Yogiji's lectures. He was happy to see me and invited me to join him in leading the chanting. I was hoping for the invitation and had brought my guitar.

I joined Guru Singh at the front of the room, sitting on the floor next to Yogiji's "teaching seat" facing the class. Even as we tuned our guitars, the electricity in the room was palpable. We began with an upbeat and popular melody that we had played dozens of times at solstices. The whole room immediately joined in, soon singing with wild abandon and joy. Scores of people continued arriving as we played, and by the time Yogiji entered the room the place was jam-packed with devoted students, their enthusiastic chanting carrying throughout the neighborhood.

Yogiji looked at me warmly, then took his seat and joined in the chanting. Yogiji's teaching seat was like a huge throne. It had a back of polished brass, whose ornate curves and scrollwork were reminiscent of the arched doorways of the Golden Temple in India. The seat was covered in soft, white sheepskin, topped by the pelt of a tiger. When he sat upon it, Yogiji truly looked like a king, an effect that was obviously intended.

There was a sense of something special about tonight. For ten minutes we continued singing, the chanting growing more and more energized. I looked out upon the sea of joyful faces. Many people had their eyes closed and were swaying back and forth to the music. Others made occasional eye contact with me, expressing their delight and welcome. Occasionally, Guru Singh and I would exchange smiling acknowledgements. At the back of the room people continued arriving, soon overfilling the ashram and spilling out onto the sidewalk. Dozens of old acquaintances in the crowd smiled or winked their hello. I basked in a glow of happiness.

Finally, at a signal from Yogiji, Guru Singh and I started to bring down the volume. Soon we were singing softly, leading two hundred gentle voices at no more than a whisper. The effect was spellbinding. "Inhale!" shouted Yogiji. The room instantly fell silent and for a moment we were suspended in that peculiar trance-like state that can only be reached through group chanting. It is an appealing sensation—a feeling of oneness with all things and with each other. Tonight, it was particularly strong, and I took satisfaction in knowing that it was, in part, my energy added to the mix that had brought everyone to such a state. I thrived on this kind of validation, especially in the kind of acknowledging glances Yogiji had given me when he first entered the room. "Exhale," he said.

"Tonight," Yogiji continued in his thickly accented English, "We welcome Peter Singh, who has moved from Washington. Stand up, Peter." (He usually left off the "Sat" from my name.) I stood up stiffly and faced the group; I had been sitting cross-legged for over 30 minutes and my knees felt shaky. "Peter is a very sexy guy," said Yogiji, "So all you women be forewarned." Everyone laughed. I blushed, taken aback at such mixed praise. "Peter," said Yogiji, addressing me, but speaking to be heard by the whole room, "You will lead the sadhana every morning, and you will lead the chanting before every class." I bowed my head in his direction, flattered at such attention. "We will keep you out of trouble by keeping you busy," he concluded. "Now sit down." Obediently, I set down my guitar against the back wall and took my place on the floor at Yogiji's feet.

This was it, I thought to myself. For years I had dreamed of moving to L.A. to study directly under Yogiji. Now I had done it and made a big splash. Yogiji had just given me special acknowledgement. I was a little confused by his pointed and demeaning comments, but, overall, I felt good that he had singled me out and had taken the time to introduce me this way. Guru Singh smiled and winked, showing his support. Any attention at all from Yogiji, whether positive or negative, was something to be cherished.

After selling my '55 Chevy, I got around L.A. on a motorcycle.

CHAPTER THIRTY-SIX

A New Livelihood

MY BUSINESS ARRANGEMENT with Balwant and Hari was not destined to last for long. Although the mechanics of my new advertising business were working well—the printing and mailing were all accomplished competently and on time—the lack of a profit motive on my part worked against the business. Because of their greed, my "partners" left me with only 25% of the profit for a business in which they did no work at all. It was around this time that I first heard the old adage "If you don't pay a man what he thinks he's worth, he'll take what he thinks he's owed." I took this to heart and made "breaking even" my target for each mailing. After five or six months of this my partners tired of the arrangement and decided to kill G.R.D. Advertising. I quickly filed paperwork with the state, creating a new business, "G.R.D. Ad Express," which allowed me a semblance of continuity as I moved out of the G.R.D. offices and set up business in my garage.

It was a lowly start. My garage was one of those back alley four-car structures built in the 1930s and '40s to serve the needs of a burgeoning population of apartment dwellers in West L.A. My "office" was the first bay, which by a stroke of good fortune also had a door to the backyard of my fourplex apartment building. My desk was a couple of old planks set on sawhorses. I ran a telephone wire from the back window of my bedroom across the yard to the garage so I could use my home number as a business phone. It was not a place that I brought clients, but it was adequate, and compared to the toxic environment at G.R.D. it was wonderful. The only real discomfort was on cold winter days. Although Los Angeles is famed for its mild weather, it commonly gets down into the 40s and 50s in the winter. My unheated and leaky garage had no insulation and provided no comfort in that kind of weather.

My 1955 Chevy's transmission had given out by this time and I gave the car away to a friend who said he would fix it and use it for himself. Instead, he promptly sold it for $50 to a junkyard. The lack of a car, however, was the reason I had space in the garage for my office, so its absence was a blessing. For transportation I bought an old Honda 400 cc motorcycle. I cut quite a figure riding around Beverly Hills in my turban and flowing white robes. To capitalize on the image, I designed a business card based on a photograph of me on the bike, shot from ground level looking up. On the huge expanse of blue sky behind me I superimposed the words "Ad Express" in letters resembling skywriting.

CHAPTER THIRTY-SEVEN

Disturbing News

AROUND THIS TIME, I made an unexpected trip to DC to "rescue" Ganga and help her move to Los Angeles. Shortly after I moved to L.A. in May 1980, things completely unraveled in DC. Larry had suddenly announced that he was divorcing Ganga and leaving Sikh Dharma. I was totally taken aback by this news. What could possibly have happened to cause Larry, once the most esteemed and respected of Yogiji's disciples, to turn his back so suddenly and walk away from it all? There was much in this situation I would never know or understand. But Ganga was beside herself. Her reputation had already been destroyed by events in India. She was unloved and abandoned by her husband, without money or means of support, and was no longer useful or even welcome in the Sikh community in DC. I reassured her that I would fly out and help drive her car and meager possessions across the country.

The trip took most of a week, and being short of funds we stayed in a shared motel room on nights when there was no Ashram nearby. Our devoted friendship was still intact, and despite the opportunities provided by the isolation and anonymity of our cross-country journey, our relationship never got physical.

On the trip, I learned more disturbing news. The Golden Temple restaurant was closing, ostensibly because Larry had been embezzling funds for years. I couldn't help wondering if it had anything to do with the "Rent and Wage" system Larry had imposed on the community four years earlier. Upon Larry's departure, Kamal, the second-in-charge who had replaced me during the Khalsa String Band tour, took over as head of the Ashram and its businesses. He later reported to me that the Golden Temple was more than $100,000 in debt to its suppliers. There was no choice, according to him, but to close its doors.

Further, the entire Ashram community was moving out of downtown DC to a newly built suburban cul-de-sac near Dulles Airport in Virginia. I thought that this was one of the worst moves possible. We could have bought the building at 17th and Q for a fraction of its future value (it was offered to me in 1971 for $25,000). The neighborhood was rapidly improving, and it was obvious that the building would appreciate dramatically in coming years. By 2015 it had appreciated to well over $2,000,000. The location was fantastic, within walking distance of stores that could provide nearly every household necessity, and just three blocks from the DC Metro stop at Dupont Circle. Further, as an area for raising children, the Dupont Circle neighborhood could hardly be better, with dozens of national museums that charged no admission, and other cultural and natural treasures like the Washington National Cathedral and Rock Creek Park within a mile or two. The cul de sac, on the other hand, nearly an hour outside of Washington, was miles away from the centralized shopping malls of suburban Virginia, and was nearly devoid of anything that would be culturally, artistically, or spiritually enriching to growing children.

The planning for moving out of DC had started while I was still living there. It began with the sale of a spacious house the Ashram had purchased in Cleveland Park during the heady days when the Golden Temple was thriving beyond our expectations. The house, with seven bedrooms and nearly as many bathrooms, was an ideal setting for our communal lifestyle, especially as more children were

CHAPTER THIRTY-SEVEN: Disturbing News

born into the community. Sat-Peter Kaur and I lived there along with five other couples, and my second daughter was born there. But the Rent and Wage system had made the place unaffordable and many of the couples with children felt that the suburbs would be a better environment for raising children.

When the decision to sell the house was being discussed, I offered to go to work for the same real estate company that had leased us the Golden Temple so I could take the listing. Larry and Kamal agreed to this arrangement and for several weeks I showed the house, but no buyers came forward. After three months, Kamal, who had been taking on more responsibilities and authority, decided to terminate the contract and list the property with another agency, putting me out of work again. When the house finally did sell shortly after my move to L.A., the buyer turned out to be the first couple to whom I had shown it. I was outraged at the loss of what would have been a $9,000 commission—enough money to have paid all my debts and put me back on my feet financially. But I was not in a position to do anything about it, and was unsure if I even had any rights under the circumstances. So, I did nothing. Kamal did try to make it right by canceling my considerable debt to the Ashram from two years of unpaid rent.

While in DC to help Ganga move, I also had a chance to discuss with Kamal the unfinished business of our '55 Thunderbird. Since moving to L.A. I had been trying halfheartedly to sell it and had come close a couple of times, but the fiberglass fender killed every prospective deal. Kamal, however, was a wheeler-dealer on a scale that I had not realized. He told me he had already sold the car at a loss to three different people, laughing that he was going to have to pay two of them back if one of them ever wanted to take delivery. There was not enough money, however, to pay back my $4,000 investment and I was not willing to press the point. For me, it was a total loss. I was just glad not to be involved in any further financial dealings with my former friend. I did wonder what kind of person would pay thousands of dollars for a car, but not take delivery. A few years later I got a little hint at the answer when Kamal and one of his "business associates" were arrested for their involvement in what was, at the time, the largest shipment of marijuana ever intercepted by the Feds.

Kamal was not alone in getting into serious legal trouble during the 1980s. The head of the Ashram in Fairbanks got arrested for smuggling new cars into Alaska and selling them as "used" in order to avoid taxes. Another enterprising Sikh in northern California was busted for a scam he was running by which he relieved old people of their life savings. Apparently, he would tell them that they had won millions of dollars in a Canadian lottery and needed only to "prepay the taxes" on the winnings in order to collect. One of my former friends in New Mexico was arrested for a similar scam. Years later, I learned that my former partners at G.R.D. had been arrested when the FBI raided their business. Were these isolated incidents, or did they reflect Yogiji's "end justifies the means" and "no karma on the telephone" sense of ethics?

CHAPTER THIRTY-EIGHT

Trying to Make it in Music

DECEMBER 8, 1980, ONE OF THE WORST DAYS OF MY LIFE, was marked by the news of John Lennon's murder. Lennon had been a musical hero and inspiration for me since the moment I heard the Beatles' first American hit, "Please Please Me," in early 1964. As he became more politically active, and I became more politically aware, Lennon steadily rose in my esteem. After the breakup of the Beatles in 1970 he went through some dark times musically, and for nearly a decade I had paid little attention to him. But in October of 1980 he and Yoko Ono released their *Double Fantasy* album, which I loved. Actually, I didn't find Yoko's tracks very listenable, but Lennon's were fantastic. The first track, "Just Like Starting Over," seemed prophetic, and indeed I was encouraged to learn that he was thinking about putting a band together and going back on tour. But just a few weeks later, an insane Mark Chapman put an unhappy end to that dream.

For me, Lennon's death was on a par with the murders of the Kennedys and Martin Luther King, Jr. As much as I had been influenced in my political thinking by the lives and speeches of the latter, my musical and emotional life had been forever altered by John Lennon's voice and soul-moving songwriting. I was devastated, as were all my musical friends within the Sikh community. However, there was an upside to the enormous sense of loss. My friend, Guru Singh, and I started playing music together in a serious way, vowing to do our best to fill the void.

Guru Singh had a long history in the west coast Folk Music scene prior to becoming a Sikh. Performing as Gerry Pond, he often shared the stage with The Grateful Dead in the mid-1960s. They opened for *him* at one point, early in their careers. He was one of the first Americans to study with Yogi Bhajan and one of the first to wear a turban. He and I had been friends from the moment we first met and played music together, and some of our collaborations had already made it onto vinyl with The Khalsa String Band's *Spiritual Nation* LP. The prospect of being able to perform together more often was one of the compelling reasons for my wanting to move to L.A., and indeed, we often joined forces for the chanting before Yogiji's classes or to perform our American devotional songs in Gurdwara.

But John Lennon's death catapulted us into a new musical dimension. We were determined to become a musical act together, and to bring our music into mainstream culture. Guru Singh still had some connections from his days as a folk singer in San Francisco, and as our repertoire grew with our own original songs, he pulled out all the stops in an effort to launch our career. Armed with some home-recorded demos he approached Joe Gannon, a music industry friend who had worked with Shep Gordon putting together Alice Cooper's stage act and tours. Joe was thrilled with our music and spent his own money taking us into a studio to make a proper demo recording. He then hired a set designer to work up some drawings of our future stage show.

Joe was confident that his many connections in the music industry were going to pay off, and we truly believed we were about to be hurled into the stratosphere of popular success. We started working with a drummer and bass player and booked a few gigs at McCabes in Santa Monica, and the Whiskey a Go Go in Hollywood, to get our musical act honed to a professional performance level. But Joe's efforts failed to pay off. He told us he had called in every favor from every person he knew in the industry and had gotten the same reaction each time. Everyone who heard our demo tape loved the music, but after taking one look at our publicity photo with our long white robes and turbans they all said "No way!"

Guru Singh and I, though disappointed, continued to play and record together for a couple more years, but the energy flagged. We recorded three albums of music that we published on tape cassettes under the name "The Brothers," but even within the American Sikh community and extended family of yoga students the tapes did not sell well. Our songs were mainly secular in nature and were not a good match for meditation or yoga classes. We tried to collaborate on a spiritual music project that Yogi Bhajan had asked me to undertake, writing and recording western versions of the *24 Ashtapadis* (poems) that make up the *Sukhmani* (Hymn of Peace)—one of the most important spiritual texts of the Sikh Faith.

I recruited many of my musician friends, asking each to take on the task of writing compositions for one or two of the twenty-four Ashtapadis. Guru Singh tried to help me but we quickly got into a terrible argument about how to produce a song written by an attractive young Sikh woman whom Guru Singh had been mentoring. Up until that point I had deferred to most of Guru Singh's musical inclinations. He was a prolific writer and had a strong persona on stage. Performing as "The Brothers" I had been perfectly happy to play an accompanist's role, providing lead guitar lines and vocal harmonies. But my ego had latched on to the assignment that Yogi Bhajan had given me, and I was not about to defer to Guru Singh or anyone else on questions of production. The unfortunate result was the sudden termination of our musical partnership. Never again, after that ugly incident, did we ever perform together.

The Golden Temple restaurant in Los Angeles was inspired by our success with the first Golden Temple in DC. Located across from the famous Los Angeles Farmers Market, it was hugely popular. While I maintained my office in the building's former garage I crossed paths with many of the place's star-studded clientele.

CHAPTER THIRTY-NINE

My Business Grows

WHEN I SET UP BUSINESS on my own after leaving GRD, I decided to gradually move out of direct mail and get into what I rather pompously called "full-service advertising." I picked up a few clients who needed display ads for publication in the Los Angeles Times. I produced a radio spot for a local pharmacy, designed and produced a children's activity book, and wrote music for an accompanying record album—and even recorded all the songs for it. I also did other small jobs in addition to the mailers I continued to assemble in the more profitable neighborhoods. Because I had no office overhead, I managed pretty well—well enough that when a small office space became available at the Golden Temple Restaurant at 3rd and Fairfax, I jumped at it. The original Golden Temple in DC that I had started in 1972 with Larry and Ganga had inspired many imitators by our 3HO colleagues in cities all over the world.

My new office was also in an old garage, but this one had been renovated and turned into a viable space with proper doors and windows. In fact, it had large picture windows facing the outside dining patio on one side and overlooking the patio's back entrance on the other. As I sat at my desk, therefore, I got a good look at everyone who came and went the back way. This included many of the Golden Temple's star-studded clientele like Annie Lennox and Michael Jackson. Michael and his bodyguard showed up for lunch almost every day and we were soon waving hello to each other each time he walked past. Emboldened, one day I stopped by his table and apologetically handed him a tape cassette with a few songs I had recorded with Guru Singh. The next day, much to my delight, Michael smiled and sang a few bars of one of the songs as he walked past my window. I was excited, but nothing more came of it.

One day a well-dressed and very self-assured man, around my age, tapped on my office window on his way out after lunch. I motioned for him to meet me at the front door of my office, opening onto the alley. Before even introducing himself, he asked, "Hey, do you do advertising work?" "Yes," I answered. "Peter Khalsa," I said, extending my hand. I always left out the "Sat" from my name in my business dealings. Some of my fellow Sikhs criticized me for this, but I pointed out that Yogiji himself usually just called me "Peter." That would shut them up. "We're a small shop," I continued, "but we offer a full range of services." "Nice to meet you, Peter. My name is Bob Bane." He paused to let the name sink in, as if I should recognize him, but I didn't. "Can you do catalogues and display ads?" he continued. "Absolutely," I responded, full of confidence. I had never done a catalogue before, but I figured it couldn't be too difficult. I could farm out to subcontractors anything I wasn't capable of doing myself. "Good!" said Bob. "I've got a friend who needs some help with a catalogue and some display ads. Would you be able to come up to his place later this afternoon?"

"Well, I'm on deadline for one of my clients in Beverly Hills," I fibbed, "But I can probably rearrange things a little. What time would you like to get together?" "Let me check with him," said Bob. "Why don't you come out? I have his number in my car." I followed Bob out to the alley where he stepped into a beautiful blue Rolls Royce Silver Ghost, found the number and proceeded to call his friend from a phone in his car. This was the first mobile phone I had ever seen, other than the one Jack Lemmon used in the 1973 movie

Save the Tiger. Bob was clearly a high roller—or at least putting on a pretty good show. Among his other accoutrements were black leather pants, patent leather shoes, and stylish Ray Ban sunglasses.

A moment later Bob stood up and asked over the top of the car if 3:00 PM was OK. "Sure," I said. Bob gave me a thumbs-up, finished his call and came back with me into my office. "Let me explain a little about my friend," he started. "His name is Pierre Marcey, and he's a major publisher of works by Salvador Dali. He uses a unique process, creating signed limited editions of hand-engraved, hand-colored etchings of Dali's greatest works. He needs a catalogue that not only displays the images, but also explains and illustrates the fine-art etching process. There will be a lot of photographs, and the look needs to be elegant and classy, but the most important thing will be the writing. Are you a good writer?" "That's my strongest suit," I told him, this time without fibbing. "Excellent. I think you're going to like Pierre. He's quite a character." Bob gave me an address just off Mulholland Drive, high in Beverly Hills, and told me he'd meet me there at 3:00. "And one more thing," he added. "Don't lowball Pierre. He wants a top-notch job. He's used to getting only the best and can afford to pay for it. If your price is too low, it will make him suspicious." "Thanks for the tip," I smiled. Bob and I shook hands warmly and he drove off in his Rolls.

At 3:00 PM sharp, I arrived at Pierre Marcey's mansion in Beverly Hills. I parked my motorcycle in the circular drive just behind Bob's Rolls Royce. The drive was graced with one other Rolls and two Jaguars. I felt out of place in my Sikh attire and second-hand motorcycle, but I boldly stepped forward and rang the bell. A beautiful dark-haired French woman opened the door and smiled. "Oh! You must be Peter! Bob has been telling us all about you. Won't you please come in? My name is Monique, and this is my husband, Jean-François." "You can call me J.F.," said Monique's husband, enthusiastically shaking my hand as I stepped through the door. "Mr. Marcey will be joining us in a few minutes, so why don't Monique and I show you around first?"

I was quite overwhelmed at being treated so well. Monique and J.F. were genuinely friendly and put on no airs. Maybe it was because they were European and a lot more cosmopolitan than I was used to, I thought. As he led me downstairs into the "work area" J.F. explained that he and Monique were Pierre's assistants. "I handle all the logistics and all the finances," he said, "So if there is ever any misunderstanding, which can happen with Pierre sometimes, just come to me. Now this is the etching studio." We entered a well-lit room at the back of the house. "And this is Pierre Spalaikovitch, our master engraver." Pierre was buried in his work with a loop, inspecting the lines on a large engraved copper plate. On hearing his name, he looked up and upon seeing me his dark features brightened. "*Ah, bonjour*" he said enthusiastically. "So, you are the advertising man?" "*Oui, monsieur*," I replied in somewhat fractured tones. "*Je suis enchante a faire votre connaisance.*"

"Oh my God!" said Monique, You speak French!" "Oui," I answered with a smile, "Very badly." "I see we will all be good friends," said J.F. Pierre observed me closely for a moment then, turning to Monique, pronounced, "*Oui, c'est un bon homme.*" "*Merci,* Pierre," I said.

J.F., Monique, and I had finished our tour of the working portion of the house and were waiting in a small study for some time before Pierre Marcey finally appeared. He was exquisitely, but casually dressed, arm in arm with a beautiful dark-haired woman whom he introduced dismissively as his cook (the following week there was another "cook" in attendance). Pierre looked me over the way a fox might regard a small chicken. "Halo," he said without shaking my hand. "You can make my catalogue?" he asked. "Of course,"

I replied, then added playfully "May I introduce myself? *Je m'appelle* Peter Khalsa." "*Oui*," he said absently, "Bob has told me." Then, turning to Monique he commanded "Bring me the photographs." Clearly, this was a man used to getting his way. Monique stepped out and quickly returned with a cardboard box full of high quality 4x5 color transparencies of Salvador Dali in a variety of intriguing poses. Some showed him in his studio, others in front of Parisian landmarks, others before some of his most famous paintings. I was astounded by this collection and assumed that Pierre had gotten them directly from Dali. I was wrong, of course, as I was about so many things.

My days working for Pierre Marcey's business were heady, creative, and challenging. I learned a great deal from Pierre Spalaikovitch about the etching and engraving process, incorporating it into the catalogue along with the photos of Dali and illustrations of Dali's images as reproduced by Pierre Spalaikovitch. I was curious about Dali's signature, which usually appeared on the lower right-hand corner of the etched prints, but was not always apparent when the prints first came off the press. But I did not ask questions.

Every two or three days I would ride my motorcycle up into the hills to Pierre's mansion with a new chapter or two for the catalogue, then wait around for Pierre to look it over. He was generally pleased with my work, but had an unsettling habit of asking everyone's opinion, giving the greatest weight to the last person asked. One day I arrived to find that everything I had brought him earlier had been thrown out. J.F. explained to me that Pierre had sought the opinion of the UPS deliveryman that morning. The poor guy's lack of interest and understanding had so enraged Pierre that he had torn my manuscript to pieces and thrown it in the trashcan. This was before the days of computers, and I had made no copy. I would have to start again from scratch. J.F. assured me that I would be paid anyway—a promise he made good on.

In fact, I was being very well paid and felt rather flush in my new prosperity. Bob, favorably impressed with the work that I was doing for Pierre, and equally impressed that I was able to work for someone so eccentric and demanding, gave me a lot of his own advertising work and referred me to other art dealers and publishers. I was commissioned to develop full-page ads for various art magazines, and to design catalogues, catalogue sheets, brochures, and logos. Before long, I was billing my clients over $20,000 per month. I farmed out much of the work, but hired a secretary and full-time graphic designer. I then moved into a larger office space on the second floor of the same building that housed GRD. I was riding high, and felt it was a kind of sweet revenge against my former "partners" to have office space on top of their heads. But, in fact, I had set myself up for a very big fall. After the big buildup leading to the New York Art Expo for which all my clients had me working overtime, business suddenly fell off to almost nothing and I was left with a $10,000 per month overhead that I couldn't pay.

CHAPTER FORTY

Shady Characters

AMONG THE MANY ART DEALERS and other shady characters whom I met while working for Pierre Marcey, the most charismatic and dangerous was T.R. Rogers. T.R. was a wiry and athletic man in his mid-forties with a penchant for exotic cars, beautiful women, and expensive and unusual clothes. Lamborghinis and Rolls Royces were his cars of choice, and he had a string of them during the time I knew him. I don't think I ever saw him in the same outfit twice, and nothing he wore—even his shoes and belts—ever cost less than several hundred dollars.

At first, I was most impressed by how friendly he was to me. He went out of his way to talk with me and showed real interest in my music and my life with the Sikh community. He started coming to my yoga classes and bringing friends, and he often invited me out to lunch at expensive restaurants. Our conversations ranged from the art business to the esoteric and philosophical, and I quickly began considering him a friend. When T.R. took trips out of town, he would leave me with his car, which really impressed Yogi Bhajan, and when my advertising business got in trouble, he stepped in and helped me transition into a new business, selling art.

But friendship with T.R. was a double-edged sword, and the short-term benefits of the art business only led me deeper into a financial and ethical hole from which I was fortunate, indeed, to escape.

The dubious provenance of so much of Dali's catalogue was a perfect medium for a man like T.R., who excelled at making up wonderful stories to add charisma and perceived value to reproductions that, if not worthless, were worth far less than the thousands of dollars for which he would sell them. I didn't know any of this when I first met him. All I knew was that he was generous to me, accepting—even admiring—of my Sikh lifestyle, and that he seemed genuinely interested in helping my business flourish. It was not until later, when my own financial well-being was so closely tied to his, and so threatened by T.R.'s business dealings, that the truth was more fully revealed to me.

One of the first signs that things were not entirely on the level with T.R. came from his girlfriend, Kathy, with whom he began attending my yoga classes. She called me on the phone one day, hysterical, demanding if I knew what T.R. was up to. I had no idea what she was talking about. "Listen to this," she said. "I'm reading from a classified ad in the Los Angeles Times. 'Driver wanted for Beverly Hills art dealer. Duties include driving Rolls Royce and keeping the boss happy.' It's got T.R.'s phone number. That f-ing bastard is two-timing me!" she fairly screamed at me. I was taken aback by her language and tone of voice. It was far coarser than anything I had experienced in my sheltered life. I was also disturbed at the possibility that T.R. could be cheating on her so brazenly and that he would use such a lame artifice for procuring sex. It didn't occur to me that T.R. was capable of grand deceptions, and that no one was immune—even me—from becoming one of his victims.

In retrospect, I realize that T.R. was using me in many ways to carry out both his personal and business agendas, but I was far too naïve to understand his devious manipulations. He called later and asked me to speak to Kathy on his behalf. He told me that the ad was not for him, but for one of the salespeople in his office for whom he

CHAPTER FORTY: Shady Characters

was doing a favor. I believed him. T.R. knew that Kathy liked and trusted me and that she held me in almost mystical esteem as her yoga teacher. I spoke to her of higher purpose, and shared my own convictions about T.R., that he was a generous and caring person with a heart of gold. I repeated what he had told me about the ad being a favor for one of his salespeople. She was convinced, and the happy outcome was that they both showed up at my yoga class the next evening, smiling and affectionate.

A few days later when I met T.R. for lunch at the Brown Derby, he was accompanied by one of the respondents to the classified ad. Sheila was young, blonde, insecure, somewhat overweight, and obviously very impressed with T.R.. She was also quite impressed with me. T.R. had given me a big buildup and she acted as if she were in the presence of Mick Jagger, or perhaps the Dalai Lama. During lunch, T.R. announced that he was taking Sheila out to the San Fernando Valley that afternoon to purchase a thoroughbred horse. "Do you ride?" I asked Sheila. "I used to take lessons when I was in high school," Sheila responded sheepishly. "She's a great rider!" T.R. enthused, as if he knew a great deal about riding and had already seen his new friend on horseback. I did not ask T.R. about Kathy. A day or two later, when I next spoke with T.R., I asked him if had bought the horse. For a moment he seemed confused, but then he laughed and said, "No, but I got quite a ride out of it!" I never saw Sheila again, but Kathy and T.R. showed up together that night for yoga class. I felt it best not to ask further about Sheila. I was uncomfortable knowing that I was now party to T.R.'s deception.

A few months later, T.R. offered me an attractive but complex business proposition. Up to that point, my business, which I called Masterworks Gallery, had done fairly well, thanks to a considerable amount of help and mentoring from T.R. His latest proposition was bigger than anything he had previously attempted. He was about to purchase an entire edition—all 1000 prints—of a "limited edition" lithograph by Salvador Dali. He said he wanted to use these prints to put me "on the map" as an art dealer. He offered to supplement my sales force with four of the "best men in the business" who would work out of my office on a commission-only basis. All I had to do was place some advertising in a few magazines to generate leads, and the high-powered salesmen would do the rest. But there was more: T.R. had a partner in the acquisition of the 1000 prints—one of his best customers—and he wanted me to join them for a business luncheon to help close the deal. "If the deal goes through," said T.R., "I'll give you $50,000." That was a lot of money in 1985!

I met T.R. and his customer, Jim, for lunch in Beverly Hills the next day. I had met Jim once before at T.R.'s office. He was middle-aged, short, and chubby, with thick-lensed glasses and a balding head. Jim had inherited his father's manufacturing business and had a lot of discretionary cash. He was very impressed with T.R.'s high-rolling lifestyle, especially T.R.'s flashy wardrobe and his "charm with the women." Like the hapless Sheila, Jim was also impressed by me, and he was unctuous in his efforts to be friendly. As we enjoyed an expensive lunch together, T.R. explained the business proposition to Jim.

"This edition was part of Dali's 'Professions' collection," T.R. began. "Dali called it 'The Dresser,' and he gave the entire edition to one of his secretaries several years ago. The secretary, whose name I have to keep confidential because he is a world-renowned figure in the art world, has kept all 1000 lithographs locked in a vault in Spain waiting until after Dali's death to sell them. Everyone knows that when a major artist dies, the value of his works skyrockets overnight! But the secretary has run into some financial difficulties and is willing to sell me the entire edition—all but 50 Artists Proofs—for $500,000. That's just $500 apiece!" I could see Jim's eyes light up at this. T.R. had already sold Jim dozens of Dali prints for $2,000 - $5,000 each. $500 sounded like a steal.

"But here's the thing," T.R. continued. "I have only $200,000 of my own money available at the moment and I've got a competitor in Europe. If I don't move on this deal today, I'm going to lose it. I need a partner, and that's where you come in, Jim. If you can put up the other $300,000 we can close this deal. You know I can sell these things for $1,500 each all day long. And with Sat-Peter and his team selling them, too, we can make a lot of money together. In fact, Sat-Peter has already started putting together the advertising campaign, right Brother?" T.R. turned to me. Jim and I were both seeing dollar signs at this point. "Well," I said, pulling out a tear sheet of a full color ad, "I've had my people design this ad for Venture Magazine, the Robb Report, Penthouse, and several others. They're all ready to run in five or six weeks, but we're near the deadline right now and I have to place the orders this week." I was still innocent of what T.R. was up to, and I was speaking with convincing sincerity.

Jim was impressed, but careful. "How long do you think it will take to sell 1,000 prints?" he asked. "Well," said T.R. "I don't want to give you false hope that we're going to do it overnight, but I'd say conservatively it will take 18 to 24 months. You'll need to consider the 25% commission I have to pay my salespeople. How about you, Sat-Peter?" T.R again turned to me. "Well," I calculated, "I'm paying my people 20% and with my overhead I don't think I could do this for less than a 30% commission without losing money."

Jim took out a pencil and did some calculations on his napkin. "Let's see, $1,500 less 30% is $1,050, less the $500 cost leaves $550 profit. Not bad...OK, I'll do it!" he exclaimed. To my amazement he pulled a cashier's check out of his coat pocket and handed it to T.R., who glanced at it to confirm the amount (it was, indeed $300,000), and slipped it casually into his shirt pocket. He then ceremoniously reached over the table and shook Jim's hand. "Welcome to the art business, Partner!" Turning to me, beaming, he shook my hand and said, "Welcome to the big time, Brother."

That afternoon I placed orders for more than $12,000 of advertising, signed a lease for an empty office adjacent to mine, called the phone company to install four new lines, and bought desks, office chairs, and secretarial supplies for the four new salesmen that T.R. was sending over to work for me. I was not concerned about the expense. I was about to get $50,000!

But the check didn't come—not the next day, and not the day after that. On Friday I called T.R. "What's going on?" I asked, obviously upset. "The prints have just arrived," T.R. enthused. "Wait 'til you see them. They're amazing! This has got to be one of Dali's greatest images. We're going to make a KILLING! So relax, I'm sending over payment this afternoon." I hung up the phone, relieved and glowing with excitement and anticipation. Two hours later one of T.R.'s employees arrived with a large package. I opened it up and found 100 prints of Salvador Dali's "The Dresser." I was totally surprised and perplexed. I called T.R.. "Hey, T.R., What's this?" I demanded. "That's your payment for helping me close the deal with Jim," he said. "Congratulations!"

"But, T.R.," I complained, now greatly agitated, "I've committed over $12,000 in CASH that I have to pay for the advertising!" "Don't worry," he soothed, "You'll make a ton more than that as soon as you start selling the prints," he said. Then his tone changed. "Hey, I didn't have to include you in this deal. I've set you up with the best salespeople in the business. I've GIVEN you $150,000 worth of prints. I've let you meet and sell art to some of my best customers. And I've taught you everything you know about the business," he said with some indignation. "I don't understand where you get off being upset."

I was quiet for a moment while I digested all this. I had to admit that everything he said was true, yet there was a very big difference between $50,000 in cash and 100 limited edition prints by Salvador Dali. "Well, OK," I said with a pathetic note of resignation. "It's true you've brought me into this deal when you didn't have to, and I'm grateful for that. It's just that I was expecting money, not prints."

"It's all going to work out," T.R. reassured me. "In fact, I'm going to send over a list of some of my best customers to help get you started." Then he laughed and said, "Well, Sat-Peter, we've just had our first 'lovers' spat,' haven't we! But we've gotten through it, and our friendship will be stronger for it."

"I guess so," I answered weakly. I didn't doubt that I could turn my inventory of 100 prints into cash over time, but it was a nasty revelation, and I couldn't help harboring the thought that T.R. had tricked me and made a lot of money with my help and at my expense. But I still hadn't imagined the extent of the deception and didn't figure it out until years later. It got a lot worse.

The following week I received a list of about 400 of T.R.'s customers and prospects. Over the next several weeks, my new sales team went through the leads and gave me encouragement that several looked like they would close in the near future. Then the advertising leads started pouring in. We received dozens of "business reply" postcards every day for weeks: hundreds of prospects who were interested in learning more about how they could make money and put their kids through college by investing in limited edition prints of "The Fashion Designer" by Salvador Dali. I turned all the leads over to my new sales team.

But I didn't provide much oversight. In fact, I wasn't even in the office much. After nearly 16 years in an unhappy marriage, I had fallen head over heels in love with a woman I met at one of Yogi Bhajan's lectures. I was infatuated and ecstatic and cared about nothing else except spending time with the woman whom I loved with all my heart and soul. Each morning at 4:00 AM I would furtively leave my apartment on Preuss Road and ride my motorcycle to Linda's house in Venice. At 7:00 AM I would ride back home, pretending that I had been at sadhana, which I had often led. After breakfast I would leave for "work," but in reality I would head back to Venice. I kept this deception going for a couple of months. My wife never noticed. I found out later that she had been having her own affair with someone she had met at the school in India.

Once every week or so I checked in with the sales team that T.R. had entrusted to me. But they took to complaining about the quality of the leads, and they made no sales. I didn't know how they could survive for weeks on end with no income, but they persevered and I was grateful for their loyalty. After two months, however, when the bills for all the advertising were becoming past due, I started paying attention to my business again. The sales team had already gone through several thousand leads without generating a single sale, and the two "top" salesmen had developed an insolent attitude towards me that I did not understand. I felt that they were holding me responsible for the poor quality of the leads. I had been so obsessed with my new love life that I was blind to the obvious—that they were stealing from under my nose. When this thought first dawned on me, I imagined they were probably taking the best leads home with them, but I later realized they had been working for T.R. all along. T.R., after all, could afford to pay them a lot more handsomely than I could, since he didn't have to bear any of the overhead costs. I was taking care of all that!

If I had been paying attention, and if I had not been such a trusting fool, I would have realized the extent of T.R.'s scam. It started with the fact that the prints did not cost him $500 each. They cost only $100. I accidentally happened upon the invoice for them one

CHAPTER FORTY: Shady Characters

day during a visit to T.R.'s office. It was lying on his desk in plain view. Jim's $300,000 investment, therefore, left T.R. with $200,000 in cash profit up front, plus 400 prints for free. He could afford to give me 100 of them as an enticement to set me up, for he would continue making money hand over fist by having my salespeople sell his 300 remaining prints.

Still innocent of how I was being used, I welcomed T.R.'s continuing friendship and the sympathy he expressed for my difficulties. In the midst of my financial meltdown, when I had to let all the salespeople go, walk out on my lease, and take a tiny office in a Venice storage locker for less than one quarter of what I had been paying in Beverly Hills, T.R. went out of town on a three-week vacation and left me his Rolls Royce to "take care of." He was fond of saying "It's just a car."

Although I was on the verge of bankruptcy, I was now driving a Rolls Royce. Yogi Bhajan was impressed. He singled me out during his lectures, telling the other students how I was a model of success. Yogiji had always said he could read our auras and see our destiny, and I could not help noticing that he was completely wrong about my situation. But I overlooked it at the time. I didn't realize that I was swimming in a sea of con men. They were surrounding me on every side. And I still trusted them. But it would all unravel soon enough. And T.R. did not have many years left to live.

Ironically, Sat-Peter Kaur's and my happiest moments were when we could be together with our children. Ironic, because the stresses in our relationship were a key reason that we sent the children to school in India in the first place. Moments of peace and happiness, however, were few and far between.

CHAPTER FORTY-ONE

Divorce

O N JULY 17, 1986, I FILED FOR DIVORCE. It was 16 years from the fateful day in 1970 when I got "married" by Yogi Bhajan on that houseboat at Staten Island. Back then I was in complete fear and awe of Yogiji. Now I just sent him a formal note on my Masterworks Gallery letterhead.

> "Dear Sir, I am writing to let you know that I am divorcing Sat-Peter Kaur. I take this action after considerable reflection and am not seeking your permission, approval, or advice, but am writing as a courtesy. Your devoted son, Sat-Peter Singh Khalsa."

It was the first time in my long relationship with him that I had ever asserted myself so strongly and, though I didn't realize it at the time, it was the beginning of the end of my relationship with both him and with the Sikh community.

I had met Linda just a few months earlier. I was standing near the back of the lecture hall in the "House of Guru Ram Das" on a balmy April evening, waiting for Yogiji to enter for one of his classes. This was one of the few times that I was not at the front of the room leading the chanting, and I was enjoying greeting friends and newcomers as they entered. As Linda came through the door, she looked my way and smiled. Our eyes met from across the room and for a second or two remained locked together. I experienced a surge of energy running through my whole being and a thrill of excitement and danger. This was new territory and I was not at all prepared for it. When she sat down, she again looked up at me. It was too much, and I could not resist. I made my way over to her as if in a trance and sat down. I don't remember how the conversation started. Everyone else was chanting, but Linda and I were whispering back and forth, our heads close together in our own intimate world. She commented on the ring I was wearing, a very large and beautiful lapis lazuli stone set in a massive gold band. I instantly slid the ring off my finger and handed it to her. It was an impulsive and highly symbolic act.

In the fishbowl world of the Sikh community, carrying on an affair was a challenging feat. But before the evening was over, I had arranged to visit Linda at her home in Venice at 4:00 AM the next morning. I do not think I slept at all that night. At 3:30 AM I arose in my customary way, took a shower, dressed, and pretended to leave for sadhana. In those days there was a "group sadhana" that took place every morning at the Kundalini Yoga center on Fairfax Avenue, four blocks to the east of my apartment on Preuss Road. I usually rode my motorcycle there and back, so it was easy to slip away at that hour and drive to Linda's house instead. Sat-Peter Kaur usually slept late.

I flew down Robertson Boulevard in the dark, my white robes flapping in the wind. I turned right on Culver and followed the blinking orange lights all the way to Venice. In less than ten minutes I parked my motorcycle and found Linda's front door. I felt like a criminal sneaking around in the dark that way, so conspicuously dressed in white robes and turban. I looked about furtively to see if any neighbors were around to notice me, and seeing none, I knocked. A moment later Linda opened the door, rubbing her eyes sleepily. She took my hand and led me inside, straight back to her bedroom.

I was uneasy at first that she was so sure of herself in initiating

CHAPTER FORTY-ONE: Divorce

My older daughter, Amrit, took the news of our divorce much more heavily than Sathari, who was only 8.

our affair, but I was so starved for love that I let her take the lead. As she took me by the hand, I felt a bit the way a child might, trepidatiously climbing aboard a roller coaster and giving up all control. Only, I was not so sure of the outcome, and feared that Linda might be a little unbalanced. Yet, I followed along in wonder. Once in her bedroom she removed my turban, allowing my hair to tumble over my shoulders and down my back. It was nearly three feet long. She looked at me in awe and admiration, luxuriating and running her fingers through my hair. In sixteen years of marriage, I had never felt appreciated in a sensual way. Instead, the relationship had been marked by resignation and a sense of obligation that was lacking true connection. I couldn't blame Sat-Peter Kaur for this any more than I could blame myself. The very foundation of our marriage was faulty and compromised, with both of us, severely damaged from our youth, pushed into a "spiritual union" at 18 and 20, respectively, by a sociopathic father figure who pretended he could see our destinies. Our suffering for all those years was mutual.

However, Linda seemed to see something in me that I had not seen in myself. It was a new and much welcome experience. Yet, I felt dizzy and unsure, and did not feel that I truly deserved such love, so freely given to me in a way to which I was not accustomed. But Linda's affection was real, and it was like a soothing balm on my heart and soul. Like a starved man, coming upon an oasis after sixteen years in the wilderness, I greedily welcomed the love she showered on me. By the time I left her home three hours later, I was completely captivated. We spent the next two months making love and getting to know each other. Each day I fell deeper into a trance. Nothing in my life, including my time with Anni, just before getting involved with 3HO, came close to the euphoria of passion and validation I experienced with Linda. But I was also acutely aware that I was living a double life, and edging ever closer to a catastrophic disruption of everything I had committed to during the past 16 years.

Our conversations were profound and stimulating, but gradually took on a counseling tone as Linda questioned and advised me about my failed marriage, my children, my relationship with Yogi Bhajan, my business, my relationship with TR, my music, my future... She revealed very little about herself, though I soon met her family and learned something of her background. She remained mysterious, but that was part of the appeal.

I gave myself entirely to Linda. I trusted her worldly wisdom. I loved her obsessively, more than anything or anyone. I loved her more than I could love myself. Being with her day and night was all I wanted, and I could see nothing else. The deeper I fell into the trance of love, the less was my own sense of self. Her opinions and viewpoints I adopted as my own. Even Linda's family accepted me with open arms. Linda had an exceptionally close relationship with her mother and had introduced her parents to Yogi Bhajan. Her mother didn't think very highly of "the Yogi" and was outspoken about it, which I found distressing. Linda convinced me to enroll in Gold's Gym and work with her trainer. I was already in pretty good shape from doing yoga for 16 years, but the daily workouts soon helped fill out my skinny frame. Yet, even as my self-confidence from the physical changes began to grow, my relationship with Linda was beginning to show signs of strain.

One morning in early July, she announced that the status quo wasn't working for her anymore. I was surprised. I thought things were going along pretty well. But Linda was not willing to be "the other woman" while I maintained the appearance of respectability within my community by staying in a false and empty marriage. I knew she was right, but I was gripped with an all-consuming fear at the thought of what I would have to do. I had made a lot of momentous decisions in my life. I dropped out of college to start a rock band, left the band to join an ashram, married someone I didn't know, left my home in DC to move to Los Angeles. But none of these was as monumental as the prospect of ending my marriage of 16 years. There were my two young children to think of, and the storm of criticism and condemnation that I would certainly incite among my friends and peers within the Sikh community. And, of course, there was Yogi Bhajan, against whose will and authority I would finally have to assert myself. I went home and thought about it. The next morning when I arrived at 4:30 AM, I announced my decision: I was going to get a divorce. I did not waste any time. Linda referred me to a divorce attorney she knew and I filed papers within a few days. I also found a guesthouse that I could rent near 3rd and Fairfax, and moved out of my apartment on Preuss Road. My path was now set, and my world began to unwind rapidly.

The divorce was ugly. Linda counseled me to pull out all the stops, which I was reluctant to do. My preference was to slip away quietly, but Linda convinced me that I owed it to my children to get custody and provide them with a proper home. I had plenty of ammunition I could use to convince the court that my soon-to-be ex should not have custody of my children, and it was not hard to twist even relatively benign facts into the picture of a sick and disturbed woman, unfit for motherhood. This hardball strategy worked, but its brutality infected my soul and affected my children in direct and indirect ways for decades to come.

My children, then 8 and 14, were still in school in India, and the only way I could communicate with them was by letter. I was not a regular writer, and the more tumultuous my life became, the more difficult it was to stay in touch in any meaningful way. They were much more regular writers, but most of their letters were formulaic, especially those from Sat Hari, the 8-year-old. Every one of them started in exactly the same way: Dear Papa, how are you? I am fine. I am happy here at school, etc., etc. Amrit's letters were more personal and informative, but neither child was free to tell me what was really going on. Unbeknownst to me, all their letters were censored by the staff. Some letters would arrive with sections erased and written over by an adult hand. The news was always rosy.

Occasionally, I would write and send them stories about elves, remembering how much my siblings and I loved the "elf stories" my own father would sometimes tell us at bedtime. In these stories it was easy to anthropomorphize the characters—most of them innocent and delightful forest animals—projecting on them the fears and anxieties that I suspected my own children were experiencing so far from home. In view of my impending divorce, I sent them a couple of stories in which the protagonist, an elf named Doofo, leads two mice through the dangers of a wolf-infested forest and human-occupied farmland where a knife-wielding farmer's wife posed a mortal danger. Eventually, in an attempt to find their way home, Doofo helps his two mice friends cross a gorge high above a raging river using the thread from his sock as a bridge. The mice make it safely across, but the thread snaps when Doofo himself tries to cross. He falls and is swept away. The "chapter" ended there, but a footnote assured my children that Doofo didn't drown and was eventually reunited with his two mice friends.

It was an oblique message, and I hoped it would help them weather the news about the divorce that would arrive a few weeks later. I thought that Sat Hari would be most strongly affected, but it was Amrit, at 14, whose letters reflected enormous shock, distress, and anger at my decision. I tried to reassure them, but the warfare of divorce had many fronts, and I was pretty sure my children were hearing extraordinarily negative assessments from other adult members of the Sikh community. I refused to fight back. How could I share with my children the damning information I was relying on in the custody proceedings?

After giving my life to Yogi Bhajan and his "mission" for 17 years, I reached a point where I could no longer overlook his faults. I realized that his mission was almost entirely self-serving. He had grown wealthy and powerful, promoting himself as a liberated "spiritual master" at the expense of his students. His exploitation of women, and his dishonesty and manipulation, to which I was a first-hand witness and sometimes a victim, finally pushed me to take responsibility for myself. It felt tragic, as things had started on such a high note in the early 1970s. Leaving was, perhaps, the hardest decision of my life.

CHAPTER FORTY-TWO

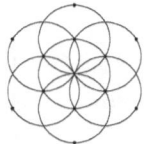

Disillusionment

As I went through the agony of divorce I relied increasingly on Linda as a counselor. Our relationship also became public and Yogi Bhajan suddenly took a great interest in us. He often invited us—commanded us, really—to visit with him in his living room where we would spend long hours. From time to time during these visits he would turn his attention to us, but most of the time we sat as witnesses while he counseled a continuous train of my fellow Sikhs and yoga students. I was astonished at the level of manipulation we witnessed, and equally astonished at the kinds of issues for which some of the students were seeking guidance and advice. Yogiji would prescribe an austere diet to a man whose wife wouldn't have sex with him, while instructing the wife to meditate two hours a day for forty days on a photo of Yogi Bhajan himself. He would advise another student how to run his business, then send yet another across the street to get job selling school supplies for GRD.

During these counseling sessions, he would sometimes call Linda over to his side and have her sit at his feet for some confidential exchange. One day, after departing from one of these visits, Linda told me that Yogiji had made a pass at her. I was dumbfounded.

"There's no way!" I complained. "He's a liberated master. It must be something you are projecting."

"Sat-Peter," she responded with firmness, "I'm a woman, and I KNOW when someone is playing with sexual energy. I'm telling you, he is making a move on me, and if you don't believe it, just watch the next time we're there."

Linda was right. I suddenly saw an aspect of Yogi Bhajan's behavior in a new and unsettling light. It wasn't just flirtatiousness that I witnessed. He really was coming on to Linda, and, apparently, doing the same thing with a lot of women. For years I had dismissed as wicked slander the stories of Yogiji's sexual exploits with his secretaries and students, but now I began to doubt his repeated denials and those of the people closest to him. Just harboring doubts, even without proof, was incredibly corrosive to my trust in him. I began observing his actions and pronouncements more critically.

One day I heard from my soon-to-be ex that Yogiji had told her I should make alimony payments in an amount that was far in excess of what I was earning each month. I was speechless. Already, after moving out, I had been voluntarily sending her a substantial monthly payment. "Why is he getting involved in my divorce settlement," I wondered. Later I had a chance to ask him privately why he had told Sat-Peter Kaur how much money I should provide her. His reply left me even more bewildered. "I'm just trying to get her off your back," he laughed. "Just promise it. You don't actually have to give it to her."

On top of the many indications over the years of Yogiji's manipulative character, this bit of cynical deception was a tipping point for me. No matter which angle I examined it from, his words reeked of dishonesty. If I took him at face value and believed that he was actually trying to help me by tricking Sat-Peter Kaur, whom I knew would soon be facing some very hard times, it was a despicable act of deception. If, however, as I suspected, he was trying to destroy me by conning me into an agreement that was far above my ability to honor, it was a double-crossing bit of treachery for which I could not forgive him.

As a result of this interaction my opinion of Yogi Bhajan

hardened into rejection, disrespect, anger—even hatred. More than once he had said that there are times when the end justifies the means—a position I always questioned—but I now realized that his moral compass was simply nonfunctioning or nonexistent. He was a man without ethical constraints for whom the truth meant nothing. It was completely opposite from the nobility and essence of his teachings that "truth is supreme," and the only path to God Consciousness.

The disillusionment was a crushing blow. For 17 years I had dedicated myself to serving the mission laid out by this man's teachings. I had looked to him as more than a father—more, even, than a spiritual teacher: I had trusted him with everything of myself, endured an unhappy marriage, subjected my children to his will, and made many of my major decisions based on his wishes, only to find out that he was, as Linda's mother had long maintained, "just a con man in white robes."

Within 24 hours I had made my decision to leave the 3HO American Sikh community. But I was unsure at first how I would do it. I did not want to go off in a huff the way so many had before me, and I did not want to get wrapped up in trying to explain to my fellow Sikhs my reasons for leaving. Inevitably, such explanations by departing students had been viewed as slander, and had resulted in an enormous backlash of negativity. Several of my good friends within 3HO had departed over the years. Gurushabad, whom I had long considered my absolute closest friend, left in about 1982. At his departure Yogi Bhajan unleashed a torrent of shocking news about my friend's sexual life, which he described in graphic and perverse terms.

I had called Gurushabad shortly after his departure, and had asked him why he left. He told me that I was not likely to believe his reasons, and that most of the devotees within the American Sikh community would not be convinced even if they saw Yogi Bhajan on film having sex with one of his secretaries. As I spoke with my friend, who had reverted to using his original name, Stephen, I tried to remain objective and dispassionate, but at the time I found his words disturbing and offensive. Nonetheless, I now knew he was right. Most of my fellow Sikhs would deny or rationalize any corrupt behavior by our spiritual teacher. I had never seen first-hand evidence of Yogi Bhajan's misdeeds with women, but I did remember being alarmed when, in speaking about the 16-year-old daughter of one of my employees, he said that the shape of her mouth was ideal for performing oral sex. But Yogi Bhajan often spoke in crude terms, and in some respects, this was part of his appeal. He had made a special effort to learn about contemporary "hip" vernacular, and he often peppered his lectures and comments with slang and salty language that both shocked and delighted his followers.

My friend, Dayal, and his unhappy wife had also "left the Dharma" not long before, but had avoided most of the typical abuse by remaining quiet. No one that I knew had heard anything about why they had left, or even that they were no longer a part of the community. They had moved away from Los Angeles and simply "disappeared." My friends, Vikram Singh and Vikram Kaur, on the other hand, had spoken out about their betrayal at the hands of Yogi Bhajan and had been the recipients of a torrent of abuse. Vikram, who had previously been the lead guitarist for Eric Burdon and the Animals, had made the mistake of agreeing to Yogi Bhajan's request that he put legal title of the San Diego Ashram in the name of Sikh Dharma. Although Vikram and his students had paid for the house, Yogi Bhajan decided to sell it and put all the net proceeds into the organization's—or his own—coffers. Vikram was outraged, but his complaints fell on deaf ears. Disillusioned, he and his wife moved away to Hawaii, while Yogiji lambasted him publicly in his absence.

CHAPTER ONE: *Disillusionment*

Even Premka, the most trusted and honored "secretary" in Yogi Bhajan's retinue for more than a decade, had left. She had long been in love with one of her fellow students and had been forced to preside over that unfortunate man's arranged marriage to a woman he did not love, or even like. Premka later confided to me that much of what had been said about Yogi Bhajan's sexual exploits with secretaries and students was, in fact, true. But that was not my concern as I contemplated how I would sever my own ties with the man whom I had loved and obeyed as my spiritual teacher for more than 16 years. I decided that the only way to do it was to gradually slip away.

I gave up my guesthouse at 3rd and Fairfax—so close to the Golden Temple Restaurant where I had kept an office for several years—and rented a small house in Venice that had an extra bedroom I could fix up for my children. Of necessity, I had already given up my office on Robertson Boulevard, just across from the Ashram on Preuss Road, and had rented a small loft in Culver City a few blocks from my new house. I started winding down my appearances at community events, including the Sunday Gurdwara services that were in many ways the focal point of community life.

One day I decided to clean up my beard and mustache. One of the core commandments of the Sikhs is to leave the body unchanged and the hair uncut. Most American Sikhs took this quite literally, and even some women with facial hair refused to remove it. I had very light facial hair to begin with—just a mustache and small beard on my chin—but I had some scraggly hairs on my cheeks and neck. I used a razor to remove these, thinking the change was inconspicuous. But one of my friends noticed it immediately and to my dismay commented on it as I was entering the Ashram that evening. I was now faced with another dilemma: should I retain the outward form of a Sikh after leaving the community? I still loved the "way of life" and inclusive philosophy taught by Guru Nanak, but decided that the

Sikh religion as it evolved under the nine subsequent Gurus, reaching its current, highly visible form under Guru Gobind Singh, was too closely identified with Yogi Bhajan. A few days later I determined to remove my beard entirely. At first, I left the mustache intact, but I was dissatisfied with the look and ended up taking that off, too. For the first time in my adult life, I had a clean-shaven face. I looked and felt about 15 years younger.

When Linda saw me with no beard and my head uncovered, she seemed pleased at first, and suggested that I should cut my hair, too. My hair had been growing since 1967 and formed a 3' braid down my back. I was rather proud of it, but agreed that I should complete the transformation. Linda made an appointment for me with her hairdresser, who chopped off the braid, bound it at the ends with rubber bands, and handed it to me. I kept it for years until it was lost in a house fire a few years later. But with short hair, Linda now seemed disturbed by the change in my appearance and the loss of my identity as a Sikh.

Although I was excited at the thought of reentering "normal" society, I, too, felt a disturbing sense of loss, and a resurgence of the identity crisis that had so plagued me in my Claude Jones days. I honestly did not know who I was anymore.

Linda had been seeing Yogiji's astrologer for some time and I had once accompanied her several months earlier. When she told him about my departure from the Sikhs he got extremely upset. Apparently, he had very little respect for Yogi Bhajan, but, inexplicably, had a very high regard for me. Linda reported that he had said I was the only person among the American Sikhs who could "save the organization" from Yogiji's destructive path. This left me even more confused. Had I made a huge mistake? Had I truly "cut" my destiny? All I knew was that I could never go back.

CHAPTER FORTY-THREE

Final Days

A SIGNIFICANT OPPORTUNITY came my way right after removing my turban and beard that gave me some hope for the future. "Daddy's Dyin', Who's Got the Will," a comedy by Del Shores, was playing at a 99-seat, equity-waiver theater in Hollywood. My friend, Rex Knowles, who was co-directing the show, and his wife, Sherry Landrum, had been taking my yoga classes for some time, and when they heard I was leaving 3HO, they suggested that I would be perfect for the part of "Harmony," a guitar-strumming drifter, who takes up with two of the show's female leads. I auditioned and was assigned as an understudy. I was quite excited, and I relished the thought of a future acting career, but realized that my birth name might present obstacles, since few people pronounced it correctly. After toying around with a lot of options, most of which sounded pretentious, I reached back into my own family's history and took one of my ancestral family names, Alexander, as my new stage name. Impulsively, I immediately filed paperwork for a legal name change.

However, the stars in my eyes dimmed when I learned that most actors in L.A. were paying the bills by taking roles in television commercials. Rex and Sherry suggested that I take some commercial acting classes. I signed up, but it did not go well. It seemed that most TV commercials at the time depicted men being about as stupid and clueless as possible. This, to me, was not an appealing way to spend my creativity and life energy—and I didn't feel I was very good at acting stupid, though I probably would have done fine if I just acted naturally. After two classes I quit the program. I was, however, having fun and making progress with my role in Daddy's Dyin'. The understudy for the role of Marlene, with whom my character was to fall in love, agreed to practice with me, and by the time of our first performance together during the Christmas season at the end of 1987, we had developed a good rapport. My first two or three performances with her went well.

But then I got called to fill in when Marlene's role was being played by the show's headliner. Although it was a week or two before the performance, she refused to rehearse with me, with the result that I got flustered by her performance—which differed substantially from what I was used to—and I dropped a key line in the middle of an intimate scene together on stage. Completely unnerved by my error, my counterpart had a meltdown in front of the audience, throwing her arms up and ending with a hysterical scream that left me literally speechless. After a very awkward pause we somehow managed to get back on track, but that was to be my last performance. Del Shores was nice enough about it, but he fired me at the end of the night, and my "career" as an actor came to an abrupt end, with nothing to show for it but humiliation and a new name.

Shortly after being fired from Daddy's Dyin', Linda gave me some news that pushed me further into misery, announcing she was ending our relationship. It took me several minutes to grasp the full impact of this proclamation. I had built my new life entirely around my love for Linda. Without her encouragement and the prospect of spending our lives together I would not have gone through with the divorce. I certainly would not have played the kind of hardball she encouraged, bringing my wife's affair into open court, and thereby creating a toxic environment that would impact my children for decades to come. Without the first-hand evidence Linda revealed of

CHAPTER FORTY-THREE: Final Days

Yogi Bhajan's corrupt ways, I might have even overlooked his other faults. It is not exaggerating to suggest that without her influence I might not have even left the Sikh community when I did. But it was far too late to change that. I had already cut the threads that had bound me for seventeen years to Yogi Bhajan and the community he had created.

Although Linda confessed that she still felt enormous affection for me, she explained that she had shared in and endured so much of the stress of the changes I was going through that the passion had gone out of the relationship for her. In addition, the financial crisis I was entering into, with the challenges to my business and looming obligations of alimony and child support, convinced her that I was not a viable long-term partner or husband. She did, however, want to keep me in her life, to remain as her friend.

As the enormity of this change in our relationship sank in, it left me reeling. I had never in my life felt so completely in love with anyone, and the sense of loss was profound beyond anything I had experienced. I don't remember how that conversation ended. I was paralyzed and deflated. For days afterwards my moods were wild and unpredictable and the slightest provocation would leave me a sobbing wreck. One day I was about to check out a small purchase at a local hardware store when I was overwhelmed by the thought that I was losing not only Linda, but her family, too. I had grown quite fond of her parents, and even some of her extended family members, all of whom had been generous and kind to me. This thought filled me with such grief that I had to turn away from the counter and flee down an aisle where I did my best to hide my tears and stifle my sobs.

I continued to see Linda occasionally for a few weeks, but she eventually started dating another man and it became too painful and awkward for me to pretend we could still go on seeing each other (though, years later, we are still in occasional contact and remain friends). I was now more completely alone than I had ever felt in my life. My former friends among the Sikhs regarded me as a fallen soul, lost to them, and unworthy of their continued friendship. I was divorced. My sense of identity was shattered, and I had virtually no friends other than Linda, whom I could no longer bear to see.

At loose ends I accepted my brother's invitation to attend his son's recital as a boy soprano in New York City. Alex and I had always been close, and he was the one family member with whom I regularly communicated throughout the seventeen years of my involvement with the Sikh community. Since my move to Los Angeles seven years earlier, however, we had seen each other in person only a few times. He knew that I was coming to New York, but was preoccupied with arrangements for the concert, and I arrived a little late. Throughout the concert I sat inconspicuously at the back of the hall.

After the recital, as the audience milled about congratulating James and his parents, I went and stood next to Alex, waiting for him to finish a conversation with one of the other guests and wondering why he seemed to be ignoring me. I was wearing an Australian cowboy hat, blue jeans, and a denim jacket. I stood there for some time and when there was a pause in the conversation interjected, "Hello Alex. James sounded great!"

On hearing my voice Alex turned in astonishment and looked at me closely.

"Oh my God!" he exclaimed, "It's PETER!"

Epilogue

My seventeen years as a Sikh had come to an end, but my difficulties were just beginning. I had no friends outside the Sikh community, and was shunned by almost all those who remained behind when I left. The woman I loved had broken up with me. I was alienated from my father and his wife, and had little connection to my siblings. I had no social networks that might provide a way to climb out of the emotional and financial pit in which I found myself. My business was a mess, with overdue rent and bills I could not pay, and I was behind on payments for the small house I was renting in Venice. Years earlier my education had been cut short, by my own choice, with only one year of college studying the "great books"—very inspirational and thought provoking, but not very useful in the materialistic world of the Reagan era. And I was almost absurdly immature and naive, as if my emotional development had atrophied when my spiritual pursuits began.

Actually, I was probably stuck at the maturity level of a 15-year-old, and though I felt the deficit, I did not have the time or even the imagination to explore and come to grips with the influences that had led me into the Sikhs in the first place, or the vulnerabilities that had made me susceptible to the narcissistic abuse meted out by Yogi Bhajan and other sociopaths.

I was vaguely aware, even in high school, that I had felt inadequate, somehow. When we had creative writing assignments, for example, many of my classmates exhibited a level of emotional sophistication and understanding that I lacked. Even the lyrics of popular music at the time left me feeling inadequate and somewhat envious. Although I was an accomplished musician, writing lyrics with subtlety and emotional impact was completely out of my reach. Further, I was at the time unaware of the fact that my whole family on my father's side—including my siblings—exhibited tendencies on the autism spectrum, and how this could have shaped my character and world view. Only many years later was I able to see in retrospect how I was impacted by this. High-functioning autism and narcissism have many tendencies in common, for they both manifest as self-centered. But narcissists are often malevolent in their behavior, callous towards the needs and feelings of others, while people on the autism spectrum are simply unaware and insensitive to social cues. In another cruel dynamic, people on the spectrum are sitting ducks for exploitation by manipulative narcissists and sociopaths, for they are often blindly trusting and lacking in personal boundaries. At the time, this would certainly have described me to a "tee"!

Yogi Bhajan was narcissistic, manipulative, and malevolent in the extreme. He routinely used so-called spiritual explanations to justify as legitimate his harmful and antisocial behavior. A favorite ploy of his, for example, was to cite some karma from a past lifetime as reason for a student to submit to his authority—or even sexual exploitation—as a part of their spiritual "destiny." What's more, he fully understood the malevolence of this behavior, for he was acutely aware of his students' vulnerabilities, their insecurities, their naivete, their need for a father figure who could help them navigate the challenges of life, and their blind devotion to him on ideologically spiritual terms as laid out in texts like *Autobiography of a Yogi* and *How to Know God*.

In spite of rejecting Yogi Bhajan's "end justifies the means" approach to life and business, and the abuse he heaped on me and many of my fellow Sikhs, my own moral compass had not found its bearings by the time I left the organization, and was about to be tested in ways I could never have imagined. I was still hopelessly naïve and insecure, and I was surrounded by manipulators, sociopaths, and even convicted criminals to whose schemes I was vulnerable. But I was also determined to BE someone, to be recognized, to be validated, praised, and loved. Thus, many of my decisions were terribly misguided and selfish—not out of malevolence, but from ignorance and the significant deficits in my development.

The adventure of self-discovery that I undertook upon my departure from the American Sikh community carried me through years of challenges and tests of my integrity—many of which I failed miserably. But, gradually, I did start learning from my mistakes. As the decades rolled by I worked hard to come to grips with my time in Yogi Bhajan's cult, slowly dispelling my anger and blame for his abuse as I came to accept my own deficiencies. Book II of this memoir documents that perilous journey, and—so far—I can attest it has a happy ending.

Acknowledgements

This book would not have been possible without the kind support of many people who have contributed editing suggestions, photographs, shared memories, and technical support. Among these are Stephen Josephs, Pamela Dyson, Suzanne Jordan, and my beautiful daughters, Amrit and Sat Hari. Chris Molé has been tremendously helpful navigating the publishing process. I am especially grateful to the many people who have helped me over the years with counseling, patience, and loving support as I struggled with life's lessons. Chief among these has been my wife and partner, Johannah Harkness, whose own work as a psychotherapist continues to provide insights.

PETER MACDONALD BLACHLY grew up in Washington, DC, the youngest of five children. His parents provided him with piano and guitar lessons from a young age, as well as a private school education made possible in part by a scholarship he earned as a boy soprano in the choir of the Washington National Cathedral.

Peter was deeply influenced by his childhood summers, which were spent on a primitive island in Maine where he learned to live "off the grid." His first memoir, *The Stone From Halfway Rock*, documents those formative early years. The multiple skills developed in his youth have led him through a varied career that has included journalism, home construction, energy efficiency consulting, environmental advocacy, and music.

Although he had left the Sikh community with only one year of college under his belt, he eventually continued his education—earning a Masters Degree in Environmental Studies—and served as executive director of a number of non-profit organizations. After moving to Maine in 2008, he and his wife, Johannah Harkness, collaborated together to write and produce a rock opera, *One Way Trip to Mars*, which was most recently performed at the Waterville Opera House in Maine. Peter and Johannah now live in Bath, Maine with a large collection of guitars, keyboards, boats, outboard motors, pet cats, ducks, and a covey of quail.

He can be reached at peter@peteralexander.us

www.ingramcontent.com/pod-product-compliance
Lightning Source LLC
Chambersburg PA
CBHW030544080526
44585CB00012B/249